Q&A

Routledge•Cavendish Questions & Answers Series

Contract Law
2009–2010

Richard Stone
LLM, BARRISTER
Professor of Law, Lincoln Law School, University of Lincoln

Routledge·Cavendish
Taylor & Francis Group
LONDON AND NEW YORK

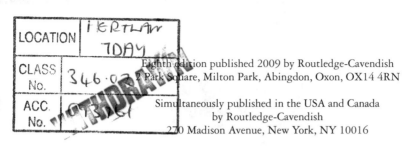
Eighth edition published 2009 by Routledge-Cavendish
2 Park Square, Milton Park, Abingdon, Oxon, OX14 4RN

Simultaneously published in the USA and Canada
by Routledge-Cavendish
270 Madison Avenue, New York, NY 10016

Routledge-Cavendish is an imprint of the Taylor & Francis Group,
an informa business

© 1993, 2009 Richard Stone

Previous editions published by Cavendish Publishing Limited
First edition   1993
Second edition   1995
Third edition   1998
Fourth edition   2001
Fifth edition   2003
Sixth edition   2005

Previous editions published by Routledge-Cavendish
Seventh edition   2007

Typeset in Garamond by
RefineCatch Limited, Bungay, Suffolk
Printed and bound in Great Britain by
TJ International Ltd, Padstow, Cornwall

British Library Cataloguing in Publication Data
A catalogue record for this book is available from the British Library

Library of Congress Cataloging-in-Publication Data
Stone, Richard, 1951 Mar. 7–
Contract law : 2009–2010 / Stone, Richard. – 8th ed.
p. cm. – (Routledge-Cavendish Q&A series)
1. Contracts – England. 2. Contracts – England – Problems, exercises, etc. I. Title.
II. Title: Questions & answers contract law. III. Title: Questions and answers contract law.
IV. Title: Q&A contract law. V. Title: Q and A contract law.
KD1554.S756 2009
346.4202 – dc22
2008031613

ISBN 10: 0–415–48167–8
ISBN 13: 978–0–415–48167–0

CONTENTS

PREFACE

Contract must be one of the most widely studied areas of English law. As well as being one of the 'core' subjects for professional purposes, it is often studied by those taking law options within a more general course, at degree level or below. One reason for this is that contract law provides a good, and in some cases essential, grounding for the study of many other legal subjects, such as commercial law, company law, consumer law, employment law and land law. Master contract and you will have a firm basis for the study of many other courses. It is also a typical 'common law' subject, which means that its rules and principles have developed largely through the decisions of the courts, rather than through statutory intervention. A comparison between the size of the Table of Cases and that of the Table of Legislation in this book illustrates the point.

This book was written with a view to helping all those studying contract. I am pleased that previous editions seem to have been well received by students. This edition contains five completely new questions and answers, and has been fully revised throughout to take account of developments in the law. The purpose of this book remains the same. It is not a substitute for attending lectures, or reading textbooks or law reports. It is hoped that it will prove a valuable supplement to those activities. Students often find that, having attended lectures, or read the books, they have difficulty in deciding what is relevant and irrelevant, what is important and less important, what needs to be committed to memory, and what can be safely regarded as background. This is a particular difficulty when students are taught contract early in their legal studies, as is usually the case. One of the objectives of this book is to help students who face such difficulties. The answers to the questions contained in this book provide a distillation of the essential points on the topics that they cover. They help to highlight the most important elements, and indicate the fundamental rules and principles that need to be learnt.

The second objective is to illustrate, by example, how to answer questions on contract law. The answer plans are important here, as well as the answers themselves. Each of the answers is around 1,500 words long, which is probably an average length for a first-year law degree essay. Exam answers may well be a little shorter and less detailed, but the overall approach should be the same. Note, however, that the answers given are not, and are not intended to be, perfect. There is probably no such thing. Nor are they the only way in which the questions given could be answered. They are, however, examples of the kind of well-structured answer that will be likely to receive good marks. They will also help to answer, it is hoped, some of the perennial student concerns, such as 'how far should I give the facts of cases?', and 'how many cases do I need to cite?' It is not easy to answer such questions in the abstract. The answers here give concrete examples of how the material should be handled.

The questions themselves are frequently adaptations of questions used in past examination papers, and are of the style used in many degree courses, including the London External LLB. Non-degree courses will often adopt a similar approach. The law is stated as it stood on 1 July 2008.

I hope that you find this book useful as a supplement to your study of the law of contract. It will not remove the need to read the textbooks and the cases, but it will help you to make better use of the information you have acquired from these sources and, I hope, achieve success in your examinations.

Richard Stone
Elston, Newark
July 2008

TABLE OF CASES

TABLE OF STATUTES

TABLE OF STATUTORY INSTRUMENTS

CHAPTER 1

OFFER AND ACCEPTANCE

INTRODUCTION

There can be few contract exam papers which do not contain a question on offer and acceptance. Students will often make this one of their 'banker' questions, but you will need to make sure that you are prepared to deal with any of the forms in which a question about offer and acceptance may be asked. The topics covered within this general heading are quite varied, but are nevertheless fairly predictable. General issues that will need to be understood include:

- the nature of an offer and an acceptance – is an advertisement an offer? What if an 'acceptance' does not match the offer precisely? What is the effect of a 'counter-offer'?

- the relationship between offer and acceptance on the one hand and 'agreement' on the other – the objective approach to determining the existence of a contract; and

- the differences between unilateral and bilateral contracts.

As will be seen from the questions in this chapter, problems concerning the communication of offer and acceptance are often asked. In particular, students will need to be familiar with:

- the 'postal rule' (*Adams v Lindsell* (1818)) – the types of communication to which it applies, and the situations in which it does not apply;

- silence as acceptance – the rule in *Felthouse v Bindley* (1862), and possible exceptions to it;

- the problems, many of them unresolved by the courts, of electronic communications, such as faxes, email and Internet contracts. Does the postal rule apply to them? If not, when and where do they take effect?; and

- the rules governing revocation of an offer, in both bilateral and unilateral contracts – can there be revocation once performance of a unilateral contract has started?

Finally, it should be remembered that a question involving offer and acceptance may also sometimes require you to touch on other issues. You may find, for example, that an offer and acceptance question (although this is not the case with those contained in this chapter) will also involve discussion of intention to create legal relations, consideration or mistake.

1

Checklist

You should be familiar with the following areas:

- the meaning of offer – the distinction from an 'invitation to treat';
- the meaning of acceptance – the distinction from a 'counter-offer', and the possibility of acceptance by conduct or silence;
- subjective and objective approaches to agreement;
- the differences between unilateral and bilateral contracts;
- the postal rule and its limitations;
- revocation of offers; and
- recall of acceptance.

Question 1

On 1 November, Albatross plc sent a letter to Budgie Ltd, with which it had been negotiating, offering it a contract to service all Albatross's birdseed processors each month for the next five years at a cost of £10,000 per annum. The letter said that Budgie should reply by return of post. Unfortunately, the letter contained an error in the address and was not delivered to Budgie until 6 November. Budgie replied at once, accepting. This letter was posted at 11 am on 6 November. In the meantime, on 4 November, Albatross had received an offer from Canary Ltd to do the servicing work for £9,000 per annum. Albatross, having heard nothing from Budgie, telephoned Canary on 5 November and offered it the contract at £8,000. Canary accepted. Albatross sent a fax to Budgie on 6 November telling it that the offer of 1 November was withdrawn. This fax was received on Budgie's fax machine at 10.45 am on 6 November, but not read by anyone until 5 pm on the same day.

Advise Albatross, Budgie and Canary.

Answer plan

This question is of a common type, raising issues about the communication of offers and acceptances, and which of two parties is entitled to enforce a contract. In answering such a question, in which the timing of events may be very important, it is a good idea to make a chronological plan – for example:

1 Nov: Albatross offer to Budgie, letter posted

4 Nov: Canary offer to Albatross, £9,000
5 Nov: Albatross counter-offer to Canary, £8,000, accepted by Canary
6 Nov: 1 Nov offer arrives
      10.45 am Albatross's fax withdrawing offer to Budgie
      11 am   Budgie's acceptance posted
      5 pm   Albatross's fax read

This should make it easier to pinpoint the issues for discussion. Particular areas to be considered here are: offers and counter-offers; the operation of the postal rule (*Adams v Lindsell* (1818)); the time of communication of electronic messages, such as faxes; and the revocation of an offer. This problem raises the issue of whether Albatross is committed to one contract, or two. The answer to this will depend on the precise time at which each contract was formed. This in turn depends on the point at which communications between the parties take effect, particularly acceptances and revocations of offers.

Answer

The English law on the formation of contracts generally requires there to be an offer and a matching acceptance. This is particularly the case with contracts made by correspondence. The offer must set out, or refer to, all of the important terms of the contract; the acceptance must indicate agreement to all these. If it does not do so, not only will it not be a valid acceptance, but it will be regarded as a counter-offer, which prevents the original offer from being accepted later (*Hyde v Wrench* (1840)). An offer can generally be withdrawn at any time before acceptance is complete.

In the problem, there are three offers, two of which are made by Albatross. One is contained in the letter to Budgie of 1 November, and the other in the phone call to Canary on 5 November (this is, strictly speaking, a counter-offer). The third offer is made by Canary in the letter received by Albatross on 4 November. This offer is rejected by Albatross's counter-offer, and so need not be discussed further.

Which of the other two offers was accepted? In both cases, there was a purported acceptance. Albatross's first offer is accepted by Budgie in the letter posted on 6 November. Canary accept Albatross's offer during the telephone conversation on 5 November. There seems no reason to doubt the effectiveness of this acceptance, so Albatross would appear to have made a binding contract for the servicing of its machines with Canary. Has it also made such a contract with Budgie?

The issue here is the time at which communications are effective when conducted by post or fax. Looking first at Albatross's offer to Budgie, this was posted on 1 November, but did not arrive until 6 November. Offers have to be actually communicated to the recipient to be effective, so this offer took effect on 6 November.

Budgie posted a reply accepting on the same day. We are not told when this was received, but this may well not matter, if the special postal rule as regards acceptances applies.

The postal rule derives from the case of *Adams v Lindsell* (1818). In this case, a letter offering some wool for sale was sent to the plaintiffs but, unfortunately, as in the problem, it was misdirected and delayed. The plaintiffs posted a letter of acceptance as soon as they received the offer. After this letter was posted, but before it was delivered, the defendants had sold the wool elsewhere. The plaintiffs brought an action for non-delivery.

The court decided that the acceptance should be regarded as having taken effect when posted. The main reason for adopting this rule was that of business efficiency. It was thought that businesses would be able to operate more effectively if, having posted an acceptance of a contract, they could then proceed on the basis that a valid contract existed immediately, rather than having to wait to receive confirmation that the acceptance had been delivered. Later cases have confirmed that the *Adams v Lindsell* rule should apply whenever it was reasonable for the offeror to expect the acceptance to be made by post (for example, *Henthorn v Fraser* (1892)). This expectation can be removed by express instructions from the offeror (as in *Holwell Securities v Hughes* (1974), in which a requirement for 'notice in writing' displaced the postal rule) or be implicit in the means of communication (for example, *Quenerduaine v Cole* (1883), in which an offer by telegram was held to imply a requirement for an acceptance by equally speedy means).

From the facts given here, there is no reason to say that the postal rule should be displaced. The offer was made through the post, and specifically asks for a reply by 'return of post'. There is no indication that actual notice of acceptance was specified. What of the fact that the letter was delivered five days after posting? This was the result of the letter being wrongly addressed by Albatross, so it should take responsibility for that. Indeed, the same had happened in *Adams v Lindsell*, so it is clear that, despite the fact that the acceptance was not sent until several days after Albatross would have expected, the acceptance must be taken to have been effective at 11 am on 6 November. If this were the only relevant communication, then Albatross and Budgie would be bound to a contract created at that point.

Albatross, however, had tried to withdraw its offer at 10.45 am on 6 November. The effectiveness of this attempted withdrawal must now be considered.

The first point to note is that the postal rule has no application here for two reasons. First, there is clear authority from the case of *Byrne v van Tienhoven* (1880) that the rule does not apply to revocation of offers. Second, the case of *Entores v Miles Far East Corporation* (1955) established that the postal rule did not apply to 'instantaneous communications' such as telex. It is submitted that this should also apply to communications by fax.[2]

If the postal rule does not apply, when exactly is a faxed revocation effective? In particular for our purposes, does it need to be read by the recipient to be effective, or is it sufficient that it is received on his fax machine?

Two cases since *Entores* have addressed this issue in respect of telexes. In *The Brimnes* (1975), the Court of Appeal agreed with the judge that the telex took effect when it was received on the recipient's telex machine, provided that this was within office hours. In *Brinkibon Ltd v Stahag Stahl* (1983), Lord Wilberforce suggested a more flexible approach, looking at all of the circumstances. On balance, it seems likely that the courts would say that Albatross's fax withdrawing its offer was effective at 10.45 am on 6 November (assuming that 6 November was a normal working day). If this is the answer given by the court, then Albatross is in a good position. It has its contract at £8,000 with Canary, and has managed to escape from its contract with Budgie. Budgie's only hope is to try to argue that the revocation of an offer by fax should not be effective until it is actually communicated. If that is so, then Albatross's attempted revocation will be ineffective and Budgie's acceptance will stand. Albatross will then be in the position of having made contracts with both Budgie and Canary, and being unable to fulfil both of them. It runs the risk of having to pay substantial damages for breaking one of the contracts. Canary is in the best position. Its contract was clearly formed on 5 November. Canary can stand aside and leave Albatross and Budgie to sort out their differences, confident in the knowledge that its contract with Albatross is without doubt enforceable.

Think points

1 An offer will lapse after the expiry of a reasonable time: *Ramsgate Victoria Hotel Co Ltd v Montefiore* (1866). Could it be argued that this has happened here, because of the delay?

2 This is not accepted by Treitel, who suggests that electronic communications may occupy an intermediary position whereby, for example, an illegible message of acceptance might still be regarded as effective: see Treitel, *The Law of Contract*, 12th edn, 2007, p 30 and Stone, *The Modern Law of Contract*, 7th edn, 2008, pp 69–72.

Question 2

Michael in Manchester wrote to Laura in Loughborough offering to sell Laura his Rolls Royce car for £20,000. On receiving Michael's offer, Laura telephoned him in order to accept. Michael, however, said that since such a large sum of money was involved he wanted written confirmation of the acceptance from Laura. He said that if Laura got her letter of acceptance to him by 11 am the next day (Tuesday), he would go ahead with the sale at £20,000. Laura at once wrote and posted a letter of acceptance, which Michael received at 9 am on the Tuesday morning. In the meantime, however, Michael had received a better offer for his car, and wrote to Laura withdrawing his offer to her. This letter was posted at 5 pm on the Monday evening, and was received by Laura at 8.30 am on Tuesday.

Discuss.

Would it make any difference to your answer if the letter from Michael to Laura withdrawing his offer had been received by her at 9.30 am instead of 8.30 am?

Answer plan

The important thing to note about this problem is that, although there are communications via the post, the postal rule (from *Adams v Lindsell* (1818)) has little role to play. The main issue relates to unilateral contracts, and whether an offer in a unilateral contract can be withdrawn once the other party has started to perform. Note also that the instruction at the end of the problem is simply 'Discuss', so you are not here looking at the problem from the point of view of any particular party, but should discuss all of the issues raised by the facts.

The topics that will need covering include:

• acceptance by telephone;
• avoidance of the postal rule;
• the nature and definition of a unilateral contract; and
• revocation of offers in unilateral contracts.

Answer

The negotiations between Michael and Laura over the sale of Michael's Rolls Royce clearly reach an agreement, in the sense that at a certain point both are willing to go through with the transaction at an agreed price. Does this mean, however, that they have a contract? Not necessarily, because the English law of contract, rather than simply looking for a 'meeting of the minds' between two parties, generally looks for the formalisation of this into a matching 'offer' and 'acceptance'.[1] Indeed, it may well happen that, in some cases, by the time an offer and acceptance have been exchanged, one of the parties is no longer in agreement, and would like to back out, but is prevented from doing so by the rules of offer and acceptance. This may be the position that Michael finds himself in at the end of this problem.

The exchanges between Michael and Laura are started by Michael's first letter, offering his car for sale at £20,000. It seems reasonable to treat this as a definite offer, rather than an invitation to treat, or an expression of willingness to contract (as in *Harvey v Facey* (1893)). In any case, the status of the original letter does not matter because Michael and Laura clearly reach agreement on the terms of the contract during their telephone conversation. The way in which a contract is made by a telephone conversation was considered by the Court of Appeal in *Apple Corps Ltd v Apple Computers* (2004). The issue before the Court was where such a contract was made. The Court took the view that it may be unrealistic to analyse contracts negotiated over the telephone into 'offer and acceptance', because the answer as to when and where the contract was made might depend on the chance as to how the conversation developed, and who ended up speaking last (and thus 'accepting' the other side's 'offer'). This approach, if applied, here, would favour Laura, in that it could be argued that a contract was finalised on the phone, and all that happens subsequently is irrelevant. Michael, however, will argue that he never reached a final agreement on the phone, and introduced a new stipulation before there was any contract, requiring confirmation of Laura's acceptance in writing. It might be possible to regard this as a condition precedent for the contract taking effect (as in *Pym v Campbell* (1856)).[2] It is submitted that the court would be more likely to treat this as giving rise to a particular type of contract – a 'unilateral contract' – as it did in the rather similar situation in *Daulia Ltd v Four Millbank Nominees* (1978), in which the defendants had promised to enter into a contract provided that the other party produced a full written agreement plus a deposit by a particular time.

Unilateral contracts are sometimes called 'if' contracts, in that rather than both parties committing themselves, one party makes an offer in the form 'if you do this, then I promise to do that'. A famous example of a unilateral contract is *Carlill v Carbolic Smoke Ball Co* (1893), in which the company, by its advertisement for its 'smoke ball', was deemed to have made an offer in the form, 'if you use our smoke ball as directed, and still catch influenza, we will pay you £100'. So, in the problem, Michael is saying, 'if you get your letter of confirmation to me by 11 am on Tuesday, I will sell you my car for £20,000'. The contract is unilateral in that, although Michael is committing himself to the sale if Laura does what he has requested, Laura has no obligation. She can supply the written confirmation if she wishes, but she is perfectly free to change her mind and do nothing, in which case Michael will have no claim against her.

As it happens, Laura decides to go ahead with the contract, and writes and posts the letter that Michael has requested. This letter is an acceptance, and the usual rule when a letter of acceptance is sent in reply to an offer made by letter is that the acceptance takes effect on posting (*Adams v Lindsell* (1818)). This postal rule has no application here, however, since the case of *Holwell Securities v Hughes* (1974) makes it clear that the rule can be avoided by a specific request for written notice. Moreover, in the context of the unilateral contract, the actual delivery of the letter to Michael is of crucial importance.

Even though the postal rule does not apply, Laura would at first sight appear to have a binding contract, in that her letter is received by Michael two hours before the 11 am deadline. At this point, however, a complication arises. Michael has changed his mind about the contract, and has tried to withdraw. His letter of revocation is received by Laura half an hour before her letter of acceptance is received by Michael. Is his withdrawal effective?

The normal rule about revocation of offers is that they will be effective provided that they are communicated before the acceptance has taken effect (for example, *Dickinson v Dodds* (1876)), and that this is so even if the offeror has said that the offer will be kept open for a particular time (*Routledge v Grant* (1828)). This is so because no consideration has generally been given in exchange for the promise to keep the offer open, and it is therefore unenforceable.

How does this apply to unilateral contracts? If applied strictly it would mean that the offeror could withdraw the offer even when the offeree was on the brink of completing the requested task. This is because the offer is not accepted, and therefore there is no complete contract until the offeree has done everything asked for. Thus, in a traditional example, the offeree who has been offered £100 if he walks from London to York could be met by a valid revocation of the offer when only a mile from his destination. Application of this to the problem would mean that Laura had no contract with Michael. The rule is one that gives great potential for injustice, and in two cases the courts have indicated that it should not be applied strictly. First, in *Errington v Errington and Woods* (1952), a father had promised his son and daughter-in-law that if they paid the mortgage instalments on a house, he would transfer it to them. Lord Denning took the view that once the young couple had started to make the payments that offer could not be withdrawn. Similarly, in *Daulia Ltd v Four Millbank Nominees* (1978) (on facts close to those in the problem), it was regarded as settled by at least some members of the Court of Appeal that, once performance of a unilateral contract had begun, the power to revoke the offer was lost. The conceptual basis for this ruling is unclear, and in neither case was the statement of principle part of the ratio, but it perhaps indicates the likely approach of the courts, at least where the offeror has notice that the offeree is trying to accept.[3] Applying this to the problem would lead to the conclusion that Michael is unable to withdraw his offer, provided that Laura indicated in their telephone conversation that she would be sending the written confirmation, and that Laura is therefore entitled to enforce the contract for sale at £20,000.

As regards the alternative situation, Laura is in an even stronger position. Revocations of offers must be communicated to be effective (*Byrne v van Tienhoven* (1880)), and so Michael's letter clearly arrives too late to prevent the contract coming into existence. Once again, Laura can insist on buying the car at £20,000.[4]

Think points

1 In other words, the courts are applying an objective rather than a subjective test for the existence of an agreement. See, for example, *The Hannah Blumenthal* (1983).

2 A condition precedent is an event that must occur before the contract comes into existence. In *Pym v Campbell* (1856), for example, an agreement for the sale of a patent was conditional on a third party approving the invention. The approval was not given, and so there was no contract.

3 It may be different in a case in which the offer is made to the world, as in *Carlill v Carbolic Smoke Ball Co* (1893).

4 What remedy would be available to Laura – specific performance, or only damages? This will depend on whether the car is regarded as being unique, or only one of a kind that could be purchased on the open market. See Stone, *The Modern Law of Contract*, 7th edn, 2008, pp 602–4.

Question 3

What is meant by 'the battle of the forms' in relation to the formation of contracts? Have the ways in which the courts have tried to deal with this problem led to satisfactory results?

Answer plan

Essay questions, while they may appear more straightforward than problems, often require just as much care in deciding exactly on which issues you should concentrate. Although it may be easy to identify the general area in which you should be writing, simply reproducing all your knowledge of that area will not gain you high marks. For that, you need to identify the precise 'angle' on the topic suggested by the question. Here, the main topic is clearly the rules concerning the formation of contracts. The particular angle is the way in which those rules apply to 'battle of the forms' situations (that is, those in which businesses negotiate by the exchange of mutually inconsistent standard terms, and it is unclear which set is to apply to the eventual contract). It is this area that should form the main focus of your discussion. Two cases in particular will need close attention – namely, *Butler Machine Tool v Ex-Cell-O Corp* (1979) and *Trentham v Archital Luxfer* (1993).

Your essay should contain the following points:

- an explanation of 'the battle of the forms';
- an outline of the rules of offer and acceptance;
- discussion of the approach adopted in *Butler Machine Tool v Ex-Cell-O Corp* (1979);
- discussion of the alternative approach suggested by *Trentham v Archital Luxfer* (1993); and
- consideration of whether the current position in this area is 'satisfactory' (and perhaps of what alternatives there might be).

Answer

The traditional approach of the common law to the formation of contracts is to look for a matching 'offer' and 'acceptance'. This is sometimes referred to as a requirement that the two elements (offer and acceptance) must be a mirror image of each other. Any significant difference in the acceptance will mean that the offer is regarded as being rejected: *Hyde v Wrench* (1840).[1] The purported acceptance may constitute a 'counter-offer', but no contract will be formed until it has in turn been unequivocally accepted. The 'battle of the forms' refers to a situation that sometimes arises when two businesses are negotiating towards a contract. Each business may well have its own standard terms, which it prefers to use as the basis of its contracts. Letters that constitute the negotiation may well have the appearance of being an 'offer and acceptance'. If, however, each letter has attached to it a set of standard terms, and the two sets are inconsistent, it may be very difficult to determine whether there is in fact a contract between the parties. This type of situation fell to be considered by the Court of Appeal in *Butler Machine Tool v Ex-Cell-O Corp* (1979). In this case, the plaintiffs had offered an item of machinery to the defendants, using their (the plaintiffs') standard terms, which included a price variation clause. The defendants replied by sending an order in their standard form, which provided for a fixed price. This order enclosed an 'acknowledgment slip', to be filled out by the plaintiffs. The plaintiffs signed and returned the acknowledgment slip, but also referred in their accompanying letter to the terms of their original offer. There were no further relevant communications between the parties. When the machine was ready for delivery, the question arose as to whether the fixed price or the price variation clause was to apply. The Court of Appeal analysed the transaction using the traditional concepts of offer, counter-offer and acceptance. The plaintiffs' original letter was an offer. The defendants' reply was not an acceptance, but because it put forward different terms (that is, in particular, a fixed rather than a variable price) it was therefore a counter-offer. The plaintiffs' return of the signed acknowledgment slip was an acceptance of the defendants' counter-offer. But what of the accompanying letter referring back to the original terms? The Court treated this as not being of any legal significance, so that there was in the end a contract on the defendants' terms. This rather cavalier dismissal of what the plaintiffs no doubt saw as an important part of their communications is perhaps indicative of the courts' eagerness, in this type of situation, to find that some sort of contract has come into existence. A strict application of the offer and acceptance principles might well lead to the conclusion that there was no contract at all. But this could be regarded as being unsatisfactory in a business context, where one or both of the parties may have spent time and money on the basis that a valid contract had been created. A further example of this type of approach may be seen in *Hertford Foods Ltd v Lidl UK GmbH* (2001), which concerned a contract for the sale of goods. Once again, inconsistent terms had been exchanged, but both parties thought that they had made a contract. In this case, the Court of Appeal was able to find that the parties had in fact reached agreement on the essential terms of the contract (that is, the goods to be sold and the price) before any of the standard terms had been put forward. Neither set of standard terms therefore applied. In particular, the claimant could not rely on a force majeure clause that appeared in its standard terms but not in those of the defendant.

At times, some members of the Court of Appeal have attempted to confront the problem of the battle of the forms more directly. In *Butler Machine Tool v Ex-Cell-O Corp* (1979), for example, Lord Denning would have preferred to find that the overall communications between the parties showed that there was an agreement and therefore a contract, without the need to divide this up strictly into offer and acceptance. He developed this argument further in *Gibson v Manchester City Council* (1979), but on this occasion his approach was specifically rejected by the House of Lords. A similar type of argument was put forward by Steyn LJ in *Trentham Ltd v Archital Luxfer* (1993). This concerned an agreement for the supply and installation of doors and windows as part of a construction contract. The work was done and paid for, but a dispute then arose, which required an analysis of whose terms governed the contract. Although there had been considerable correspondence and a number of telephone calls, there was no clear matching offer and acceptance. The trial judge held that there was acceptance by performance. Steyn LJ in the Court of Appeal agreed that this was a possible analysis, but went on to suggest that in a fully executed transaction, a contract could be found to have come into existence without the need for a precise analysis in terms of offer and acceptance. The other members of the Court agreed with Steyn LJ's judgment. *Trentham*, despite the fact that it seems to revive an approach rejected by the House of Lords in *Gibson v Manchester City Council*, indicates the possibility for arguing that, at least in certain contexts and in particular when a transaction has been completed, the courts should not be too concerned to find an offer and acceptance. Provided that there was clearly an agreement that there should be a contract between the parties (even if all of the details have not been worked out), the courts should try, wherever possible, to give effect to that.

The problems of fitting all transactions into the precise 'slots' of offer and acceptance, in both the consumer and business contexts, have been recognised by the English courts at least since the comments to this effect by Lord Wilberforce in *The Eurymedon* (1975). Nevertheless, despite the recognition of the problem, the tendency has been to try to use the traditional concepts wherever possible. What are the advantages, if any, of this over the more broadly based approach to finding agreement advocated by Lord Denning and, to some extent, by Steyn LJ? One purported advantage might be that of certainty, which the courts often put forward as a reason for adopting a particular approach towards contracts. It is felt that businesses in particular will favour clarity about the legal rules that will apply to their transactions in general over flexibility that might lead to a more 'just' solution on particular facts. Such unpredictability is thought to be undesirable.

The major disadvantage of the traditional approach, however, is that, applied strictly, it will be likely to lead in a 'battle of the forms' case to an answer that neither party would advocate – that is, that there was no contract at all. Hence the adoption of various strategies indicated in the various cases (outlined earlier in this essay) by which the courts have tried to find a contract, despite the difficulties of identifying a matching offer and acceptance.

The desirability of mechanisms having this effect is illustrated by the fact that they appear in the **Vienna Convention on the International Sale of Goods**, the **United States Uniform Commercial Code** and the **Principles of European Contract Law**. These documents provide, for example, that an 'acceptance' which contains additional, but not material, alterations may still be effective as an acceptance, and that, in the case of the **European Principles**, where there are conflicting conditions, a contract may be made on such terms as are common to the offer and acceptance. To date, however, the English courts (and in particular the House of Lords) have not fully grasped the nettle of recognising that the 'battle of the forms' requires an explicit modification of the traditional offer and acceptance rules. Until they do, the English law in this area cannot really be said to be satisfactory.

Think point

1 You might also refer here to the case of *Pars Technology Ltd v City Link Transport Holdings Ltd* (1999) as an example of a case in which the Court of Appeal did not allow a minor difference in terms to prevent a contract arising. See Stone, *The Modern Law of Contract*, 5th edn, 2002, p 39.

Question 4

Carl was browsing the Internet when he came across a site, run by OperaClassics, which was offering a set of CDs of the complete Wagner Ring Cycle at the price of £120. In accordance with the information on the site, Carl immediately sent an email to OperaClassics ordering a set of the CDs, and giving his credit card details. About 30 minutes later he found another site, run by DirectOpera, which was offering the same set of CDs for £75. He selected this set and then moved to the website's 'checkout' page. Here he was asked to fill out a form, giving his details, including his credit card number. He was then presented with a page setting out the details of his order and asking him to click on the 'confirm order' icon if he wished to proceed. Carl did so. He then immediately sent a second email to OperaClassics cancelling his previous order. Five minutes later he received an email from Opera-Classics in response to his original email, confirming that his order was being processed.

The next day Carl received an email from DirectOpera explaining that the price of £75 had been posted in error, and that the real price was £135. He also received a further email from OperaClassics stating that his second email had come too late; the processing of his order was continuing, and his credit card would be charged with £120.

Advise Carl, who wishes to hold DirectOpera to the price stated on the website, and does not wish to proceed with the transaction with OperaClassics.

Answer plan

This question requires you to apply the general principles governing the formation of contracts to the particular situation of contracting over the Internet. The dealings with OperaClassics raise the issue of contracting by email; those with DirectOpera raise the issue of contracting via a company's website.

The most important matters to be considered are as follows.

- Are the advertisements contained in the websites 'offers' or 'invitations to treat'?
- If Carl's first email to OperaClassics was an offer, was his withdrawal communicated before it had been accepted?
- If there is a contract between Carl and OperaClassics, what is the effect of the **Consumer Protection (Distance Selling) Regulations 2000**?
- Was there a concluded contract with DirectOpera for a sale at £75? If so, what constituted the offer and the acceptance?

> • What is the effect, if any, of the **Electronic Commerce (EC Directive) Regulations 2002** on this issue?

Answer

Carl has taken steps towards entering into contracts with two Internet companies for the purchase of a set of CDs. He now wishes to enforce one of these contracts and escape from the other. In deciding how to advise him, it will be necessary to consider the ways in which the rules about formation of contracts, and in particular the rules of offer and acceptance, apply to Internet transactions. There are no reported cases specifically dealing with the area of Internet contracts, so it will be a question of applying the relevant general principles to the situations set out in the problem.

In both situations, the starting point is the advertisement of goods on a website, at a stated price. The initial question is, therefore, whether these advertisements constitute 'offers' capable of 'acceptance', or whether they are simply 'invitations to treat'. A relevant authority is *Partridge v Crittenden* (1968), in which an advertisement was placed in a newspaper advertising bramblefinches for sale at 25 shillings each. It was held that this advertisement was not an 'offer' but simply an invitation to treat. Assuming that the placer of the advertisement only had a limited supply of the bramblefinches, he could not have intended to be bound to anyone who responded to the advertisement. Such responses would thus constitute offers to buy, which the advertiser would be free to accept or reject as he chose. A contrast can be drawn with the American case of *Lefkowitz v Great Minneapolis Surplus Stores* (1957), in which an advertisement stated that three mink coats were available at a shop at a special price – 'first come, first served'. This was held to constitute an offer, which could be accepted by being one of the first three people to claim a coat. In the case of both OperaClassics and DirectOpera, the form of the advertisement seems to be in line with that in *Partridge v Crittenden* rather than in *Lefkowitz v Great Minneapolis Surplus Stores*. The advertisements should therefore be viewed as invitations to treat rather than offers.

Turning now to Carl's dealings with OperaClassics, it is clear that Carl's initial email is an offer to buy the CDs at the advertised price. This is accepted by Opera-Classics in their first email to Carl. In the meantime, however, Carl has sent them a withdrawal of his offer. The answer to whether there is a contract between Carl and OperaClassics depends, therefore, on whether Carl's revocation of his offer is effective; if it is not, then OperaClassics' acceptance will be effective to create a contract. Carl's only possibility of escaping this obligation will then lie under the **Consumer Protection (Distance Selling) Regulations 2000**.

The case law on revocation of offers establishes that offers can be withdrawn at any time prior to acceptance (*Payne v Cave* (1789)), provided that the withdrawal is communicated to the offeree. The latter point was confirmed by the decision in *Byrne v van Tienhoven* (1880), which concerned the revocation of an offer by telegram. Applying this to the dealings between Carl and OperaClassics, if Opera-Classics received Carl's email before it sent its email confirming his order, then his revocation will be effective, and there will be no contract. This assumes, however, that the email is deemed to be communicated to OperaClassics as soon as it is received on its email system, and available to be read. OperaClassics might wish to argue, on the other hand, that Carl's email was not communicated, and therefore not effective, until it was read by someone at OperaClassics. There is no case law that settles this issue. In *Entores v Miles Far East Corp* (1955), it was held that, in relation to 'instantaneous' communications, they take effect at the place where they are received. In *The Brimnes* (1975), it was held that a telexed withdrawal was effective when it was printed on the recipient's telex machine, not when it was actually read. In *Brinkibon Ltd v Stahag Stahl* (1983), however, the House of Lords refused to confirm any hard-and-fast rule, taking the view that the intentions of the parties and 'business practice' must be taken into account in deciding when such a communication is effective. If it is sent out of normal office hours, for example, it might not be treated as being communicated until the point when the office would be expected to reopen. These cases were concerned with telexes. Should the same approach apply to email? There seems no good reason why not, unless it is felt that emails are not in practice read as quickly as telex communications. In the absence of other authority, the test should probably be that the email communication should be taken to be read at the point when the sender would reasonably expect this to occur. When sending an email to a business in normal office hours, it would generally be reasonable to expect that it will be read almost as soon as it arrives.

If this approach is applied to the problem, then, in the absence of any more precise information about when the emails were sent, received and read, it would favour Carl, since OperaClassics' acceptance of his offer is not received by him until after the point when his withdrawal would have been received by OperaClassics.

There is one other issue, however, which needs brief consideration: whether the 'postal rule' derived from *Adams v Lindsell* (1818) applies to emails. This states that an acceptance sent by post, where post is a reasonable means of communication, will take effect on posting rather than receipt. If this is applied here it would require even further investigation as to the precise timings of the various communications. Fortunately, it was made clear in *Entores v Miles Far East Corp* that the postal rule does not apply to instantaneous communications. It is generally agreed that this will cover email, and so the time of communication, rather than the time of sending, is the relevant time. This will not therefore help OperaClassics.

Overall, then, as regards Carl's dealings with OperaClassics, he can be advised that on the facts as stated he has effectively withdrawn his offer before it was accepted by OperaClassics. He is not bound to the contract with the company, and is entitled to instruct his credit card company not to make the payment to OperaClassics.

However, even if the analysis of Carl's dealings with OperaClassics leads to the conclusion that there is a contract, he will probably be able to escape from this by virtue of the **Consumer Protection (Distance Selling) Regulations 2000**. These apply to contracts made by a 'consumer' (this will cover Carl) when there is no face-to-face contact with the seller of goods or supplier of services. They will therefore apply to most Internet transactions. Where they do apply, the consumer is given the right to cancel the contract by giving written notice. The right lasts until seven days after goods have been received. Carl will therefore be able to escape from any contract with OperaClassics by exercising his rights under these Regulations.

Turning to Carl's dealings with DirectOpera, in this case Carl is trying to argue that there is a contract, based on the originally quoted price of £75. As has been established above, the advertisement on the website is an invitation to treat. Carl responds to this by filling in and submitting a form detailing his order and the method of payment. This may be regarded as an offer to buy the goods at the stated price. At this stage, DirectOpera would be free to accept or reject Carl's offer. If, for example, it was unhappy with his credit card details, or had at this stage realised that a mistake had been made with regard to the price quoted, DirectOpera could have withdrawn from the transaction. What happens, however, is that it displays a page setting out the details of Carl's order and asking if he wishes to continue. This is not an acceptance of Carl's offer, since it is allowing him the opportunity to back out. It might well be regarded as a further offer to enter into a contract on the terms stated. Carl could then be treated as accepting this offer by clicking on the 'confirm order' icon. DirectOpera will no doubt wish to argue that this was not an acceptance, but simply a restatement of Carl's offer, which DirectOpera was still free to accept or reject. On the basis of the general approach by the English courts to questions of offer and acceptance, there seems no reason why there should be this further stage. All the terms of the contract have been agreed, and the presentation of the page setting out Carl's order would surely be taken by a reasonable person as indicating that DirectOpera was prepared to contract on these terms.

The **Electronic Commerce (EC Directive) Regulations 2002** may, however, give some support to DirectOpera's preferred analysis. **Regulation 11(1)(b)** states that a service provider (which in this case would be DirectOpera) shall make available to the recipient of the service (that is, Carl) 'appropriate, effective and accessible technical means allowing him to identify and correct input errors prior to the placing of an order'. **Regulation 12** then provides that 'order' in **reg 11(1)(b)** means 'the contractual offer'. DirectOpera will thus wish to argue that the screen that it displays in response to Carl's initial 'order' is simply fulfilling the requirements of **reg 11(1)(b)**, and that **reg 12** means that this must be taken as preceding 'the contractual offer'. The 'contractual offer' then becomes Carl's clicking of the button confirming that he is happy with the terms set out on the page presented to him. So although the

Regulations do not on their face purport to affect the rules of offer and acceptance, it is clearly arguable here that a different result will obtain under the Regulations than would have been the case at common law. At common law, as argued above, Carl's clicking of the button could be treated as an acceptance; under the Regulations it is treated as 'the contractual offer' – which DirectOpera is therefore free to accept or reject. The result is, since the Regulations must prevail over the common law, that Carl will probably not be able to claim his CDs at the 'bargain' price.

Question 5

Julia, who lives in New Street, owns a first edition of George Orwell's novel, *1984*. On Monday, she contacts her friend, Winston, who collects rare books, and asks if he would be prepared to buy it for £2,500. Winston says that he would like to buy it, but needs a few days to get the money together. Julia says that she will keep her offer open until 12 noon on Friday, but that if Winston cannot come up with the cash by then, she will look elsewhere for a buyer.

On Wednesday evening, Winston is in the pub, when he sees his friend Eric, who is also interested in rare books. He tells Eric that he is going to buy Julia's copy of *1984*. Eric tells Winston that he has just seen O'Brien, who is a book dealer. He says that O'Brien had told him that he had just agreed on the telephone to buy a first edition of *1984* from a 'lady who lives in New Street', and that he was going to pick it up the next day at 4 pm.

On Thursday morning, Winston manages to obtain £2,500 in cash and goes to Julia's house at 12 noon. Julia tells Winston that she has already sold the book to O'Brien, and so cannot sell to Winston.

Advise Winston.

Answer plan

There are three main issues in this question, as follows.

- What is the effect of a statement that an offer is to be held open until a particular date? – *Routledge v Grant* (1828) is a relevant authority.
- Can a statement that an offer will be held open in this way amount to a unilateral contract? – The case of *Daulia Ltd v Four Millbank Nominees* (1978) will be the most relevant authority.
- Is an indirect notification of the withdrawal of an offer effective? – The case of *Dickinson v Dodds* (1876) will need consideration.

The following order of treatment is suggested:

- identification of the issues;
- statement of general rules re:
  - keeping offers open;
  - revoking offers;
- application of general rules to the particular facts:
  - Julia not obliged to keep the offer open, unless perhaps it constitutes a unilateral contract;
  - revocation of offer communicated via Eric may well be effective – provided that Eric is a reliable source;
- conclusion as to advice to Winston:
  - probably needs to argue that it is a unilateral contract, if he is to be able to prove a binding contract with Julia for the sale of the book.

Answer

This problem is concerned with the situations in which offers can be revoked. In particular, it raises questions about the extent to which a promise to keep an offer for a particular period is binding, the manner in which revocation of an offer is communicated, and whether an offer in a unilateral contract can be revoked.

The basic rule is that an offer can be revoked at any time before it has been accepted. In this case Julia has told Winston that she will keep her offer open until noon on the Friday, but then appears to have agreed to sell it to O'Brien before that date. Is she bound by her promise to keep the offer to Winston open? This issue was dealt with in the case of *Routledge v Grant* (1828), in which it was held that a promise of this kind will not generally be binding. The reason is that the promisee will generally not have provided any consideration for the promise. If Winston had given Julia £5 in return for her agreeing to keep the offer open, then he would have provided consideration, and would be able to hold her to the promise. So it seems Julia is free to revoke her offer; to be effective, however, a revocation of an offer has to be communicated to the offeree. A decision by the offeror to withdraw the offer, and even the making of an alternative contract with a third party, is not sufficient, if the offeror has not informed the offeree of this. The requirement of communication can be deduced from the decision in *Byrne v van Tienhoven* (1880), in which it was held that a telegram containing a revocation did not have effect until it was received by the offeree. If Julia had telephoned Winston, or sent him letter, and he had received the phone call or letter before midday on the Friday, then, subject to the possibility of there being a unilateral contract (discussed below), it seems that she would have been able to withdraw her offer to him. She does not do this. On the other hand, Winston is given information by Eric on the Wednesday evening that appears to indicate that Julia has already sold the book. The information is not explicit, but it is highly unlikely that there would be more than one 'lady who lives in New Street' trying to sell a first edition of *1984* at the same time. Is the receipt of this information sufficient to amount to notification to Winston that Julia has withdrawn her offer? The relevant authority in relation to this type of situation is the case of *Dickinson v Dodds* (1876). In this case the facts were similar to those of the problem. On 10 June, Dodds offered to sell a property to Dickinson, with the offer to be held open until 12 June. On 11 June, Dickinson learnt from a third party that Dodds was negotiating with Allan. Dickinson made several attempts on the afternoon of 11 June and the morning of 12 June to communicate his acceptance to Dodds, but Dodds had already sold to Allan before he was aware of Dickinson's acceptance. It was held that the offer had been withdrawn before Dickinson had effectively accepted. Two points emerge from this. First, it does not seem to matter how the revocation comes to the attention of the offeree – provided that the offeree is aware that the offer has been withdrawn, it cannot be accepted. Second, in *Dickinson v Dodds* it seemed to be enough that the offeree was aware that the offeror was *negotiating* with a third party for the revocation to be effective. He did not need to know that the property had actually been sold elsewhere. Both of these points are unhelpful to Winston. He has fairly clear information that Julia is dealing with a third party over the book – even though this comes third-hand, via O'Brien and Eric. Moreover, the information is that Julia has actually completed a contract with O'Brien, rather than simply negotiating with him.

Winston might try to suggest that the conversation with Eric, taking place in a pub, was not necessarily one which involved reliable information, and so should not result in it being treated as an effective withdrawal. In *Dickinson v Dodds*, the source of the information was not simply an acquaintance, but someone who had been involved in the offeree's business. It is unlikely, however, that a court would place much weight on this distinction, as it was not a point given any emphasis in *Dickinson v Dodds* itself.

A further possibility that Winston could pursue would be to suggest that there was in effect a contract made on the Monday. The contract was not, however, one in which Julia bound herself to sell the book to Winston, but a unilateral contract in which she said: 'If you come to me with £2,500 in cash on Friday, I promise to sell the book to you.' If this analysis was possible, then Winston could draw analogies with the cases of *Errington v Errington and Woods* (1941) and *Daulia Ltd v Four Millbank Nominees* (1978). In *Errington*, a father had told his son and daughter-in-law that if they paid-off the mortgage on a house that he owned, he would transfer ownership to them. It was held that once they had started to make the mortgage payments, this offer could not be withdrawn. In *Daulia*, the parties were negotiating over the sale of a property. The seller told the prospective buyer that if he turned up the next morning with a signed contract and a banker's draft, the seller would go ahead with the sale. The Court of Appeal, although deciding the case on other grounds, suggested that the seller would not have been able to withdraw this offer without giving the offeree a proper chance to complete his side of the arrangement.

Applying this to Winston's case, he would need to argue that there was a unilateral contract of the kind outlined above, and that Julia was aware that he was attempting to fulfil his side of it. If that was accepted, then on the basis of *Errington v Errington* and the *obiter dicta* in *Daulia Ltd v Four Millbank Nominees*, he could argue that Julia was not free to make any contract with O'Brien until 12 noon on the Friday, or until Winston indicated to her that he was no longer attempting to raise the money. It has to be said, however, that the court might well not regard the conversation that took place on the Monday as leading to a unilateral contract, because it is not clear that what Winston was trying to do would amount to consideration for Julia's promise. In *Errington*, the payment of the mortgage was a clear benefit to the father; in *Daulia*, the benefit would have been a quick sale, with all of the burden of putting together the documentation undertaken by the purchaser. Here, it is much less clear what benefit there would be to Julia in this arrangement. It may well be that the unilateral argument will fail on this basis.

A final argument that might be put forward for Winston is that the conversation on Monday resulted in a binding bilateral contract for the sale of the book at £2,500, with Winston simply being given time to pay. The way that the discussions are reported, however, would not support such an analysis, since it is in terms of Julia 'keeping the offer open' rather than giving Winston time to pay on an agreed contract.

In conclusion, therefore, it seems unlikely that Winston will be able to compel Julia to sell him the book, since her offer has probably been effectively withdrawn by the time Winston tries to accept. His best possibility is to argue for a unilateral contract, but as has been indicated, even this line does not have a high likelihood of success. On balance, the most likely outcome is that Winston will be left without a remedy.

CHAPTER 2

INTENTION AND CONSIDERATION

INTRODUCTION

The two other elements, apart from offer and acceptance, which the courts look for in relation to the formation of contracts, are intention and consideration, and the questions in this chapter deal with these.

The issue of intention to create legal relations is very straightforward. There are two basic rules:

- if the contract is a 'domestic' agreement, then there is a presumption that there is no intention to create legal relations (*Balfour v Balfour* (1919)); and
- if the contract is 'commercial' in nature, then there is a presumption that it is intended to be legally binding (*Edwards v Skyways* (1964)).

All that needs to be done is to apply these to the facts of any problem asked, and consider whether there is any reason why the presumption should be rebutted. Because it is such a simple issue, questions about intention will rarely, if ever, stand alone, but will be contained within some other topic. Here, intention is linked with consideration, which is quite common in contract questions.

The topic of consideration, by way of contrast, is definitely difficult. Some aspects are, however, reasonably straightforward. It is not too difficult to learn the rules and the cases relating to:

- the difference between 'adequate' and 'sufficient' consideration – what kinds of actions or promises can or cannot amount to consideration – the general irrelevance of the value of consideration (for example, *Chappell v Nestlé* (1960));
- past consideration – the reformulation of the rules relating to this in *Pao On v Lau Yiu Long* (1979) needs to be learnt and understood; and
- existing obligations as consideration – whether owed to the public, a third party, or the other contracting party. Here, the case of *Williams v Roffey* (1990), and its effect on *Stilk v Myrick* (1809), will need to be considered.

Where things start to become more difficult, however, is in relation to the variation of contracts, and how the doctrine of consideration applies to this. Once again, the implications of *Williams v Roffey* (1990) need to be considered, but more generally the whole topic of 'promissory estoppel' must be faced. Promissory estoppel is a topic that students do not like. If you are going to prepare yourself to deal with questions on consideration, however, it is something with which you will have to get to grips. Four out of the five questions in this chapter raise promissory estoppel issues in one way or another. The points that need to be understood are:

- the basic elements of the doctrine as laid down by Lord Denning in *Central London Property Trust v High Trees House* (1947);

- the origins of the doctrine in the nineteenth-century 'waiver' cases, such as *Hughes v Metropolitan Railway* (1877);

- the limitations on promissory estoppel derived from post-*High Trees* cases, such as *Combe v Combe* (1919) ('shield not a sword') and *D & C Builders v Rees* (1966) (must be equitable to use it);

- the relationship between *High Trees* and the cases on part-payment of debts, such as *Pinnel's Case* (1602) and *Foakes v Beer* (1884); and

- the unresolved problem of whether the doctrine is only suspensory of rights, or whether it can have an extinctive effect.

None of these points is easy. In relation to some of them, it has to be accepted that there is no clear answer from the case law, and you must therefore argue from general principles. You should not be afraid to do this. Whatever the conclusion arrived at, if the argument is presented carefully, logically and consistently with the cases, it will be likely to obtain high marks.

Checklist

You should be familiar with the following areas:

- intention to create legal relations – the presumptions applying to domestic and commercial agreements;

- the meaning of 'consideration';

- the difference between 'adequate' and 'sufficient' consideration;

- past consideration, and when it can be effective;

- existing duties, and when they can amount to good consideration for a fresh promise. The rules relating to public duties, contractual duties owed to a third party, and contractual duties owed to the promisor, all need to be understood; and

- promissory estoppel – its origins, development and limitations.

Question 6

On Friday, Laura visited Sarah's hairdressing salon, because she wanted her hair to look special for a party she was going to that evening. When Sarah had finished, Laura was so pleased with what she had done that she said that she would give Sarah an extra £20. She then found that she did not have enough money with her to do so, and said she would call in on Monday to give it to Sarah.

On Saturday, Laura agreed with her friends, Ted and Simon, that they would go the local greyhound racing track that evening. When they were on their way to the track Ted said: 'If any of us makes a killing, let's say more than £100 over the evening, how about we share the winnings?' The others both agreed that this was a good suggestion. At the track, Simon was lucky in all his bets, and at the end of the evening had won £600. He then denied that he had agreed to share his winnings, and refused to make any payment to Laura or Ted.

On Sunday, Laura visited her neighbour, an elderly man called Brian. Brian was lonely because his wife had gone to visit relatives in Australia, and would be away for two months. Brian said that if Laura would come and sit with him every Sunday afternoon while his wife is away, he would, in return for her kindness, give her his valuable grandfather clock, which he knew that Laura had always admired, but which Brian's wife had always disliked.

On Monday, Laura seeks your advice as to (a) whether she is obliged to pay the £20 to Sarah (since Laura is now short of money after her visit to the dog track), (b) whether she can compel Simon to pay her a share of his winnings, and (c) whether Brian's promise to give her the clock is legally binding.

Answer plan

This question involves issues of intention to create legal relations and consideration, arising out of three potential contracts.

(a) The offer to pay Sarah the £20 raises the issue of past consideration. The basic principle, as stated in, for example, *Re McArdle* (1951) needs to be stated, followed by discussion of whether the exceptions to it, as set out in *Pao On v Lau Yiu Long* (1980) can apply here. There is no issue of intention to create legal relations really here – the relationship between Laura and Sarah is commercial, and there is no reason why an agreement that has the other characteristics of a contract should not be binding.

(b) The main issue here is intention to create legal relations. The agreement to share the winnings is made in a social setting, so the presumption is likely to be that it was not intended to be legally binding. The case of *Simpkins*

> *v Pays* (1955) and the recent Court of Appeal decision in *Wilson v Burnett* (2007) will need discussion.
>
> (c) Again, one of the questions in relation to Brian's promise will be whether it is intended to be legally binding. There is also, however, the question of whether Laura is providing any consideration. 'Kindness' is unlikely to be enough – see *Thomas v Thomas* (1842) – since consideration is generally said to require some economic value. Is Laura providing something that falls into this category?

Answer

There are three potential contracts to consider here, and they will be looked at in turn. The issues that arise for discussion are (i) whether there was valid consideration for the promises that were made, and (ii) whether the promises were intended to create a legal relationship.

(a) The first promise to consider is Laura's to Tracy, where she says that she will give her £20 because she is so pleased with the way in which Tracy has done her hair. The relationship between Laura and Tracy is a commercial one – Tracy is providing a service for a fee – and so it will be presumed that any agreement in contractual form will be intended to be legally binding: *Edwards v Skyways* (1964). The main problem here is the question of consideration. Laura has made a promise to pay £20. What is the consideration provided by Tracy for that promise? The answer is that it is doing Laura's hair. But Tracy has already completed that task before Laura makes her promise. This raises the issue of 'past consideration'. The general approach of English law to this issue is that if a promise is made after work has been done, or some other benefit conferred, that work or benefit is not consideration for the promise, which is therefore unenforceable. This is a result of the idea of contract involving a mutual exchange. How can work be given in return for a promise if the promise is not made until after the work is completed? An example of the application of this rule is *Re McArdle* (1951). Two members of a family, who were living in a house that had been left jointly to them and other members of the family, did some improvements on it, and then sought promises to contribute to the costs of the work from their relatives. It was held that they could not enforce the relatives' promises to pay, since they were given after the work was completed. The work was therefore past consideration and could not be relied on.

The courts have recognised, however, that this rule can operate harshly in certain circumstances and have therefore formulated an exception to it. The principles derived from the earlier case law have now been restated in *Pao On v Lau Yiu Long* (1980) in the following way:

(i) the act must have been done at the promisor's request – this derives from *Lampleigh v Braithwait* (1615);

(ii) the parties must have anticipated at the time the work was done that it was to be paid for – this derives from *Re Casey's Patents* (1892); and

(iii) the promise must have been legally enforceable if it had been made in advance.

Applying these requirements to Laura and Tracy, it is clear that if Laura had promised Tracy before she started that she would pay her extra if she was very pleased with the result, this would have been enforceable. Requirement (iii) is clearly met. The other two are more debateable. Although Laura asked Tracy to do her hair, she did not presumably ask her to make a specially good job of it. Similarly, although it was expected that the work would be paid for, was it expected that Laura would pay extra if it were done particularly well? In relation to both of these aspects there are doubts that the requirements set out in (i) and (ii) are met.

On balance, it is submitted that since Tracy would not have expected to be paid extra for doing a very good job, the promise by Laura should be considered to be unsupported by consideration, and therefore unenforceable by Tracy.[1]

(b) The main issue in the agreement between the three friends is not one of consideration. They were each promising to share their winnings, and a mutual exchange of promises of this kind will be sufficient to satisfy the requirements of consideration: *Dunlop Pneumatic Tyre Co Ltd v Selfridge & Co Ltd* (1915). The difficulty for Laura and Ted is whether the agreement can be said to be intended to create legal relations.

The legal principles in this area derive from the case of *Balfour v Balfour* (1919). In this case, a husband and wife had to separate because the wife was not well enough to travel back to the husband's place of work (Ceylon). The husband promised to pay her £30 per month. When he failed to keep up the payments, she sued. The court held that she could not succeed because there had been no intention to create legal relations.[2] Lord Atkin said that in the case of social and domestic arrangements, there was a presumption against there being an intention to create legal relations. This presumption could be rebutted but in this case there was no evidence to suggest that it should be, and the wife's action therefore failed.[3]

This case has been taken as the basis of a general principle that agreements made in domestic or social contexts are presumed not to be binding. In this case, therefore, the burden will be on Laura to prove that the agreement between the three friends was intended to be binding. Two cases with similar facts to the problem need to be considered: the first is *Simpkins v Pays* (1955). Three women who lived in the same house regularly entered a newspaper competition, submitting three entries on the one form, and sharing the cost of the entrance fee. When one of the entries won, the other two women claimed that there was an agreement to share any winnings. The court held in their favour, deciding that the arrangement went beyond the kind of informal agreement that might exist in a family context. There was a clear understanding as to what was to happen in the event of a win, and this was enforceable. This case is obviously helpful to Laura. The second one is less so. In *Wilson v Burnett* (2007) three young women who worked together decided to have an evening at the local bingo hall. One of them won a national prize, worth over £100,000. The other two claimed that there had been a prior agreement between the three that any prize of over £10 would be shared between them. The Court of Appeal upheld the trial judge's decision that there was no binding agreement. It took the view that the women's 'chat' about sharing winnings had not crossed the line to where it could be regarded as intended to create a legally binding relationship. The claimants had not satisfied the burden of proof required to overturn the presumption.

Applying this to Laura, it seems that she may well have difficulties with her claim. The discussion was related to a 'one-off' situation, rather than a long-standing arrangement as in *Simpkins v Pays*. The nature of the agreement is also rather sketchy, on the basis of the facts in the problem. Was it supposed to be a straight three-way split of any winnings, or some other division? Given that the burden is on Laura to overturn the presumption of non-enforceability, it seems unlikely that she will be successful.

(c) The third situation concerns Brian's promise to give the clock to Laura. This is in the form of a unilateral contract – that is, Brian will only have to fulfil his promise once Laura has done what he has requested. Two possible questions arise. First, did Brian intend his promise to be legally enforceable? Second, will Laura's actions provide valid consideration?

On the first point, the general principle has been set out in the answer to (b). It is probably correct to regard this as a 'domestic' arrangement between friends, and so the burden will be on Laura to prove that it was intended to be binding. She has more chance of doing so here than in (b), in that Brian appears to be genuinely wishing to make a definite agreement, and is asking for something from Laura in return. This brings us to the second issue, which is whether Laura will be deemed to have provided good consideration.

The doctrine of consideration is fundamental to English contract law. It requires that, for a promise to be binding, something must be given or done in exchange by the promisee. One of the requirements of consideration is sometimes said to be that it must be of some economic value. For example, in the case of *White v Bluett* (1853), it was held that a son who promised to stop complaining provided no consideration for a promise by his father not to enforce a promissory note. In *Thomas v Thomas* (1842), it was held that doing something 'in consideration of' the other party's wishes was not sufficient, because consideration must have some value. Brian has referred to giving her the clock in return for Laura's 'kindness'. This will clearly not be enough in itself to establish consideration. There is more to the proposed agreement than this, however. Laura is being asked to give up her time to sit with Brian on a number of Sunday afternoons. This is a service that Brian could pay someone to provide. Laura is being asked to provide it without payment, but she is being offered the clock on the conclusion of the arrangement. This commitment of time by Laura would seem sufficient to constitute consideration. As long as Laura fulfils her side of the arrangement, and sits with Brian as requested, she will have a strong argument for insisting that he gives her the clock.

In conclusion, the first two situations do not seem to involve contractual obligations. In (a), Tracy has not provided any consideration for Laura's promise, whereas in (b), it is unlikely that there is any intention to create legal relations. The third situation, however, probably is intended to be legally binding, and Laura's actions (if carried out) will be sufficient to constitute valid consideration.

Think points

1 Do you think that the answer would be different if Laura had made it clear from the start that she wanted Tracy to try to do something special with her hair, although without explicitly promising to pay her extra if she did so?

2 Can you think of any other reason why Mr Balfour's promise might not be enforceable? Two members of the Court of Appeal thought that it was unlikely that Mrs Balfour provided any consideration for her husband's promise.

3 Would it have made a difference if the marriage had been breaking down at the time that Mr Balfour made his promise? Yes, as is shown by *Merritt v Merritt* (1970), in which the presumption against intention was overturned.

Question 7

Charles contracts to supply Peter with 10,000 widgets per month for 24 months, for a fixed sum of £20,000, payable in advance. After six months, the market price of widgets unexpectedly doubles, due to the outbreak of war in Ruritania (the main widget-producing country). Peter, hearing that as a result of this Charles has started to cancel similar contracts, suggests to Charles that he will be prepared to take 7,000 widgets per month in satisfaction of their contract. Charles agrees, and delivers 7,000 widgets per month for the next five months. The war in Ruritania then ends and the market price of widgets collapses. Peter now demands: (a) the 15,000 shortfall in widget deliveries in relation to the past five months; and (b) 10,000 widgets per month for the rest of the contract.

Advise Charles.

Answer plan

This question raises in a fairly straightforward way the issue of equitable waiver, or promissory estoppel. Note that the problem does not involve part-payment of a debt. The dispute is about the number of widgets to be supplied, not the amount to be paid for them. There is thus no need to discuss *Pinnel's Case* (1602) or *Foakes v Beer* (1884), or their relationship to promissory estoppel.

In this and similar questions, however, it is important to consider whether there is a binding variation of contract supported by consideration, as well as discussing the promissory estoppel issue.

The topics to be covered are therefore:

• the possibility of a binding variation;

• the requirements for promissory estoppel;

• the limitations of promissory estoppel – in particular, whether it is suspensory or extinctive in effect; and

• if promissory estoppel is suspensory, how its effect is terminated.

Answer

The dispute between Charles and Peter raises the issue of how a contract can be varied once it has been agreed. To explain this, and how it affects this situation, it will be necessary to consider the related issues of the doctrine of consideration and the concept of promissory estoppel.

The standard approach of English contract law is to say that a variation of an existing contract will only be binding if there is consideration to support it. In other words, the change in obligations must not be one-sided. If the reduction of the number of the widgets delivered had been accompanied by a drop in the purchase price, there would be no argument that the new arrangements were enforceable by both sides. Both Peter and Charles would have changed their position, and there would in effect be a new binding contract on the new terms. Turning to the facts of the problem, can we find any consideration for Charles' agreement to supply a smaller quantity of widgets? At first sight, the answer would seem to be 'no'. Charles has not agreed to a reduction in price, or any other change of the agreement with Peter, which would be a benefit to Peter, or a detriment to Charles. On the contrary, the change appears to be made for Charles' benefit. On closer examination, however, the position is not so straightforward. The reason why Peter suggests the reduction is that he hears that Charles is cancelling similar contracts, and he presumably wishes to avoid this happening to his contract. Two possibilities exist here. The first is that the contract between Charles and Peter contains a provision that would allow Charles to cancel it without being in breach. If this is the case, then there is a strong argument for there being a binding variation. The benefit to Peter would be keeping the contract alive in some form, rather than being in a situation in which he might have had to look elsewhere for his entire supply of widgets. There is also detriment to Charles in that he is still getting a lower price for his widgets than he might get on the open market. The second possibility is that if Charles cancels the agreement, it would be a breach of contract. Here, the argument for the change amounting to consideration is weaker. It is not, however, ruled out altogether. In *Williams v Roffey* (1990), the Court of Appeal was prepared to accept that the benefit to a contracting party (the defendant) of preventing the other side from failing to complete the contract could be good consideration for a promise by the defendant of extra payments on completion. If this line of reasoning is accepted, then there is an argument for saying that there is a binding variation here.

Two further points need to be noted. First, it is important for the argument for a binding variation that the initiative for changing the contract came from Peter. If Charles had come to Peter and said 'if you don't agree to a change, I am going to cancel our agreement', this would have amounted almost to duress, and the courts would be unlikely to look sympathetically on Charles' claim for a binding change. This point was regarded as important in *Williams v Roffey*. Second, if there is a binding variation, this means that Charles can reject both of Peter's claims. The contract will have been varied with permanent effect, and if Peter wishes to return to the previous terms he will have to negotiate another mutually acceptable variation.

Let us now turn to the situation if it is decided that there is no consideration and, therefore, no binding variation. Here, Charles will only have a basis for resisting Peter's claim if he can invoke the doctrine of promissory estoppel. It has been recognised by the courts for over a hundred years that in certain circumstances an indication by a contracting party, by words or actions, that he is not going to insist on his strict contractual rights can be binding on him, at least to some extent. In *Hughes v Metropolitan Railway* (1877), the actions of the plaintiff had led the defendant reasonably to believe that a period of notice to quit that had been issued had been waived. The defendant had relied on this, and the House of Lords took the view that the plaintiff could not simply bring the waiver to an end and impose the notice to quit without more ado. This idea of 'equitable waiver' has developed into the modern doctrine of 'promissory estoppel' following the decision of Denning J in *Central London Property Trust v High Trees House* (1947). As stated in that case by Denning, the doctrine is that 'a promise intended to be binding, intended to be acted upon, and in fact acted upon, is binding insofar as its terms properly apply'. The promise that Denning was considering here was to reduce the rent on a block of flats during part of the Second World War, which had led to many of the flats being unoccupied.

Denning felt that this promise was binding, in that the landlord should not, at the end of the war, be able to go back on it, and claim the full rent for the war years.

As stated above, Denning's definition is too wide. Taken at face value, it would destroy the whole doctrine of consideration.[1] Various limitations to the doctrine have now been recognised.

First, there must be an existing legal relationship between the parties – probably, but not inevitably, a contract. In other words, the doctrine is concerned with the variation of legal obligations, rather than their creation. This links in with the second limitation, that promissory estoppel can only be used 'as a shield, and not as a sword'. This famous phrase comes from *Combe v Combe* (1951). A husband who was divorcing his wife made a promise to pay her £100 per annum. When he failed to do so, she sued. The judge at first instance allowed her to succeed, although she had provided no consideration for the promise, on the basis of promissory estoppel. The Court of Appeal held that this was a misuse of the doctrine, which could not create new legal rights.

The third limitation is that the doctrine will only be applied where it would be inequitable to allow the promisor to go back on the promise. Two cases are relevant here. In *D & C Builders v Rees* (1966), Lord Denning said that the doctrine should not be used where the promise had been extracted by improper pressure. The defendants had persuaded the plaintiffs to accept less than they were owed by a threat that if they did not accept they would get nothing. In *The Post Chaser* (1981), there was no impropriety on the part of the promisee, but Lord Goff thought that there was such a short period between the making of the promise and its withdrawal (a matter of days) that it was not inequitable to allow the promisor to escape from it.

The final possible limitation is that the doctrine only suspends rights, rather than extinguishing them. This is certainly what happened in *Hughes* and in *High Trees*. It is not clear whether this is a general rule, however, or something that depends on the individual circumstances of each case. One other point needs to be clarified. The promise itself may be expressed to be only applicable for a limited period. This was what Lord Denning meant by referring to the promise being binding 'as far as its terms properly apply'. In *High Trees*, the promise was taken to have been stated to be applicable only while the Second World War continued and the flats were not fully occupied. Once these conditions ceased to exist, the original terms automatically revived. If no limit is placed on the promise when it was made, it may still be terminable by notice. This was the case in *Tool Metal Manufacturing Co v Tungsten Electric Co* (1955). The House of Lords held that the initiation of a previous action amounted to notice that the promise (to accept a reduced royalty) was being withdrawn. For continuing contracts that involve periodic obligations, it seems then that rights which would have otherwise accrued during the currency of the promise will be lost; for the future, the previous position may be revived, either by the automatic termination of the promise or by giving notice.[2]

Applying this to the problem, we find a promise intended to be binding, intended to be acted upon, and in fact acted upon. It is a variation of an existing legal relationship, and Charles wishes to use it as a shield not a sword. The two remaining issues are related to the suspensory nature of the doctrine, and whether it would be inequitable to allow Peter to go back on it.

Dealing with the second issue first, it is significant here, as it was in relation to the argument about consideration, that the request for the change came from Peter. Had Charles in any sense been holding Peter to ransom, then Lord Denning's comments in *D & C Builders v Rees* might well have applied. This is not the case, however, and there seems no reason on the facts why equity should allow Peter to escape from his promise.

This leaves the issue of the duration of the promise. Peter may well wish to argue that the promise was only intended to last as long as the war in Ruritania continued. If that is right, he can insist on a return to 10,000 widgets per month for the future. There is no suggestion on the facts as given, however, that the promise was made in this form. This will mean, therefore, that Peter will have to give reasonable notice of his intention to return to the original terms, as in *Tool Metal v Tungsten*. What constitutes 'reasonable notice' must be a question of fact in each case. Looking at the overall duration of this contract, it is suggested that notice of two months would be perfectly reasonable.

In conclusion, the advice to Charles is that he does not have to provide the 15,000 shortfall in deliveries. This is because there has either been a binding variation, or Peter is estopped from going back on this part of his promise. As regards the future, there are three possibilities:

(a) there has been a binding variation, and so Charles can continue to supply 7,000 widgets a month for the rest of the contract;

(b) there is a promissory estoppel, which will come to an end at the end of the war in Ruritania – Charles will in this case have to return to 10,000 widgets a month immediately; and

(c) there is a promissory estoppel, determinable on Peter's giving reasonable notice – which would probably be two months.

It is submitted that, on the basis of the facts given, there is no clear evidence of consideration to support a binding variation, or that the promise was expressed to last only for the duration of the war. As a result, (c) above would seem to be the most likely outcome to this dispute, and Charles should be advised accordingly.

Think points

1 This may have been Denning's intention – see his comments on the case in *The Discipline of Law*, 1979, Pt 5 – but he backed away from going this far in later cases.

2 How does this apply to single obligation contracts? If promissory estoppel has any effect, it must surely be to extinguish the obligation completely.

Question 8

'The doctrine of promissory estoppel cannot be regarded as casting doubt on the decision in *Foakes v Beer* (1884). If that case were to occur today, the House of Lords would decide it in exactly the same way.'

Discuss.

Answer plan

This is a fairly straightforward essay question, in which the main topic is the doctrine of 'promissory estoppel'. The particular issue on which your answer should focus, however, is the relationship between that doctrine and the part-payment of debts, and in particular the extent to which the principles applied in *Foakes v Beer* would still be used if similar facts were to arise today.

To answer the question properly, it is of course necessary to have a reasonable understanding of the facts of *Foakes v Beer*, and the reasons that the House of Lords gave for deciding it in the creditor's favour. The extent to which promissory estoppel has developed into a concept that might now provide a direct challenge to this decision must then be discussed.

The following order of treatment is suggested:

• a description of *Foakes v Beer*;
• an outline of the development of promissory estoppel;
• the particular significance of promissory estoppel for part-payment of debts;
• the relationship between promissory estoppel and *Foakes v Beer*; and
• the likely attitude of the House of Lords to *Foakes v Beer* today.

Answer

Foakes v Beer (1884) concerned an action to recover interest on a judgment debt. Mrs Beer had obtained judgment against Dr Foakes. They made an arrangement under which Dr Foakes was to pay off the debt by instalments. When he had completed the instalments, Mrs Beer sued to recover interest on the debt. In holding that she was entitled to recover, the House of Lords confirmed a rule that had originally been stated in *Pinnel's Case* (1602). This was that part-payment of a debt on the due date can never be satisfaction for the full amount owed. If, however, the creditor agrees to early payment or payment by means of goods (even though worth less than the full amount), or even payment on the day at a different place, then the debt will be discharged. The reason for this is that payment in a different form will provide consideration for the promise to accept less than was owed.

The confirmation given to this principle by the House of Lords in *Foakes v Beer* ensured its acceptance[1] until the intervention of Denning J in *Central London Property Trust v High Trees House* (1947). The owners of a block of flats in London agreed that the lessees could pay a reduced rent during the Second World War because of the difficulty in subletting the flats. When, after the war, they brought an action to enforce the contract on its original terms, Denning J indicated that they would not be able to recover for the 'war years', although they could subsequently revert to the original agreement. Denning's statement on this issue was clearly obiter, since the action brought only applied to the period after the end of the war, but it was regarded as a challenge to the decision in *Foakes v Beer*. According to the original contract, the defendants in *High Trees* owed money to the plaintiffs for the war years. There was no consideration for the promise to accept less. Under *Foakes v Beer*, therefore, the plaintiffs appeared to have an unanswerable case.

Denning, however, felt that the effect of *Foakes v Beer* could be circumvented by using an equitable doctrine that he traced back to the case of *Hughes v Metropolitan Railway* (1877). In this case, the owners of some houses gave notice to the tenants to carry out repairs within six months. If the repairs were not done within that period, the landlord was entitled to forfeit the lease. Shortly after the notice was given, however, the parties entered into negotiations for the sale of the property to the tenants. These negotiations collapsed, and the landlord sought to forfeit the lease in accordance with the terms of his original notice. The House of Lords said that he could not. His actions in entering into the negotiations had to be taken as indicating that he was 'waiving' the notice while the negotiations continued. The courts of equity would not allow him to go back on this indication of waiver, on which the defendant had relied. In effect, the notice to repair was suspended while the negotiations were going on, and time only began to run again when they ceased.

In *High Trees*, Lord Denning took this principle from *Hughes v Metropolitan Railway*, which has since come to be known as 'promissory estoppel', and applied it to the case before him. He said that in both cases there had been a promise made that was intended to be binding, intended to be acted on, and in fact acted on. Such a promise should be binding, insofar as its terms properly apply. The novelty of this approach was that it extended the notion of equitable waiver into the area of part-payment of debts, where it had previously been assumed to be inapplicable because of the authority of *Foakes v Beer*. Denning met this objection by arguing that *Foakes v Beer* was decided on common law principles, ignoring the role of equity. In the light of the fact that *Foakes v Beer* was decided after the 'fusion' of law and equity by the **Judicature Acts 1873–5**, and that some of their Lordships expressed regret at the outcome, it seems hard to accept that they would have overlooked what Lord Denning seems to regard as an obvious escape route from the harshness of the common law rule.

There is, however, no doubt that promissory estoppel has been accepted as being applicable to variations of contract which involve the payment of money. In *Tool Metal Manufacturing Co v Tungsten Electric Co* (1955), it was accepted that the variation of the amount payable on a royalty was enforceable under the doctrine. It may be significant, however, that, as in *High Trees*, *Tool Metal v Tungsten* was concerned with a continuing contract involving periodic payments. It is possible to argue in such cases that promissory estoppel has only a suspensory effect and is, therefore, less directly in conflict with *Foakes v Beer*. This is true in the sense that the parties could at the end of the war (in *High Trees*), or upon giving notice (*Tool Metal v Tungsten*) revert to the original terms of their agreement. On the other hand, the shortfall in the money which under the original agreement would have been payable during the variation is clearly regarded as being irrecoverable. In that sense, therefore, a debt is being satisfied by part-payment.

A more direct challenge to *Foakes v Beer* would arise if promissory estoppel were found to be applicable to a debt comprising a single sum of money. There is no reported case in which this has happened. The nearest to it is *D & C Builders v Rees* (1965). The plaintiffs had done work for the defendants. After pressing for payment, they were told by the defendants that if they did not accept a lesser sum in settlement of the account they would get nothing. The plaintiffs agreed to take this smaller sum, but then sued for the balance. It was argued that their action should fail on the basis of promissory estoppel. Having promised to accept a lesser sum, the plaintiffs should not be allowed to renege on that promise. The Court of Appeal decided in favour of the plaintiffs. Only Lord Denning considered the promissory estoppel issue in any detail. He was clearly of the view that promissory estoppel could operate in this situation. It is, however, an equitable doctrine, and the defendants had acted inequitably in pressurising the plaintiffs into accepting the lesser sum, so Lord Denning refused to allow them to rely on promissory estoppel. The rest of the Court of Appeal were content simply to apply the principles from *Pinnel's Case* and *Foakes v Beer*, and hold the defendants liable because they had provided no consideration for the promise to accept the lower amount.

Moreover, the Court of Appeal has more recently confirmed, in *Re Selectmove* (1995), that it remains bound by the principle in *Foakes v Beer*.

Is the statement in the question correct? Would *Foakes v Beer* be decided in the same way today? It is clear that the strict rule about part-payment of debts has been weakened by *High Trees* and decisions that have followed it. As we have seen, however, the doctrine of promissory estoppel has been found most useful in relation to continuing contracts, rather than one-off contracts. Given the approach taken by the majority in *D & C Builders v Rees*, it seems likely that Mrs Beer would still be successful in recovering the interest on her debt.

Think point

1 Won't part-payment be likely to be more beneficial to the creditor than trying to enforce his strict rights through legal action? This point was noted by some of the judges in *Foakes v Beer* itself, for example, Lord Blackburn, but the approach taken in *Pinnel's Case* took precedence.

Question 9

Armadillo plc makes a contract with Movit Ltd, under which Movit agrees to transport 3,000 rolls of material from Armadillo's warehouse in London to Armadillo's factory in Leicester. The contract specifies that the material is to be delivered at a rate of 150 rolls per week for 20 weeks. The contract price is £20,000. Just before deliveries are to start, Movit realises that it is only possible to carry 100 rolls at a time on its lorry. It asks Armadillo to agree to deliveries being made over 30 weeks. Armadillo, which is suffering from a fall in business, agrees. After five weeks, Armadillo signs a very valuable contract for the production of T-shirts, which will require its factory to operate at full capacity. Armadillo asks Movit to return to delivering 150 rolls per week, and says that it will pay an extra £5,000 on completion of the contract. Movit hires an additional small lorry and completes the contract at 150 rolls per week. Armadillo, which is now in financial difficulties, refuses to pay more than £20,000. Movit accepts and is paid this, but now wants to bring an action to recover the additional £5,000 that it says it is owed.

Advise Movit.

Answer plan

At first reading, some problems, like this one, look more complicated than they actually are. There are really only two points of dispute here, although they are interlinked. They are: (a) whether the first variation of the contract (that is, regarding the number of rolls to be delivered) was either a binding variation or enforceable under the doctrine of promissory estoppel; and (b) whether there was any consideration for the promise to pay the additional £5,000. The answer to the second question will depend to some extent on the answer to the first. It will also involve consideration of the effect on the case of *Stilk v Myrick* (1809) of the decision in *Williams v Roffey* (1990).

Note that although the facts of this case are in some respects similar to those of *Atlas Express v Kafco* (1989), which is a duress case, no issue of duress really arises here.

Answer

Movit Ltd is seeking to recover the £5,000 additional payment that it was promised by Armadillo. The difficulty that Movit faces is in arguing that there was consideration for this promise. Armadillo may well claim that, in delivering 150 rolls per week, Movit was doing no more than it was already contractually obliged to do, and so, on the basis of the rule in *Stilk v Myrick* (1809), cannot enforce the promise of extra payment. To discover if Movit has any answer to this argument, it is necessary to examine in detail what happened between the parties during the course of this contract.

The first problem arises when Movit discovers the difficulty with the capacity of its lorry, and asks for a variation of the agreement. It is clear that at this point Armadillo would be entitled to refuse to entertain any change, and to insist that deliveries follow the pattern agreed in the contract. Movit would have had no cause for complaint had this been the line taken. Instead, however, Armadillo agrees to the change. Is this a binding variation of the contract? It is quite clear that if the parties to a contract agree to a variation that is mutually beneficial, this will be binding on both of them. In other words, consideration would exist to support the change in terms. Was there any consideration given here for Armadillo's agreement to accept delivery at a slower rate over a longer period? The answer would seem to be 'no'. Armadillo did not vary its side of the bargain in any way – there is, for example, no reduction in the amount to be paid to Movit. The only possibility would be if it could be said that, because of the fall in its business, it is to Armadillo's benefit that the contract is varied in this way. It is likely that something more than indifference on the part of Armadillo will need to be shown. If, for example, the continuation of deliveries at 150 rolls per week would mean that Armadillo would have to find storage space for some of them in Leicester, then avoiding this could be said to be consideration. It might still be objected that this benefit would be incidental, and would not move from the promisee, as is normally required. The Court of Appeal, in *Williams v Roffey* (1990) (which will be discussed in more detail later), appears to have relaxed this requirement somewhat. Even so, it is submitted that the odds are against Movit being able to establish a contractually binding variation.

If the change does not operate in this way, then it is necessary to consider whether it takes effect as a promissory estoppel. The modern form of the doctrine of promissory estoppel is derived from the judgment of Denning J (as he then was) in *Central London Property Trust v High Trees House* (1947). It states that where a promise is made that varies existing contractual obligations between the parties, and that promise is intended to be binding, intended to be acted upon, and is in fact acted upon, then it will be binding insofar as its terms properly apply. There are two principal limitations on this. First, the promissory estoppel cannot be used to found a cause of action (it can only be used as a shield not a sword: *Combe v Combe* (1951)).

Second, it must be inequitable to allow the promisor to go back on the promise (*D & C Builders v Rees* (1965); *The Post Chaser* (1981)). There seems to be no reason here why Armadillo's promise to take the smaller deliveries should not be regarded as giving rise to a promissory estoppel.

We now need to turn to the second change in the contract. After five weeks, Armadillo asks Movit to revert to 150 rolls a week, and agrees to pay £5,000 extra. This is the promise that Movit now wishes to enforce. To do so, it will need to show some consideration for Armadillo's promise of the extra money. Armadillo will no doubt claim that, far from providing consideration, Movit was only doing that which it was contractually obliged to do. Three possibilities need to be considered.

First, if the original change was a binding contractual variation, Armadillo will have no defence to Movit's claim. Movit would then have a contractual right to continue to deliver 100 rolls per week. Its surrender of that right would clearly be good consideration for the promise to pay the extra £5,000.

Second, if the first change was not a binding variation but a promise enforceable under the doctrine of promissory estoppel, Movit might argue that in not relying on the promissory estoppel it was again providing good consideration for the promise to pay £5,000. The problem with this is that promissory estoppel is often only suspensory in its effect (*High Trees* (1947); *Tool Metal Manufacturing Co Ltd v Tungsten Electric Co Ltd* (1955)). In other words, Armadillo might well be entitled to bring the promissory estoppel to an end by giving notice (as in *Tool Metal v Tungsten*). What is appropriate and reasonable notice will be a question of fact in each case. Here, given the relatively short length of the entire contract, very little notice might be required. This would make it more difficult for Movit to argue that the consideration for the promise of £5,000 was the waiver of its right to insist on notice of the termination of the promise to accept 100 rolls per week.

A further difficulty with Movit's reliance on promissory estoppel might appear to arise from the fact that it would be the claimant in the action to recover the £5,000. As we have seen, promissory estoppel can only be used as a shield and not a sword, but in fact Movit's claim would not be based on the promissory estoppel. The basis of the claim would be Armadillo's promise, and promissory estoppel would only be used to resist Armadillo's defence that the terms of the original contract were still binding.

The third possibility arises if neither of the first two arguments succeeds. Is there any possibility for Movit still to be able to succeed in an argument that the promise of £5,000 is enforceable? There are two cases that must be considered here: *Stilk v Myrick* (1809) and *Williams v Roffey* (1990).

In *Stilk v Myrick*, some members of the crew of a ship deserted part-way through a voyage. The captain promised the remaining crew extra money if they got the ship home safely. When they arrived back, however, the shipowners refused to pay. The crew's action to recover the additional payment failed, because it was said that they provided no consideration. They were already contractually bound to get the ship home safely, and performing this existing contract could not amount to consideration for a new promise from the same promisor.[1] This was taken to establish the general rule that existing contractual obligations owed to the promisor could not be good consideration. This would clearly be fatal to any claim by Movit outside the first two possibilities noted above. In *Williams v Roffey*, however, the Court of Appeal seemed to weaken, if not destroy, the *Stilk v Myrick* principle. The main contractors on a contract for the refurbishment of a block of flats promised one of the subcontractors, who was on the point of abandoning the contract through financial pressures, extra money if they continued with the contract. When the subcontractors sued to recover some of these promised payments, the defendants, the main contractors, resisted on the basis that no consideration had been provided. The Court of Appeal, however, said that there was consideration in that it was to the benefit of the defendants that the contract should continue. They would not then have the trouble and expense of finding others to complete the work. They would also avoid having to make payments under the main contract in relation to delay in completion.

The case shows a much wider approach to consideration than that in *Stilk v Myrick*. Movit might well be able to argue on similar lines that it was to Armadillo's benefit that Movit should go back to 150 rolls per week, and that if it had not done so Armadillo might have had to try to obtain additional transport from elsewhere. Since, in this case, as in *Williams v Roffey*, the initiative for the increased payment came from the promisor, and was not in any way the result of pressure from the promisee, there would be no reason not to hold the promisor to it.

In conclusion, then, Movit's possibility of recovering the £5,000 will depend on its being able to show consideration for the promise to pay it. It might do this by arguing:

(a) that the initial change was a binding variation; or

(b) that its relinquishing of promissory estoppel rights provided consideration; or

(c) that the benefits to Armadillo in continuing the contract at 150 rolls per week provided consideration, on the basis of the approach taken in *Williams v Roffey*.

Of these three, it is submitted that (b) and (c) are the arguments most likely to succeed.[2]

Think points

1 Might there have been another basis for the decision in *Stilk v Myrick*, in that it might be thought undesirable that crew members should have the possibility of 'holding the captain to ransom', in relation to increased pay? One of the reports of the case does indeed suggest that it was public policy rather

than the doctrine of consideration that decided the case. Nevertheless, it has long been taken as authority for the proposition stated here.

2 Note that Movit may need to rely on *Foakes v Beer* (1884) as regards its action for the £5,000, having accepted the £20,000. Armadillo might resist on the basis of promissory estoppel, but it is submitted that the case is analogous to *D & C Builders v Rees*, and so Armadillo would be unlikely to succeed with this argument.

Question 10

Sarah is going abroad for three months. She asks Laura, who is a police officer and who lives in the same street, to keep an eye on her house for her while she is away. Sarah says that she will pay Laura £100 for doing this when she returns. Sarah has an expensive art magazine delivered fortnightly. She arranges with the paperboy, Kevin, that while she is away he will post this through the letter box in the back door, rather than leaving it in the front porch, which lets in the rain. She pays him £10 to do this.

On her return from abroad, Sarah finds that Kevin has left the magazines in the front porch, and that half of the copies have been badly damaged by rain. It will cost Sarah £25 to replace them.

Laura asks Sarah for her £100. Sarah explains that she is overdrawn at the bank and is short of money. She does, however, have £80 in traveller's cheques. She offers these to Laura, saying: 'I'm afraid you are not going to get any more out of me.' Laura accepts the traveller's cheques, but on discovering the following week that Sarah has just taken a very well-paid job, now wishes to recover the additional £20.

Advise Sarah.

Answer plan

This problem focuses on the issue of the circumstances in which the promise to perform, or the performance of, an existing obligation can amount to good consideration. The question of intention to create legal relations should also receive at least brief discussion. The three potential contracts, or variations of contract, must be considered in turn, as follows.

- Laura – the initial arrangement with Laura is in the form of a contract: 'You look after my house, and I will pay you £100.' The only problem is that Laura, as a police officer, may be said to be under a public duty to do this already. The case of *Glasbrook v Glamorgan CC* (1925) will need discussion, as will the extent to which Laura can be said to be doing more than her obligations as a police officer require of her.

- Traveller's cheques – the answer to this part of the problem will depend in part on whether the initial arrangement with Laura is contractual. Assuming that it is, then the question is whether it can be discharged by the payment of £80 in traveller's cheques in place of £100 cash. *Pinnel's Case* (1602), *Foakes v Beer* (1884) and *D & C Builders v Rees* (1966) will all need discussion. The questions will be whether the cheques can be considered as something different from cash, and whether the doctrine of promissory estoppel affects this type of situation.

- Kevin – the agreement with Kevin is also potentially contractual. It may be argued, however, that Kevin provides no consideration, because he is doing no more than he is already bound to do under his contract with the newsagent. *Shadwell v Shadwell* (1860), *The Eurymedon* (1975) and *Pao On v Lau Yiu Long* (1979) are the relevant authorities here.

Answer

The arrangements that Sarah has made with Laura and Kevin raise the issue of what amounts to good consideration, so as to create a contractual obligation. There is also the question of whether there is an intention to create legal relations. Finally, the offer of the traveller's cheques in payment of a debt requires investigation of the rules relating to part-payment of debts.

Looking first at the question of intention to create legal relations, the rules are that in a 'domestic' agreement there is a presumption against such an intention (*Balfour v Balfour* (1919)), whereas in 'commercial' agreements there is a strong presumption the other way (*Edwards v Skyways* (1964)). The problem is identifying the category into which the arrangements in this problem should fall. As regards Laura, the fact that Sarah is promising to pay as much as £100 suggests that this is something more than an informal social transaction. Similarly, as regards Kevin, he is already engaged in paid work connected with the delivery of papers and magazines to Sarah. It is submitted, therefore, that both arrangements should be regarded as 'commercial' and therefore presumed to be intended to be legally binding. There is nothing in the facts that would suggest that this presumption should be rebutted, and so the advice to Sarah should be that she has made binding contracts with Laura and Kevin, unless they fail on the issue of consideration.

It should also be noted that we are not told Kevin's age. If he is under 18, and therefore a minor, it is likely that any contract will be unenforceable against him. As no mention is made of his age, however, it will be assumed that he is over 18 and, therefore, has full contractual capacity.

We now turn to the issue of consideration. Sarah has made an arrangement for Laura to keep an eye on her house while she is away. In return, Sarah has promised £100. The question is whether Laura's promise to keep an eye on the house is good consideration for Sarah's promise of payment. There would be no doubt that it is, were it not for the fact that Laura is a police officer. It may be argued that, as such, she already has a public duty to 'keep an eye on' other people's property, and that in doing this for Sarah she is therefore not providing consideration. In *Collins v Godefroy* (1831), it was held that a promise to pay a witness for attending a trial was unenforceable because the witness provided no consideration. Attending to give evidence was a public duty, and could not form consideration for a private contract. In *Glasbrook v Glamorgan CC* (1925), however, an exception to this was noted. The owners of a mine, where there was a strike taking place, sought police presence to guard the mine. The police were prepared to send a mobile force, but the owners insisted that the police should be billeted on the premises. They promised to pay for this, but later reneged on this promise, arguing that it was unenforceable. They claimed that the police provided no consideration, because it was their public duty to keep the peace. The court rejected this. The police, by providing the protection beyond what they thought was necessary, had exceeded their public duty. By doing more than was required, they had provided good consideration.

As between Laura and Sarah, therefore, the question is whether Laura has exceeded her public duty. The answer would almost certainly be 'yes'. Although police officers do have a general duty to prevent crime, this does not extend to keeping an eye on particular properties. Laura, by agreeing to do this for Sarah, has gone beyond her normal public duty, and has therefore made a binding contract. The only doubt about this would arise if it was felt that it was contrary to public policy to allow police officers to make private contracts of this kind. It could be argued that this, rather than the strict requirements of consideration, is the true reason why agreements to perform a public duty are unenforceable. On the authority of the *Glasbrook* case, however, and the fact that Laura is going beyond her normal duties, it is suggested that the courts would regard this as an enforceable contract.

This answer affects the position as regards Sarah's offer of the traveller's cheques. Clearly, if the original arrangement with Laura was not a binding contract, any payment by Sarah is *ex gratia* rather than contractual, and so Laura would have no legal claim to the extra £20. If, however, as we have concluded, there was a contract, we must consider the effect of Sarah's part-payment. The starting point is *Pinnel's Case* (1602). This suggested that payment of less than the amount owed on the due date could not be good consideration, although the acceptance by the creditor of early payment of a lesser amount, or a chattel (no matter what the value) instead of cash, would be sufficient. This was confirmed by the House of Lords in *Foakes v Beer* (1884). The question then is whether the traveller's cheques, which have a cash value less than the debt, can be regarded as something different from cash, and thus sufficient to discharge the debt.

A case that is relevant in this context is *D & C Builders v Rees* (1966). The plaintiffs were owed money for building work. Being desperate for cash, they accepted a cheque for less than was owed from the defendants, agreeing that this was in satisfaction of the debt. They later sued for the balance and were allowed to recover. The Court of Appeal had to consider whether payment by cheque was different from cash payment. There were old authorities that suggested that this was so. The Court of Appeal were unable to see that there was any such distinction, and overruled the earlier cases. They could not, however, overrule *Sibree v Tripp* (1846) (a case that said that a promissory note was sufficiently different from cash to amount to good consideration) because it was a decision of a court of equivalent authority (that is, the Exchequer Chamber). They therefore ruled that a cheque was distinguishable in law from a promissory note. This was because a cheque was only conditional payment, in that the debt was not discharged until the cheque was honoured, whereas the promissory note was unconditional, and discharged the debt immediately. The question here, then, is whether the traveller's cheques should be regarded as more like cash, or a promissory note, or indeed goods. There is no direct authority, but it is submitted that since the traveller's cheques are only exchangeable for their face value in cash, or the equivalent in goods or services, there are no grounds for treating them as anything other than cash. They will not, therefore, provide good consideration for Laura's promise to accept them as discharging Sarah's debt.

Can Sarah argue that she is nevertheless protected by promissory estoppel, as derived from the case of *Central London Property Trust v High Trees House* (1947)? In other words, can she claim that, whether or not there was consideration, Laura should not be allowed to go back on her promise to accept the lesser amount? The relevant authority is again *D & C Builders v Rees*. It was accepted by Lord Denning in this case that promissory estoppel could apply to single debts, as well as to ongoing payments, as in *High Trees*. He emphasised, however, that promissory estoppel is an equitable doctrine, and on the facts the promisees had not acted equitably. Here, it may well be the case that, since Sarah now has a good job, and it is only a week since the £80 was paid, there is nothing inequitable in allowing Laura to go back on her promise and claim the additional £20 that she is owed.[1]

Finally, it should be noted that, in *Re Selectmove* (1995), the Court of Appeal refused to apply the more flexible approach to variation of contracts taken in *Williams v Roffey* (1990) to the situation of the remission of a debt, and reaffirmed *Foakes v Beer*.

As far as her relationship with Laura is concerned, therefore, the advice to Sarah is that she is probably obliged to pay the additional £20. Turning to the agreement with Kevin, Sarah will presumably wish to recover the £10 that she paid him, plus £25 to cover the cost of replacing her magazines. To do this, she will need to show that there was a binding contract between them as to the arrangement for putting the magazines through the back door. Kevin may object that he was under an existing contractual obligation with the newsagent for which he works to deliver the magazines to Sarah, and that therefore there is no consideration for her promise of payment. Sarah has two possible answers to this. The first is to say that, in the same way as in the agreement with Laura, Kevin did in fact promise to do more than his existing duty. The agreement was not simply to deliver the magazines; her arrangement with him required them to be delivered to a particular place, and so went beyond his normal obligation. Even if this was not the case, however, Sarah would probably still be able to succeed. The question of existing contractual duties owed to a third party was considered in *Shadwell v Shadwell* (1860), in which getting married was held to be good consideration for a promise of an allowance from the plaintiff's uncle, despite the fact that the plaintiff was already legally bound to go through with the marriage ceremony.[2] This, therefore, established the principle that the same promise or act could be good consideration for more than one contract. More recently, and in a commercial context, the Privy Council in *Pao On v Lau Yiu Long* (1979) accepted the point as not being in dispute, relying on the earlier decision of the same court in *The Eurymedon* (1975).

It seems, then, that Sarah will be able to establish a binding contract with Kevin (providing that he is aged over 18) and, therefore, will be able to recover damages from him for his breach of their agreement.

Think points

1 Does 'inequitable' necessarily mean 'using undue pressure'? It seems not, in that in *The Post Chaser* (1981) the short space of time between a promise and its withdrawal formed the basis for a decision that it was not inequitable to allow the promisor to go back on the promise.

2 Would *Shadwell v Shadwell* be dealt with in the same way today? No, because a promise of marriage is no longer legally binding. There would be no issue of an existing obligation in this situation now.

CHAPTER 3

PRIVITY

INTRODUCTION

The doctrine of privity of contract is related to the issues of the creation of contractual obligations looked at in Chapters 1 and 2, in that it is concerned with the question of who has rights and liabilities under a contract. It is sometimes argued that some aspects of the doctrine are just another way of stating the rule that consideration must move from the promisee, and so questions may sometimes involve looking at both consideration and privity issues. More commonly, in the past, questions have tended to relate to the two sides of the basic privity doctrine, that is:

- that a person cannot sue on a contract made for their benefit if they were not a party to it; and

- that a person cannot have obligations imposed on them by a contract to which they are not a party.

The first part of the doctrine, relating to the conferring of benefits, was the subject of major reform in the **Contracts (Rights of Third Parties) Act 1999**. This Act was based on the recommendations of the Law Commission Report No 242, *Privity of Contract: Contracts for the Benefit of Third Parties* (Cmnd 3329), and applies to contracts made on or after 11 May 2000. Although the old law may still be applicable to some contracts, most questions on privity will now require you to show an understanding of the new legislation. You may well be asked, however, whether the reform is satisfactory, and this will also require knowledge of the previous law. All of the questions and answers in this chapter touch on one or more aspects of the new legislation.

It is relatively unusual to find a question that deals solely with the second aspect of the privity doctrine: the imposition of obligations. Generally, questions on this area will be linked with one on the conferring of benefits, very often in the form of a two-part question. It is important, therefore, to have a good grasp of the whole privity area if attempting questions on this topic.

Two privity-related issues that are not dealt with in detail in this chapter, but of which you may need to take account, depending on the details of the syllabus for your course, are:

- exemption clauses and privity; and
- privity and the tort of negligence (for example, the implications of the case of *Junior Books v Veitchi* (1983)).

The reasons for not looking at the second issue in this book are: first, although the area is discussed in some of the textbooks, it is not an issue that appears with any frequency on exam papers; and second, the subsequent trend of House of Lords decisions on negligence has meant that the *Junior Books* line of argument is of much less significance than at one time it appeared likely to be.

Checklist

You should be familiar with the following areas:

- the basic doctrine of privity, derived from *Tweddle v Atkinson* (1861), *Dunlop v Selfridge* (1915) and *Beswick v Beswick* (1968);
- the two aspects of the doctrine, relating to the conferring of benefits, and the imposition of obligations, on a third party;
- the major reform to the first part of the doctrine contained in the **Contracts (Rights of Third Parties) Act 1999**;
- the devices previously used to avoid the first part of the doctrine – for example, trusts, agency and collateral contracts; and
- the more limited exceptions to the second part of the doctrine: for example, restrictive covenants (*Tulk v Moxhay* (1848)), and their application in the shipping cases, and the use of tortious remedies, as in *Lumley v Gye* (1853).

Question 11

Answer both parts.

(a) Outline the effects of the **Contracts (Rights of Third Parties) Act 1999**. To what extent does this Act mean that the devices previously used to confer benefits on a third party are no longer needed?

(b) In January, Peter sells his Rolls Royce to David for £30,000. One of the terms of the contract is that Peter will have the use of the car for the first week of August, when it will be used for his daughter's wedding and subsequent honeymoon.

In March, David sells the car to Jane. When Peter hears of this, he seeks your advice as to whether he will be entitled to the use of the car in August, as originally planned.

Advise Peter.

Answer plan

As is common with questions on privity, the two parts of this question relate to the two aspects of the doctrine. Part (a) is concerned with the situations in which a third party can sue to obtain the benefit of a contract, whereas in part (b) the focus is on the extent to which a person can be bound by the terms of a contract to which he or she is not a party.

In part (a), the main body of the answer will be concerned with the provisions of the 1999 Act. As to the second part of (a), there is no need to go into detail on the 'devices previously used'. Some indication of them will be needed, but attention should be concentrated on the issue of the extent to which they will still be available or necessary now that the 1999 Act is in force.

In part (b), the issues will be:

- whether the approach in *Tulk v Moxhay* (1848) can apply to this type of situation; and

- if not, whether a tortious remedy may be available.

Answer

Part (a)

The doctrine of privity of contract says that only a party to the contract can sue on it. This principle was recognised in *Tweddle v Atkinson* (1861), and confirmed by the House of Lords in *Dunlop v Selfridge* (1915), and again in *Beswick v Beswick* (1968).

The fact that as a result of this doctrine a third party who was intended to benefit from it could not sue to recover the benefit was the subject of much criticism. The Law Commission recommended in 1996 that the law should be reformed, and this was put into effect by the **Contracts (Rights of Third Parties) Act 1999**.

As recommended by the Law Commission, the Act gives a third party the right to enforce a benefit where the parties to the contract intended to give him an enforceable legal obligation. The mere fact that a contract may incidentally benefit a third party is not enough; there must have been an intention to create a legal right.

This objective is achieved by **s 1** of the Act. It identifies two situations in which a third party will be held to have an enforceable right. The first, and most straightforward, is where the contract expressly states that such a right is given. The second arises where a term in the contract purports to confer a benefit on the third party, but does not explicitly say that this is to be legally enforceable. The effect of **s 1** is to say that such a benefit will be legally enforceable unless 'on a proper construction of the contract' it appears that it was not the parties' intention that the benefit should be enforceable by the third party. In other words, wherever the contract purports to confer a benefit, there is a rebuttable presumption of enforceability. If the parties do not wish such a presumption to be given effect, then the easiest way is to say so in the contract. In the absence of such a statement, the courts will presumably apply a test based on what reasonable contracting parties would be taken to have intended by the term in question. Where it is found that there is an intention to give a legally enforceable right, the third party will be able to enforce the beneficial term of the contract in exactly the same way as a party to the contract.

An example of the application of these provisions is to be found in the Court of Appeal decision in *Laemthong International Lines Co Ltd v Artis (No 2)* (2005). The receiver of goods being carried by sea was not in possession of the correct documentation (that is, the bill of lading) to obtain delivery. It issued a letter of indemnity to the charterers of the ship on which the goods were being carried, so as to be able to receive the goods. The charterers issued a similar letter and sent it with the receiver's letter to the owner of the ship. The owners instructed the master to unload the cargo. The ship was then seized by another party, who claimed to be in possession of the bill of lading. The shipowners sued the receiver on the letter of indemnity, which it had issued to the charterers. The Court held that the letter was intended to benefit the shipowners (that is, to protect them in the situation that in fact occurred), and there was no evidence sufficient to overturn the presumption that it was intended to be legally enforceable. This case shows the strength of the presumption and indicates that it may be difficult to overturn.

There is no need for the third-party beneficiary to be in existence at the time of the contract, provided that there is adequate identification in it. Unborn children, future spouses and unincorporated companies can all be given enforceable rights in this way.

In general, the parties to a contract can negotiate changes at any time. How does this apply to a situation in which a contract gives a third party a legally enforceable right? Does the third party have to agree to any change? The Act deals with this situation in **s 2**. This allows the contracting parties to override any third-party rights by including a clause saying that any consent to a change is not required, or setting out its own procedures for such consent. In the absence of such a clause, however, **s 2** provides that the parties to the contract will lose the right to withdraw the benefit promised to the third party if one of three conditions is satisfied.

The first is that the third party has communicated to the promisor his or her assent to the term. The second is where the third party has relied on the term and the promisor is aware of this. The third is where the third party has relied on the term and the promisor could reasonably be expected to have foreseen this. Reliance does not have to be detrimental reliance, as long as the third party has acted on the promise. Relying on the promise of a sum of money by buying goods, which have subsequently doubled in value, would be sufficient for these purposes.

Section 3 of the Act deals with the availability of defences. Subject to any specific provisions to the contrary in the contract, the promisor will be able to raise against the third party any defences that would have been available against the other party to the contract (the 'promisee'). So, if the promisee has induced the contract by undue influence or misrepresentation, the promisor will be able to use that as a defence to any action by the third party. Equally, if the third party has acted wrongly, or owes money to the promisor from previous dealings, these matters can be used by the promisor in response to any action by the third party.

The right of the promisee, as opposed to the third party, to enforce the promise (as happened, for example, in *Beswick v Beswick* (1968)) is preserved by s 4. If the promisee has succeeded in an action against the promisor, however, this must be taken into account in any subsequent action by the third party, so that the promisor is not faced with double liability.

To what extent does the **1999 Act** mean that devices previously used to avoid the doctrine will no longer be needed? The courts have in the past used, for example, trusts (*Re Flavell* (1883)), agency (*The Eurymedon* (1975)) and collateral contracts (*Shanklin Pier v Detel Products* (1951)) as ways of giving third parties rights. They have also recognised a limited scope for the promisee to recover damages on behalf of a third party (*Jackson v Horizon Holidays* (1975); *Linden Gardens v Lenesta Sludge Disposals* (1993)). **Section 7** of the Act says that all rights or remedies existing apart from the Act are preserved, so these approaches could still be used if necessary. Moreover, there are certain contracts that are not covered by the Act. These include contracts on a bill of exchange or other negotiable instrument, contracts of employment (as against the employee) and certain contracts of international carriage. In relation to the last category, the exception does not apply to exclusion clauses. Otherwise, where the Act does not apply, by virtue of **s 7**, then there is still scope for using other means of giving rights to third parties. In general, however, it is clear that the **1999 Act** now constitutes the most important exception to the traditional doctrine of privity insofar as the conferring of benefits on third parties is concerned.

Part (b)

This part of the question is concerned with the situation in which a person disposes of property, but wishes to maintain some control over it. It is a well-established principle in land law that this can be done by means of restrictive covenants: *Tulk v Moxhay* (1848). The question arises as to whether a similar principle can be applied to property other than land. The answer appeared to be 'yes' in certain shipping cases, such as *Lord Strathcona SS Co Ltd v Dominion Coal* (1926). The Privy Council held in this case that a person who had a time charter of a ship could enforce it against a new purchaser who had notice of it. The decision was, however, strongly criticised in *Port Line v Ben Line* (1958), and it seems that this line of argument will not now be followed. This does not mean, however, that Peter is necessarily without any remedy.

In certain situations, tortious remedies can be used to impose contractual obligations indirectly on third parties. The case of *Lumley v Gye* (1853) is one of the leading authorities. Here, the defendant, who encouraged an opera singer to break an exclusive contract to sing for the plaintiff, was held liable for the tort of wrongful interference with contractual rights.[1] This remedy has also been held to be available where goods are sold subject to a restriction on their disposal. In *BMTA v Salvadori* (1949), the purchaser of a new car agreed not to sell it for a year without first offering it to the plaintiff. The defendant bought the car with knowledge of this restriction, and was again held liable in tort.

Will this tortious remedy be of any use to Peter? The situation is not identical to those we have considered so far, but it is clear that there is a continuing contractual obligation as between Peter and David as to the use of the car in August. If it is unavailable, David will be in breach of contract. A remedy in damages is, however, unlikely to be satisfactory to Peter. He presumably wishes to have this particular car available for his daughter's wedding. What he will wish to do is to be able to obtain an injunction to restrain Jane from acting in a way that will infringe his contractual rights against David. On the basis of the cases noted above, he may be able to do this if he can show that when Jane bought the car from David she was aware of Peter's contractual claim to its use in August. If she was, then to act in a way that prevents Peter having access to the car will amount to the tort of wrongful interference with Peter's contractual rights, and he may well be able to obtain an injunction to prevent her from so doing.

A final possibility, suggested by the case of *Swiss Bank Corp v Lloyds Bank* (1979), is that Peter may have a remedy in equity if, as is quite likely, his contract with David is specifically enforceable. It was suggested in this case that in such a situation there was an equitable interest in the property that was the subject of the contract, as a result of the specifically enforceable obligation relating to it. This interest would operate against third parties who acquired the property, unless they did so in good faith, and without notice of the restriction on its use. Again, to have a remedy, Peter would have to show notice on the part of Jane, although here it could be constructive notice, whereas for the tortious remedy it has to be actual notice.

It seems, then, that Peter has some chance of successfully gaining access to the car, but he will need to establish that Jane had notice, possibly constructive, preferably actual, of the restriction on its use.

Question 12

In *Lloyd's v Harper* (1880), Lush LJ said: 'I consider it to be an established law that where a contract is made with A for the benefit of B, A can sue on the contract for the benefit of B, and recover all that B could have recovered if the contract had been made with B himself.'

To what extent does English law now allow a claimant suing on a contract to recover for losses suffered by a third party?

Answer plan

This essay is concerned with an issue that has been of considerable controversy, at least since 1975. To answer it, you will need to deal with:

• the attempt by Lord Denning in *Jackson v Horizon Holidays* (1975) to use the quote from Lush LJ as establishing a general right to recover damages for a third party;

• the disapproval of this approach by the House of Lords in *Woodar Investment Development Ltd v Wimpey Construction (UK) Ltd* (1980), and the consequent limitation of the scope of the *Jackson* decision;

• the renewed life given to recovering damages for a third party in a commercial context by *Linden Gardens Ltd v Lenesta Sludge Disposals Ltd* (1993); and

• the review of the concept by the House of Lords in *Alfred McAlpine Construction Ltd v Panatown Ltd* (2000).

Note that the issue being dealt with here – A, the contracting party, recovering damages for the loss of B, a third party – is not directly dealt with by the **Contracts (Rights of Third Parties) Act 1999**, but its enactment may mean that there is less need to seek to rely on such an action in the future.

Answer

Generally speaking, a party to a contract who sues the other party can only recover for his or her own losses. The doctrine of privity has operated to discourage the award of damages for losses suffered by anyone other than a party to the contract. Nevertheless, the law has, since at least 1975, recognised some exceptions to this general principle. The exact scope of those exceptions is still a matter of some uncertainty, despite recent reconsideration of the area by the House of Lords.

The starting point for the discussion of the modern law on this area is the case of *Jackson v Horizon Holidays* (1975). In this case, there had been a disastrous family holiday, and the father, who booked it, was suing the travel company. The Court of Appeal allowed the father to recover damages in respect of the losses suffered by the rest of the family. In doing so, Lord Denning relied heavily on the above quote from Lush LJ in *Lloyd's v Harper* (1880). He felt that where one person made a contract that was clearly intended to benefit others – as with a holiday, or a meal in a restaurant – the contracting party should be able to recover damages reflecting the loss of the other intended beneficiaries. The successful claimant would then be in a position to compensate the others from the damages recovered. Other members of the Court of Appeal, in particular James LJ, were more circumspect. He accepted that the father in *Jackson* was entitled to the enhanced level of damages awarded at first instance. He felt, however, that this could be justified on the basis that the discomfort suffered by the rest of the Jackson family was part of the father's loss. On this analysis, the loss was Mr Jackson's, and he would be under no obligation to compensate the rest of the family from the damages that he received.

The decision in *Jackson* was reconsidered by the House of Lords in *Woodar Investment Development Ltd v Wimpey Construction (UK) Ltd* (1980). This was a different type of contract to that in *Jackson*, in that it was a commercial construction transaction. Under it, Wimpey had agreed to pay £150,000 to a third party, Transworld, on completion of the contract with Woodar. The question before the court was whether Woodar, in an action against Wimpey for breach of contract, could recover the £150,000 promised to Transworld.[1] Reliance was placed on the statement by Lord Denning in *Jackson v Horizon Holidays* as supporting the possibility of such recovery. The House of Lords, however, held that Woodar should not be able to succeed in such an action. In coming to this conclusion, the Lords made it clear that in their view Lord Denning had made improper use of the quotation from Lush LJ, in that he had taken it out of context.

As Lord Russell pointed out, Lush LJ's statement was clearly made in the context of a fiduciary relationship between A and B, such as principal and agent. Where A (as agent) contracts with C for the benefit of B (A's principal), there is no particular difficulty in recognising that A may sue on behalf of B. This falls far short, however, of recognising a general right to recover losses suffered by a third party to the contract.

Despite these criticisms of Lord Denning, the House of Lords in *Woodar v Wimpey* did not go so far as to say that *Jackson v Horizon* was wrongly decided. They felt that the decision could be upheld, either on the basis suggested by James LJ, that the discomfort of the rest of the family was part of the father's loss, or that there were some special situations that called for special treatment. These cases were situations in which one person acts on behalf of a group by, for example, ordering a meal in a restaurant, or hiring a taxi for the group. In such situations, it was obvious that a breach of contract would affect all members of the group adversely. An issue that was left open, however, was whether a claimant who successfully obtained damages on this basis would be obliged to pass on the compensation to the other members of the group. Lord Denning clearly thought that he or she would, but the award of damages in *Jackson* did not impose any obligation of this kind. The position was therefore unclear, and remained so after *Woodar v Wimpey*.

There the matter rested for the next 13 years, until the House of Lords again returned to the issue in *Linden Gardens Ltd v Lenesta Sludge Disposals Ltd* (1993). This concerned a building contract in which the original employer had assigned its interests to a third party, but in such a way that the third party gained no legal right to sue on the contract. The original employer therefore sued the contractor for defects in the work. It was argued that since these defects had occurred after the assignment of the employer's interests, it had suffered no loss. It would have appeared that the application of *Woodar v Wimpey* would support the defendant's arguments. The House of Lords, however, drew an analogy with cases in shipping law, where it is clearly established that the shipper of goods can sue on the shipping contract in relation to the loss of goods, even if at the time the ownership of the goods has been transferred to a third party. They felt that this principle could be applied to the case before them. The contractor knew that the employer was not going to occupy the premises itself and could therefore foresee that defects in the work would be likely to adversely affect whoever acquired the premises. On that basis, the case fell within one of the exceptions to the general rule that recovery of losses suffered by a third party is not possible.

There have been two subsequent cases in which this issue has been further developed. The first was *Darlington BC v Wiltshire Northern Ltd* (1995), another building contract case, in which the Court of Appeal held that the fact that there was no transfer of the property concerned did not prevent the application of the approach taken in *Linden Gardens*. It was necessary to provide a remedy to prevent an otherwise meritorious claim for defective work falling down the 'black hole', with neither the employer nor the third party being able to recover from the contractor.

The second case is *Alfred McAlpine Construction Ltd v Panatown Ltd* (2000). Once again, this concerned a major construction contract. The employer, P, had engaged the contractor, AM, to build premises on land owned by a third party, U. In addition to the contract between P and AM, there was at the same time executed between AM and U a 'duty of care deed' (DCD). This gave U an action against AM for negligent performance of the construction contract, but was not identical to the obligations under the main contract (for example, it contained no provision for arbitration). When defective performance took place, P sued AM. AM's defence was that P had suffered no loss, and so could not recover. The case was different from the situations in *Linden Gardens v Lenesta* and *Darlington v Wiltshire* in that the third party, U, here had an independent cause of action under the DCD. There was therefore no question of defective performance falling down the 'black hole' referred to in the *Darlington* case.

P's response to this was to rely on a broader ground for recovery put forward by Lord Griffiths in *Linden Gardens*. This was based on the view that in this type of situation the employer suffers a loss, for which substantial damages can be recovered, simply because proper performance has not been supplied. The question of ownership of the property concerned is irrelevant. An analogy was drawn with a husband who contracts for work to be done repairing the roof of a house that, in fact, belongs to his wife. There should be no doubt that, in the event of defective performance, the husband can sue the contractor and recover substantial damages.

The majority of the House of Lords in *Alfred McAlpine v Panatown* was not, however, prepared to follow Lord Griffiths' lead. Accepting the argument put forward by AM, they held that the existence of the DCD was fatal to P's claim. Thus, an employer in this type of situation is only able to recover substantial damages when the property in question belongs to a third party if that third party has no independent right of action against the contractor. The existence of the **Contracts (Rights of Third Parties) Act 1999**, of course, means that such an independent action is now far more likely to arise.

One issue that is left unresolved is the question of whether, if damages are recovered for losses in relation to property owned by a third party, the successful claimant is obliged to pass this on to the third party. There are comments in all of the cases that point in one direction or the other, but no clear statement of the position. This may well fall to be the subject of further litigation.

Overall then, the position remains that, in general, a contracting party cannot sue to recover damages in relation to losses suffered by a third party. There are, however, some very important exceptions to this. First, as in *Jackson v Horizon Holidays*, it may be possible to recover when a person is contracting for a group, and it is clear that all members of the group will suffer if there is defective performance. Second, there is the situation involving carriage of goods, in which the shipper of the goods may recover even though the goods have been transferred to a third party. Finally, there are the situations recognised in the three recent cases concerned with construction contracts. Here, the employer of a contractor can sue and recover substantial damages for defective performance, even if that performance relates to property that is not owned by the contractor. This is subject to the limitation that the possibility of such recovery will disappear if the third party has an independent cause of action.

Question 13

The Seven Dwarves live in a row of cottages in Dingley Dell. Snow White lives next door. Because the cottages are in a valley, they have very poor television reception. This could be improved if a television aerial could be sited at the top of the hill, on land owned by Cruella, and then linked to the cottages. Snow White visits Cruella, and persuades her to erect an aerial at the top of the hill. Cruella demands an immediate payment of £1,000 to cover the cost of this, and as the price of her agreement. Snow White and Cruella enter into a written contract to this effect, and Snow White pays the £1,000. Snow White then collects £125 from each of the Dwarves. Unfortunately, before work can begin on the construction of the aerial, Snow White dies as a result of choking on a piece of apple. Her will names Cruella as her executrix. Cruella is now refusing to construct the aerial.

Advise the Seven Dwarves.

Would your answer be any different if Snow White had named the Seven Dwarves as her executors?

Answer plan

The issue here is whether the Seven Dwarves have any rights in relation to the contract made between Snow White and Cruella. They do not appear to be parties to this contract, even though its effect is to provide a benefit for them. The first part of the answer will need to consider whether the Dwarves can take advantage of the reform of the law of privity contained in the **Contracts (Rights of Third Parties) Act 1999**. The difficulty here may be in establishing that the contract identified the Dwarves as beneficiaries of the contract, and that it was intended to give them a right of action. Cruella is likely to dispute this unless the contract is clearly worded so as to favour the Dwarves.

If the **1999 Act** does not apply, then other methods of avoiding the doctrine of privity should be considered (for example, trusts or agency), but none seems likely to be very helpful.

The alternative facts, placing the Dwarves in the role of executors, require consideration of the decision in *Beswick v Beswick* (1968), on the basis of which the Dwarves may be able to achieve a remedy of specific performance against Cruella.

Answer

The untimely death of Snow White has left the Seven Dwarves with a problem. She had negotiated a contract with Cruella that had the potential of benefiting them, in terms of improved television reception. Although they had paid a contribution towards this to Snow White, they were not parties to the contract, and so may have difficulty enforcing it against Cruella.

The traditional English doctrine of privity meant that only those who were parties to a contract could take action on it. Even if the agreement was clearly intended to benefit a third party, that person would not be able to enforce it. In *Tweddle v Atkinson* (1861), the plaintiff was not able to enforce an agreement made between his father and father-in-law to make a payment to him on the occasion of his marriage. The basic principle was confirmed in *Dunlop v Selfridge* (1915) and *Beswick v Beswick* (1968).

The traditional position has, however, been radically affected by the **Contracts (Rights of Third Parties) Act 1999**, which allows third parties in certain circumstances to enforce benefits due to them under a contract to which they are not a party. It is necessary to consider whether this will assist the Seven Dwarves in enforcing the contract against Cruella.

The main reforming provision of the **1999 Act** is s 1. This allows a third party to enforce a contract in two main circumstances. First, such enforcement will be possible where the contract states that the third party is to have a legally enforceable right under it. Second, a right of enforcement may also arise where the contract purports to confer a benefit on a third party, but without stating specifically that the third party is to be able to enforce it. In this situation, it will be necessary to look at the agreement closely to determine its effect. **Section 1(2)** of the Act provides that a clause purporting to confer a benefit on a third party will not be enforceable by that party if it appears on a 'proper construction' of the contract that that was not the intention of the parties. In other words, where the contract purports to confer a benefit, there is a presumption that it is to be enforceable, unless a contrary intention appears from the contract. How does this apply to the dispute between Cruella and the Seven Dwarves? One problem is that we do not have details of the wording of the written contract entered into by Cruella and Snow White. If that contract names the Seven Dwarves and states that they are to have an enforceable right under the agreement, then there is no problem. Although under the common law the Dwarves would have had difficulty enforcing such a right, even when stated explicitly, the 1999 Act means that they will be able to take action against Cruella just as if they were parties to the original agreement.

The second possibility is that the contract is stated to be for the benefit of, for example, all the residents of Dingley Dell, but does not make it clear that such residents are to be given a right to enforce the agreement. It does not matter that the Dwarves are not mentioned by name; as long as the intended beneficiaries are sufficiently identified as, for example, the members of a particular class, then that satisfies the requirements of s 1(3) of the 1999 Act. The question will then become whether the presumption that such third parties will be able to enforce is rebutted by the rest of the contract. Again, it is not possible to answer this question without having the details of the wording of the agreement. It seems unlikely, however, that Snow White, who clearly entered into the contract intending it to be for the benefit of the Seven Dwarves, would have included wording that prevented them from being able to enforce it. The likelihood, therefore, is that in this situation, as in the first, the Dwarves will be able to take legal action to require Cruella to perform her part of the contract, or at least to pay damages for non-performance. This conclusion is perhaps reinforced by a recent Court of Appeal decision on the 1999 Act – *Laemthong International Lines Co Ltd v Artis (No 2)* (2005). The receiver of goods being carried by sea was not in possession of the correct documentation (that is, the bill of lading) to obtain delivery. It issued a letter of indemnity to the charterers of the ship on which the goods were being carried, so as to be able to receive the goods. The charterers issued a similar letter and sent it with the receiver's letter to the owner of the ship. The owners instructed the master to unload the cargo. The ship was then seized by another party, who claimed to be in possession of the bill of lading. The shipowners sued the receiver on the letter of indemnity, which it had issued to the charterers. The Court held that the letter was clearly intended to benefit the shipowners (that is, to protect them in the situation that in fact occurred), because it referred to the charterers' 'agents'. Even though the shipowners were not mentioned directly, they came within the category of 'agent'. Moreover, there was no evidence sufficient to overturn the presumption that it was intended to be legally enforceable. If a similar approach is taken here, the Dwarves will be able to use the Act to enforce their claim.

The third possibility is that the contract makes no mention of the Seven Dwarves, or the residents of Dingley Dell. This will make the Dwarves' position much more difficult. The Act follows the recommendation of the Law Commission that the simple fact that a third party will benefit from the performance of a contract should not in itself give a right of action under it. The example used by the Law Commission was an agreement between a highway authority and a construction company for the building of a new road. This may well benefit all those whose journeys are made easier by the existence of the new road, but it would not be correct to give them all a right of action against the construction company should the road prove to be defective, or the project delayed. If, then, the contract between Cruella and Snow White makes no reference, direct or indirect, to the Seven Dwarves, they will not be able to use the 1999 Act to take action against Cruella.

If that is the situation, are there any other ways in which the Dwarves can avoid the doctrine of privity? Of those used in the past, it does not seem likely that on the facts a trust (as in *Les Affréteurs Réunis v Walford* (1919)) or a collateral contract (as in *Shanklin Pier v Detel Products* (1951)) could be constructed so as to give a remedy. If the contract had given continuing rights over Cruella's land, then it is possible that **s 56** of the **Law of Property Act 1925** could be brought into play. In *Beswick v Beswick* (1968), however, the House of Lords made it clear that **s 56** was not relevant to contracts that were not concerned with interests in land. Here, the contract is simply for the erection of the aerial by Cruella, and does not involve any land law rights.

Another possibility might be to argue that Snow White was acting as agent for the Dwarves in making the contract with Cruella. It would not matter that she had not made this explicit to Cruella, since it is quite possible for an agent to act on behalf of an undisclosed principal (that is, the Seven Dwarves) so as to bring that person into a contractual relationship with the other party (that is, Cruella). The difficulty here is that there is no evidence that the Dwarves had delegated Snow White to negotiate with Cruella. Snow White appears to have been acting entirely independently in going to Cruella, and it is only subsequently that she seeks a contribution towards the contract from the Dwarves. The Dwarves may well have a difficulty, therefore, in basing a claim on agency.

Overall, it seems unlikely if the Dwarves do not come within the scope of the 1999 Act that they will be able to use any of the other devices to take action against Cruella. They are probably even more unlikely to succeed given that, with the passing of the 1999 Act, the courts may well be more reluctant than they have been in the past to use what have often been rather artificial devices to avoid the perceived injustice of the strict application of the doctrine of privity. Given that the parties to a contract can now avoid the doctrine by wording their agreement appropriately, there is much less incentive for the courts themselves to try to find ways around it.

Turning now to the alternative scenario, where Snow White has named the Dwarves as her executors, their position will be considerably stronger. First, of course, they may still be able to use the 1999 Act if the contract between Cruella and Snow White allows this. If this is not the case, however, they may still be able to require Cruella to go through with the agreement on the basis of the approach adopted in *Beswick v Beswick*. In this case, a nephew had promised his uncle, on acquiring the uncle's business, that he would, after his uncle's death, pay an annuity to his aunt. The nephew failed to make the payments. His aunt had, however, been appointed administratrix of her late husband's estate. In that capacity, the House of Lords held that she was entitled to step into her husband's shoes, and seek an order of specific performance from her nephew. Can the same argument apply here? One of the conditions for the courts' being prepared to grant an order of specific performance is that damages would be an inadequate remedy. In *Beswick v Beswick*, this was felt to be the case because the uncle's estate would only have been entitled to nominal damages, since it had suffered no financial loss. The position is slightly different in the problem, in that Snow White was herself going to benefit from the contract with Cruella. This might suggest that her estate could recover more than nominal damages from Cruella for the breach. It might even be arguable that this is a contract of the special type recognised in *Woodar v Wimpey* (1980), in which a party may be able to claim damages on behalf of others who were intended to benefit from the performance of the contract. It was suggested that this category of contracts could include holiday contracts (*Jackson v Horizon Holidays* (1975)), meals in restaurants and hiring a taxi for a group. Could it also include a contract that has the effect of providing improved television reception for a group of people? This is possible, but, on the other hand, the benefits are not easily quantifiable in monetary terms. There is no indication of a way in which the Dwarves, by spending money in some other way, could achieve the improved reception. It is a strong possibility, then, that on applying the basic test of 'are damages an adequate remedy?', the answer would be 'no'. This would then allow the Dwarves, as executors of Snow White's estate, to obtain an order of specific performance requiring Cruella to construct the aerial, thus achieving the benefit they are seeking.

Finally, if all else fails, the Dwarves should be able to recover from Snow White's estate the £125 they each paid, on the basis of a restitutionary action.

CHAPTER 4

CAPACITY

▌INTRODUCTION

Capacity is considered at this point as one of the factors that is needed before an enforceable contract can be made. Alternatively, of course, the issue can be looked at from the opposite point of view: that is, incapacity can be regarded as a 'vitiating factor' that prevents a contract being enforced. Whichever approach is taken (and it really does not much matter which), the rules relating to capacity are a reflection of the fact that the law of contract recognises that in some situations people need protection from themselves, in that they may enter into agreements that are not to their benefit, because they are not capable of properly understanding the implications of what they are doing. The argument may seem a little dubious where the 'incapable' individual is an intelligent 17-year-old, but the law can only operate practically by the use of broad categories and fixed borderlines.

Three principal types of incapacity are recognised in English law:

- being under the age of 18 (a 'minor');
- being mentally incapacitated; and
- being intoxicated.

Most of the law relates to the first category, and this is the one about which questions are most commonly asked.

Checklist

You should be familiar with the following areas:

- the presumption of unenforceability against a minor;
- the meaning of 'necessaries' in the context of both goods and services – as regards goods, the provisions of the **Sale of Goods Act 1979** should be noted;
- the meaning of a 'beneficial contract of service';
- the provisions of the **Minors' Contracts Act 1987**; and
- the principles applying to the intoxicated or mentally incapacitated – in particular, the issue of awareness of the other party as to the incapacity at the time of the contract.

Question 14

McKendrick comments that, despite the enactment of the **Minors' Contracts Act 1987**, 'the rules of law remain in need of further rationalisation in an effort to provide a better balance between, on the one hand, the protection of minors and, on the other hand, the interests of those who deal in all good faith with them' (*Contract Law*, 7th edn, 2007).

Do you agree?

Answer plan

The focus of the answer to this problem must of course be the changes made by the **Minors' Contracts Act 1987**. You should not attempt this question unless you have at least a reasonable idea of the position prior to 1987, and the reforms that the Act introduced. Simply describing the provisions of the **1987 Act** will not be enough to fill a whole essay. You will need, in addition, to look more generally at the rules that protect minors, and those that protect people who deal with minors. McKendrick is clearly of the view that there is currently an 'imbalance'. You are specifically asked whether or not you agree with this. Whichever conclusion you come to (and you will not be marked down simply on the basis of the line you take) must be supported by argument.

The following approach is suggested:

- an outline of the rules protecting minors;
- an outline of the rules protecting those dealing with minors;
- an outline of the changes made by the **Minors' Contracts Act 1987**;
- a discussion of possible remaining areas of 'imbalance'; and
- a conclusion.

Answer

English law adopts a paternalistic approach to the question of minors' contracts (a 'minor' being any person under the age of 18). Those under the age of 18 are thought to need protection from exploitation by unscrupulous traders, so the presumption is that all contracts made by minors are unenforceable against them. There are, however, a number of exceptions to this general rule. Some of these, as we shall see, however, are themselves designed for the benefit of the minor. The **Minors' Contracts Act 1987 (MCA)** altered the rules applying to minors' contracts, with the aim and effect of improving the position of those who deal with minors. The changes were not extensive, however, and many of the rules that applied before 1987 continue to operate in the minor's favour. The first major exception to the general rule of unenforceability relates to contracts for 'necessaries'. The reasoning here is that a total rule of unenforceability would act to the minor's disadvantage. If traders knew that any contract with a minor would involve the risk of the minor deciding not to honour it, they would be reluctant to enter into such contracts at all. As a consequence, the minor would have difficulty acquiring the basic requirements of everyday life, such as food or clothing.[1] The concept of necessaries, both goods and services, was explained in some detail in *Chapple v Cooper* (1844). It means not only things that are absolutely necessary for survival, but those that are required for a reasonable existence. Food and clothing are obviously covered, but medical assistance and education also fall into this category. Once the goods or services are of a kind that can be put in the general category of 'necessaries', there is then a further question as to whether they are appropriate to the particular minor. Whether a silk dress can count as a necessary will depend on the minor's normal standard of living. It will also depend on whether the minor is already adequately supplied with goods or services of this kind: *Nash v Inman* (1908) and s 3 of the **Sale of Goods Act 1979** (re goods). It should be noted that *Nash v Inman* made it clear that the trader who is ignorant of the minor's situation will not be protected. The decision is made by looking at matters entirely from the minor's point of view. The second major category of enforceable contracts is that of 'beneficial contracts of service': in other words, employment contracts. It is recognised that the minor should be able to earn a living, but if such contracts were void or voidable, he or she might have great difficulty in finding anyone prepared to offer employment. The contract as a whole must be beneficial, however. In *De Francesco v Barnum* (1889), a very restrictive apprenticeship was held not to be binding on a girl dancer.

There are also certain contracts that are voidable, in the sense that they will be enforceable unless repudiated by the minor before attaining the age of 18, or within a reasonable time thereafter: *Edwards v Carter* (1893). The main ones are: contracts relating to an interest in land, for example, a lease; obligations of shareholding, for example, to pay the 'calls'; partnership agreements; and marriage settlements.

From this, it can be seen that there are considerable risks in contracting with minors. The provisions of the **MCA** now need to be considered. The main effect of s 1 of the **MCA** is to repeal the provision of the **Infants Relief Act 1874**, which prohibited the minor from ratifying an unenforceable contract after attaining majority. The reason for this was the wish to prevent minors from being pressurised into making enforceable an agreement that was previously unenforceable. There was an anomaly, however, in that the minor could be bound if a fresh agreement, supported by consideration, was made after majority. The change in the **MCA** means that once the minor has attained majority, the law recognises that the need for protection disappears, and the individual must be allowed to decide whether to accept a particular obligation or not.

The **Infants Relief Act 1874** had also caused some conceptual problems by its statement that certain contracts, including contracts for goods other than necessaries, should be 'absolutely void'. This clearly did not correspond to reality, in that a contract for the sale of non-necessary goods, if carried out, was regarded as effective to transfer the ownership of the goods and the money. If it had truly been 'absolutely void', then this would not have happened. **Section 1** of the **MCA** repeals the relevant provision, so that such contracts can now have limited legal effect.

Perhaps the most important provision of the **MCA** for the person contracting with a minor is **s 3**. Under the law prior to the **MCA**, the person who supplied non-necessary goods to a minor ran a great risk. It should be remembered that the contract is unenforceable whether the supplier knows that the other party is a minor or not. Moreover, even if the supplier knows the minor's age, ignorance of the fact that the minor is already adequately supplied with the relevant goods will not prevent the contract being unenforceable: *Nash v Inman*. Under the pre-**MCA** law, the supplier who had supplied non-necessary goods on credit could recover nothing unless the minor had fraudulently induced the contract. In other words, the minor could retain the goods, and was not obliged to pay anything for them. Now, **s 3** of the **MCA** allows a restitutionary remedy. It states that, where a contract is unenforceable against a defendant, or has been repudiated because the defendant is a minor, the court can, where it is 'just and equitable to do so', order the defendant to return any property received under the contract, or other property representing it, to the claimant. Thus, non-necessary goods can no longer be retained, and the minor cannot be unjustly enriched. If, however, the goods have been consumed or otherwise disposed of without being exchanged for other property, the supplier will still have no remedy.

The final provision of the **MCA** that should be noted is **s 2**. This deals with the situation in which a contractor is aware that the other party is a minor, and so seeks a guarantee from an adult third party. Prior to the **MCA**, such contracts were thought to be void. **Section 2** now makes it clear that they are enforceable against the guarantor.

From the above, it can be seen that the **MCA** has improved in various ways the position of a person dealing with a minor. Are there still areas in which there is, as McKendrick suggests, a need for a better balance between the parties? There are two areas in which the law might be thought still to operate harshly on those who contract with minors. First, **s 3** of the **Sale of Goods Act 1979** provides that even where goods supplied fall into the category of necessaries, the supplier can still only recover a 'reasonable' price rather than the contract price. Once the enforceability of a contract is recognised, there seems to be no strong reason for not allowing it to have full effect. Moreover, no equivalent rule seems to apply in relation to services or contracts of employment – there is no obligation, for example, to pay reasonable wages.[2]

Second, the law still operates strictly against those who act without knowing that the other party is a minor, or who are unaware of the fact that goods supplied are either inappropriate to the minor's lifestyle or surplus to the minor's reasonable requirements. In such a situation (unlike the equivalent position in relation to other types of incapacity, such as mental incapacity or intoxication), the ignorance of the contractor provides no basis for compensation.

Although the **MCA 1987** has removed a number of anomalies, and to some extent improved the position for those who contract with minors, McKendrick is probably right, for the reasons noted above, in asserting that there is still room for improvement and 'further rationalisation'.

Think points

1 Is there in fact much risk for the trader in, for example, a straightforward purchase of goods for cash?

2 Would a contract that paid totally derisory wages be regarded as 'beneficial' for the minor?

Question 15

Sue Smasher was a promising young tennis player. In July 2007, when she was aged 16, she entered into two separate agreements, both of which were to run until July 2010:

(a) with Lew Lobb, a noted tennis coach, whereby he undertook to organise her training and decide in which tournaments she should play. In return, Sue agreed to act on Lew's advice and to pay him 20 per cent of her winnings from tournaments; and

(b) with Drivepowa Ltd, whereby Sue promised to use its sports equipment in all tournaments, in return for Drivepowa's paying all of her travelling expenses.

In July 2008, Sue disobeyed Lew's instruction to play in the Tournament of the Century in the USA, where the total prize money was £1.5 million, and returned to England to defend her title at the Eastmouth Championships, where the total prize money was only £20,000. Because these championships would receive far less publicity than the Tournament of the Century, Drivepowa refused to pay her air fare from the USA. Sue therefore decided not to use its rackets any more, and ordered ten 'Diamond' rackets from Hitfirm plc. These rackets had a genuine diamond fixed into the handle, and cost £1,000 each. After five rackets had been delivered, but before any had been paid for, Sue decided to retire from professional tennis.

What is the position as to the enforceability of Sue's contracts with Lew Lobb, Drivepowa Ltd and Hitfirm plc?

Answer plan

Since Sue is under the age of 18 when she makes the contracts, she has limited capacity.

The three contracts raise different issues related to contracts with minors:

- Lew Lobb's contract concerns the enforceability of a contract for services, which will depend on whether those services are 'necessary';
- Drivepowa has broken its contract – here, the issue is whether such a contract is enforceable by a minor; and
- the contract with Hitfirm is for goods – are these goods necessaries? If so, what are Hitfirm's rights? If not, can it recover the rackets already delivered?

The best way to deal with problem questions of this type is to give a short introduction dealing with the general issues arising in the area, and then to take each contract in turn.

Answer

Under English law, minors – that is, people under the age of 18 – have limited capacity to make contracts. Sue Smasher has made three contracts: two when she was aged 16; one when she was aged 17. Two of these have been broken, one by Sue and one by the other contracting party. One of them is still partially executory. Each of them needs to be considered individually as to the rights and remedies that may be available.

The basic approach of the law is to say that contracts are not enforceable against minors, but then to allow some exceptions to this. The two main exceptions are:

- contracts for 'necessary' goods and services; and
- 'beneficial' contracts of employment.

The issues that then arise are: (a) what is meant by 'necessary'; (b) what is meant by 'beneficial'; and (c) what are the consequences if the contract falls within one of the exceptions – that is, is it then fully enforceable against the minor, or is the remedy more quasi-contractual or restitutionary? Both (a) and (c) will need to be considered here, but probably not (b), as we will see.

The first contract to consider is that with Lew Lobb. At first sight, this might seem to come within the category of an employment contract, since it relates closely to Sue's career as a professional tennis player. On closer inspection, however, it is clear that Sue is not employed by Lew. He is simply providing her with the benefit of his advice and experience, in return for a share of her winnings. In other words, he is providing her with 'services'. A similar conclusion was reached in a case concerning an 'agency' contract entered into by the footballer Wayne Rooney when he was a minor: *Proform Sports Management Ltd v Proactive Sports Management Ltd* (2007). The question, then, is whether the services provided by Lew Lobb are 'necessary' services.

The approach to the definition of 'necessaries' in English law has two elements, one objective, the other subjective. The objective element asks whether what has been supplied comes into the general category of something that is necessary. As Alderson B said in *Chapple v Cooper* (1844), 'things necessary are those without which an individual cannot reasonably exist', such as food, clothing, lodging and education. The subjective element asks whether the particular thing supplied is appropriate to the particular minor who has received it. Just because food is a necessary, it does not mean that a contract to buy caviar is a contract for necessaries. This issue is considered further below, in relation to the contract with Hitfirm plc.

As regards the contract with Lew Lobb, this might well be regarded as a contract for necessaries on the basis that it is analogous to a contract for education. The relevant authority is *Roberts v Gray* (1913). In this case, the defendant was an aspiring billiards player, who made a contract to go on a world tour with the plaintiff, who was an experienced player. The Court of Appeal had no difficulty in regarding this as a quasi-educational contract, and therefore within the scope of a contract for necessaries. If that is the case here, then Sue's contract with Lew Lobb should also be enforceable.[1] The issue then arises as to what the consequences are of Sue's failure to follow Lew's instructions, thus breaking the contract. In *Roberts v Gray*, it was argued by the defendant that the plaintiff should only recover on a *quantum meruit* basis, rather than full contractual damages. The Court refused to accept this, and allowed the plaintiff to recover his full losses, even though the contract in this case was almost entirely executory.[2] It seems, then, that Lew will be able to recover, for example, for the lost opportunity of taking a 20 per cent share of the much higher prize money available at the Tournament of the Century.

Turning now to the contract with Drivepowa, the position appears to be much more straightforward. There is no indication that Drivepowa has specified in its contract with Sue that she should play in any particular tournaments. That being so, Drivepowa's failure to pay Sue's air fare from the USA would be a breach of contract. Sue has treated this as a repudiatory breach, and has ordered tennis rackets from another firm. Whether or not the contract with Drivepowa is a contract for necessaries (which is arguable) is thus probably irrelevant, since it is Sue who is likely to be suing Drivepowa rather than vice versa. It is accepted that even in relation to contracts that are unenforceable against the minor, the minor can enforce against the other party. Sue should be able to recover the cost of her air fare from Drivepowa, and should face no further action from the company.

The third contract to consider is that with Hitfirm plc. Here, the issue is whether the tennis rackets are 'necessaries'. The leading authority is *Nash v Inman* (1908). A university student placed an order for 11 fancy waistcoats with a tailor. These were supplied, but the student refused to pay. The tailor sued, but the student claimed that, as he was a minor, the contract could not be enforced against him. The Court of Appeal held that, although clothing was clearly something that came within the category of necessary goods, the trial judge had been justified in ruling that the waistcoats were not necessaries. This was because the student was already adequately supplied with waistcoats, and there was no evidence that they were appropriate to the lifestyle of the student. **Section 3** of the **Sale of Goods Act 1979** similarly states that necessary goods are those 'suitable to the condition in life of the minor . . . and to his actual requirements at the time of sale and delivery'.

How does this apply to the case of Sue and Hitfirm plc? Tennis rackets would not normally be considered 'necessaries'. But presumably, since Sue uses them to earn her living, in this situation they may come under the heading of 'tools of the trade'. The issue then becomes whether the 'Diamond' rackets are appropriate to Sue's 'condition in life'. If she were a very successful tennis player, then probably rackets of this kind, costing such a large sum each, would be appropriate. Since she is only 'promising', they may not be. Moreover, it may well be the case that Sue is still adequately supplied with Drivepowa's rackets, so that this element of the test would not be satisfied either.

If the rackets are not necessaries, s 3(1) of the **Minors' Contracts Act 1987** gives the court power to order her to return to Hitfirm the five that have been delivered, if it is just and equitable to do so. There seems no reason why she should not be so ordered here. She will have no other obligation under the contract however. If, on the other hand, the rackets were regarded as necessaries, which it is suggested is unlikely, s 3 of the **Sale of Goods Act 1979** says that the minor must pay a reasonable price for goods 'sold and delivered'. This would mean that she would have to pay a reasonable price, which might be less than £5,000, for the five rackets she has received, but would not be obliged to take delivery of, or pay for, the remaining five.[3]

In summary, therefore, it looks as though Sue will have to pay some compensation to Lew Lobb for her breach of the contract with him. She, in her turn, will be able to recover damages from Drivepowa for its refusal to pay her air fare. The most tricky issue relates to the 'Diamond' tennis rackets. She may be obliged to return them, or she may have to pay a reasonable sum for the five that she has received. What is certain is that she will have no obligation as regards the five that she has ordered, but which have not yet been delivered.

Think points

1 Would Lew Lobb's contract be beneficial to Sue if, say, it provided that he would take 75 per cent of her winnings? In that case could it be argued that, although ostensibly for necessaries, it should be unenforceable because of harsh or onerous terms?

2 Would a contract of the *Roberts v Gray* type be better dealt with as an employment contract? Some commentators have argued this – for example, Cheshire, Fifoot and Furmston, *Contract Law*, 15th edn, 2007 p 552; cf Stone, *The Modern Law of Contract*, 7th edn, 2008, pp 239–40.

3 What would have been the position if the contract had been for the supply of necessary services? *Roberts v Gray* is authority that a payment of a reasonable sum for what has been supplied will not be recoverable. Is there any reason why goods and services should be treated differently in this respect.

Question 16

To what extent does the law provide sufficient protection for those who enter into a contract with a person who, through age, mental illness or intoxication, may be said to lack the capacity to make a binding agreement?

Answer plan

This is a straightforward essay question dealing with capacity. Note, however, that it is not limited to the position in relation to minors, but brings in mental illness and intoxication as well. There is no point in attempting this question unless you are aware of the basic principles of these areas. Inevitably, because of the fact that there is more law to be discussed, much of the essay will be devoted to minors' contracts, but an essay that ignored the other two aspects altogether would be likely to be heavily marked down.

The law relating to all three areas needs to be outlined. The question then asks you to say whether there is sufficient protection for the other contracting party in this situation. In other words, you are asked to look at the position not through the eyes of the minor or other 'incapacitated' individual, but through the eyes of the person contracting with them. One issue that will certainly need to be considered here is the extent to which knowledge of the incapacity is necessary before it affects the other party's ability to enforce an agreement. The rules as to recovery of property transferred under an unenforceable agreement will also need to be discussed.

Answer

In order to answer this question, it is necessary to outline the basic rules that apply to each of the three situations: that is, minors, mental illness and intoxication. The greater part of the law in this area is concerned with minors' contracts, but we shall start with the other two.

As regards mental incapacity, persons whose mental state is such that their affairs are under the control of the court by virtue of the **Mental Health Act 1983** cannot contract on their own behalf at all, and any purported contract will be void. Those who are not subject to the control of the court, but are, as a result of mental incapacity, shown to be unable to appreciate the nature of the transaction, may also not be bound by the contract. Here, however, this will only be the case if the person can show that the other contracting party was aware of the incapacity: *Imperial Loan Co v Stone* (1892). If that is so, then the contract will be voidable at the option of the mentally disordered person. However, even if there was such awareness on the part of the other party, the mentally disordered person may still have some liability if what was to be supplied comes into the category of 'necessaries'. This issue is considered in more detail in relation to minors' contracts, below.

The approach to the intoxicated contractor is very similar. In other words, the drunken individual will be bound to the contract unless it is shown that the other party was, at the time of the contract, aware that they were contracting with someone incapable, through inebriation, of understanding the nature of the transaction: *Gore v Gibson* (1843). Once again, however, if 'necessaries' have been supplied, there may still be some liability.

The most detailed set of rules, however, are those applying to minors' contracts. A minor is a person under the age of 18. The basic rule is that contracts made by such a person are unenforceable against the minor. A person contracting with a minor is, therefore, in a risky position.[1] Some contracts are, however, enforceable. There are two main categories:

- contracts for 'necessaries'; and
- beneficial contracts of employment.

Contracts for necessaries include contracts for goods or services. Necessary goods are defined in **s 3** of the **Sale of Goods Act 1979** as goods suitable to the condition in life of the minor, and to the minor's actual requirements at the time of sale and delivery. The approach of the courts to this definition has been to say that there are certain categories of goods that come within the scope of necessaries: that is, food, clothing, etc. Once it is determined that the goods are of this type, then the two tests from the **Sale of Goods Act** must be applied: that is, are they suitable to this particular minor, and does the minor have enough of them already? The first part of the approach (that is, are the goods capable of being necessaries?) is clearly objective, and will not vary from case to case. The **Sale of Goods Act** tests are subjective, and will vary depending on the minor concerned. As was stated in *Chapple v Cooper* (1844), which contains one of the fullest statements of the courts' position on this issue, articles of mere luxury will never be necessaries, but luxurious articles of utility may be in some circumstances. In *Peters v Fleming* (1840), it was accepted that an undergraduate student could claim that a watch was a necessary, but whether one that had a gold chain was appropriate to his lifestyle was a matter for the jury. In *Ryder v Wombwell* (1868), however, the court held that a pair of diamond and ruby cufflinks and a silver goblet could not possibly be necessaries.

As to the issue of 'adequate supply' in *Nash v Inman* (1908), in which the items concerned were 11 fancy waistcoats, it was held that the onus was on the supplier to show that the minor did not have an adequate supply of waistcoats. In applying both tests, it seems that the knowledge, or lack of knowledge, of the supplier as to the minor's position as regards lifestyle, or supply of the goods in question is irrelevant.

The above approach to necessary goods has been applied in much the same way to services. In other words, certain types of service, such as provision of lodging, education, or medical treatment, are regarded as within the category of 'necessaries'. Whether they are such in a particular case again involves looking at the needs and reasonable expectations of the minor concerned.

The second main category of enforceable contracts is beneficial contracts of employment. A minor needs to be able to earn a living, but must be protected from exploitation.[2] Contracts of employment are valid, therefore, but they must, judged overall, be beneficial. So, in *De Francesco v Barnum* (1889), a very restrictive contract for apprentice dancers was held invalid. The girls concerned were bound for seven years, were required not to marry, and had no guarantee that they would be provided with work during the contract. On the other hand, the contract must be looked at as a whole. In *Clements v London & NW Railway* (1894), a railway porter was employed under a contract that contained an accident compensation scheme that provided lower rates of compensation than the statutory scheme, which would otherwise have applied. However, the contractual scheme covered a wider range of accidents, so the court was not prepared to say that it was not overall a beneficial contract.

What then is the position of the person who contracts to supply goods and services to someone who may lack capacity? The first thing to note is that there is a distinction between contracting with minors and contracting with those suffering from mental incapacity and drunkards. In relation to the latter two categories, the contractor will only be unable to enforce the contract if he or she was aware of the lack of capacity on the other side. If the contract is made in ignorance of the disability, it will be fully enforceable.

Such ignorance on the part of the other contracting party will not, however, prevent a minor escaping from the contract. The balance here is more in favour of the minor.

Second, when goods that are necessaries are supplied to a person lacking capacity, the supplier will not necessarily recover the full price. The **Sale of Goods Act 1979** only requires that a 'reasonable' price should be paid: **s 3(2)**. Here, again, the supplier is in the worse position. Moreover, the **Sale of Goods Act** makes it clear that this only applies to goods actually delivered. If the contract is wholly or partly executory, then, even if the goods are necessaries, the supplier can claim no damages for failure to take delivery.[3]

The position seems to be different as regards necessary services. In *Roberts v Gray* (1913), the court allowed recovery of damages for what was largely still an executory contract for the supply of services. The same is true of a beneficial contract of service, which is regarded as being fully binding.

What of the person who supplies non-necessary goods or services? As far as goods are concerned, **s 3** of the **Minors' Contracts Act 1987** allows the court to order the return of such goods, or other property representing the goods.[4] This will not apply, however, when the incapacity is mental or caused by intoxication. Here, the supplier seems to have no remedy. The same would appear to be the case in relation to all types of incapacity when it is services rather than goods that have been supplied.

Finally, it should be noted that a trader who knows that the other party is a minor can achieve some protection by requiring an adult to give a guarantee. Such guarantees are made enforceable against the adult, by virtue of **s 2** of the **Minors' Contracts Act 1987**, even if the contract with the minor is unenforceable. The conclusion in answering the question posed as to the sufficiency of protection for those who contract with those lacking capacity must be that there are some imbalances. In relation to mental incapacity and intoxication, the contracting party is probably sufficiently protected, because of the requirement of knowledge. In relation to minors, however, the supplier of goods or services may not know that the other party is under the age of 18. Moreover, in relation to all types of incapacity, it seems hard that goods or services can lose their status as necessaries simply because, without the knowledge of the supplier, the other party is already adequately supplied with goods of that type. In these respects, the law seems to be stretching perhaps too far in the way of protecting the incompetent contractor. The provisions of the **Minors' Contracts Act 1987** have helped to make things a little less risky for the person who contracts with those under the age of 18, but the advice must still be that a person should be very wary of contracting with someone who does not appear to know what they are doing, or appears to be under the age of 18. When goods or services are to be supplied in such a situation, it will always be the safest course to insist on payment in advance. If credit is given, it may be that the contract will be avoided, and there will then be no means of redress.

Think points

1 How are the majority of contracts made by children? They will generally involve straightforward and simultaneous exchanges of money for goods. Questions of enforceability will rarely arise in this context.

2 But note the reluctance of the courts to give effect to trading contracts, as, for example, in *Cowern v Nield* (1912), which makes things difficult for the underage business person.

3 Could specific performance be ordered? It would seem not. It is not generally available in relation to contracts for the supply of goods, and it would be surprising if it was ordered with any greater freedom in relation to contracts with minors.

4 Does this include money received when the minor has sold the goods to a third party? The statute is not specific on the point, but money should be regarded as being included within 'property', so that it would be recoverable.

CHAPTER 5

CONTENTS OF THE CONTRACT

INTRODUCTION

In this chapter, we turn from looking at the question of whether there are any contractual obligations between the parties to the content of any such obligations. In other words, where there is a contract, how do the courts determine what the terms are?

There are two main issues to be considered here:

- the status of pre-contractual statements; and
- the question of 'implied terms' under statute and, more particularly, at common law.

The first of these requires knowledge of the rules by which the courts decide whether a particular statement made during negotiations is to be regarded as part of any subsequent contract, and the use of the collateral contract. If a statement is not part of the main contract or a collateral contract, then the possibility of an action for misrepresentation should be considered. This requires looking at:

- the requirements for a statement to be regarded as a 'misrepresentation'; and
- possible remedies under the common law and the **Misrepresentation Act 1967**.

Sometimes, a contract question will call for discussion of liability for negligent misstatements under *Hedley Byrne v Heller* (1964). This complicated topic, however, is more appropriately dealt with in tort, and there is no detailed discussion of it in any of the suggested answers in this chapter. Note also that there is further discussion of the law relating to misrepresentations in Chapter 7.

In relation to implied terms, the most commonly used examples of statutory implied terms are **ss 12–15** of the **Sale of Goods Act 1979**. Detailed knowledge of these sections will not, however, generally be required in answering questions in a basic contract course. They are, however, discussed further in Chapter 15. Under the common law, the following issues in particular need to be understood:

- the *Moorcock* test;
- the 'officious bystander' test; and
- the approach of the House of Lords in *Liverpool City Council v Irwin* (1977).

Two issues related to the contents of the contract are not dealt with here:

- incorporation of terms – this is covered in Chapter 6, in relation to exemption clauses, but remember that the rules of incorporation potentially apply to all clauses, as shown by the decision in *Interfoto Picture Library v Stiletto Visual Programmes* (1989); and

- the distinction between 'conditions', 'warranties' and 'innominate terms' – this is dealt with in Chapter 11, in connection with performance and breach.

Checklist

You should be familiar with the following areas:

- the distinction between 'representations' and 'terms', and its importance;

- remedies for misrepresentations under the common law;

- remedies under the **Misrepresentation Act 1967**;

- the concept of the collateral contract;

- statutory implied terms; and

- terms implied at common law – the *Moorcock* test, the 'officious bystander' test and *Liverpool City Council v Irwin* (1976).

Question 17

'. . . in business transactions what the law desires to effect by the implication [of a term] is to give such business efficacy to the transaction as must have been intended by the parties.' (Bowen LJ in *The Moorcock* (1889))

Does this still accurately represent the courts' approach to the implication of terms? Does Parliament, as, for example, in the **Sale of Goods Act 1979**, take a different approach?

Answer plan

There are two main aspects to this question: (a) the consideration of the approach of the courts to implied terms; and (b) the comparison with the approach of the legislature. There is no reason why these two aspects should not be dealt with separately, almost as if you were writing two short essays rather than one long one. The issues you will need to consider are as follows.

Part (a)

- The meaning of the *Moorcock* test at the time it was first used
- The development of rules regarding implication of terms – the 'officious bystander' test, etc
- The effect of the decision in *Liverpool City Council v Irwin* (1976)

Part (b)

- The types of terms implied in the **Sale of Goods Act 1979**
- The reason for implying them
- Comparison with the reasons for common law implication

Answer

From time to time, the parties to a contract may find that, for some reason, their agreement will not in practice work as they intended. One reason for this may be that there is a gap in the contractual terms that they have expressly agreed. One or other of the parties may then wish to argue that a term should be implied to fill that gap. Sometimes, the custom of a particular trade or place of business may indicate what term is to be implied (for example, *Hutton v Warren* (1836)), but that is not what we are primarily concerned with here. *The Moorcock* (1889) was concerned with the extent to which terms could be implied in the absence of any external source for such a term. The case concerned a contract that involved the plaintiff's ship mooring at the defendant's wharf on the Thames. The Thames being a tidal river, at low tide the ship, as both parties knew would be the case, settled on the river bed. Unfortunately, the ship was damaged, because of the nature of the river bed at that point. There was no express term as to the suitability of the river bed for mooring the ship there. It was held that a term could be implied to that effect. It was assumed that this must have been the intention of the parties; without such a term, the contract was effectively unworkable.

This type of implication is often referred to as 'implication in fact'. This indicates that what the courts are trying to do is decide, as a matter of fact, what the parties' unstated intentions were as to that particular aspect of the contract. The difficulty arises in trying to pin down that intention. In *The Moorcock*, it was based on the idea of 'business efficacy'; in other words, what is necessary for the contract to work.

The courts will not generally imply a term simply because it appears to be 'reasonable'. It cannot be assumed that the parties would have agreed to something reasonable, rather than necessary.

Later cases have looked for other ways of determining the intention of the parties. The most famous of these alternative approaches is the 'officious bystander' test. This was first stated in *Shirlaw v Southern Foundries Ltd* (1939). It operates by imagining what would have happened if, at the time of the contract, an 'officious bystander' had suggested the particular term that it is proposed should now be implied. If the likely reaction of the parties would have been a testy 'of course', because what was being put forward by the bystander was so obvious that it should go without saying, then the courts should be prepared to imply the term. As can be seen, this is simply another way of trying to determine what the parties must have intended at the time of contracting.

A different approach was taken by the House of Lords in *Liverpool City Council v Irwin* (1976). They were faced there with tenancy contracts relating to a block of flats, in which nothing was said about who was responsible for maintenance of the common parts of the block and, in particular, the lifts and rubbish chutes. The House of Lords implied a term that the landlord should take reasonable steps to keep the common parts in good repair. It cannot be said that such a term was necessary to make the contract work, in the *Moorcock* sense. It would have been quite possible to have a tenancy agreement in which responsibility for the common parts was shared among all the tenants of the block. Nor would the officious bystander test be likely to provide an agreed answer. What the House of Lords was doing here was in effect saying that: (a) the agreement was incomplete (it contained very little at all about the obligations of the landlord); (b) it was an agreement of a type that was sufficiently common that the court could decide that certain terms would normally be expected to be found in such an agreement; and (c) the term implied was the one that the House thought was reasonable in relation to the normal expectations of the obligations as between landlord and tenant.[1] This is sometimes referred to as a 'term implied in law', rather than in fact. It is imposed on the parties by the courts, rather than reflecting what they would have agreed on if they had thought about the matter at the time of the contract. The distinction between the two approaches was very clearly analysed by Lord Denning in *Shell v Lostock Garages Ltd* (1977). In contracts that are of such a common type (for example, sale of goods, landlord and tenant, employment) that the courts are able to identify typical obligations, the *Liverpool v Irwin* approach may be used to fill in the gaps.[2] If the agreement is not of this type (as was the case in *Shell v Lostock Garages*), then the test of necessity derived from *The Moorcock* would have to be used.

How do these two approaches relate to the approach of the legislature in the **Sale of Goods Act 1979**? This Act contains a number of implied terms in **ss 12–15**. Most of them relate to the quality of goods sold. For example, **s 13** implies a term that goods should match their description, and **s 14** that they should be of satisfactory quality. We are clearly dealing here with terms implied in law, rather than in fact.

The terms will be implied whatever the intentions of the parties at the time of the contract. They are not there for business efficacy, but because these are regarded as the normal obligations of a contract for the sale of goods. To this extent, the implication of terms in the **Sale of Goods Act** would seem to have close links with the approach in *Liverpool v Irwin*, particularly as interpreted by Lord Denning in *Shell v Lostock Garages*. Closer analysis, however, shows that the **Sale of Goods Act** goes further than this. It is not simply that the statute fills in the gaps with typical terms. If this was all, then, as is the case with the *Liverpool v Irwin* type of implication, it could be avoided if the parties included a specific term to deal with the matter. In contrast, the **Sale of Goods Act** terms are always implied, and only in very limited circumstances can the parties agree not to be bound by them. Only business contractors (as opposed to consumers) are allowed to agree to modification of these implied terms, and then only if the courts think that it is reasonable (see **s 6** of the **Unfair Contract Terms Act 1977**). The object of the implied term here is not to make the agreement work, but to protect purchasers, and, in particular, consumer purchasers, from the harshness of the common law rule of *caveat emptor* ('let the buyer beware').

In conclusion, it can be said that the quotation from *The Moorcock* does still represent the courts' approach to implication of terms, but it does not give the whole picture. There is now the different approach taken in *Liverpool v Irwin*, which is not based on business efficacy, nor on the intention of the parties. This newer approach is similar to that taken by Parliament in the **Sale of Goods Act 1979**, but the terms implied by that statute go further than the common law in imposing obligations on the parties, in the interests of protecting the weaker party in a sale of goods transaction.

Think points

1 Is this a test of 'necessity'? Lord Wilberforce in *Liverpool City Council v Irwin* claimed that it was – but it looks more like 'reasonableness'.

2 Would the fact that a number of contracts are all made in identical terms give rise to the operation of implication on the *Liverpool CC v Irwin* basis? 'No' was the answer given in *Ashmore v Corp of Lloyd's (No 2)* (1992).

Question 18

Fred is a farmer, growing vegetables, which he sells to local organic food shops. He is looking for a different type of fertiliser to use in growing cabbages, and has seen advertised a product called MasterGro, made by Growers plc, which it is claimed can increase yields by 10 per cent. He emails Growers plc asking if it can confirm that its product is approved for use in organic farming. He receives an email from Graham, a sales representative at Growers, stating that MasterGro is approved by the British

Organic Farming Association (BOFA). Fred then contacts his local wholesaler, Spreaders, and asks if it is able to supply MasterGro, whether it can confirm that it increases yields, and whether it is aware of any problem with its use for cabbages. Spreaders replies that it is an 'approved supplier' of MasterGro, that all users whom it has supplied report increased yields, and that it does not have any record of problems with its use in relation to cabbage growing. Five days later, having done some further research into MasterGro on the Internet, Fred places an order with Spreaders for 20 tonnes of MasterGro.

Despite using the fertiliser as directed, Fred finds that his cabbage yield is down by 10 per cent, and that the crop is of poor quality. He has now discovered that the BOFA removed its approval from MasterGro the week before Fred contacted Growers. This means that Fred will be unable to sell his cabbages to his usual buyers. He has also discovered that only 50 per cent of users of MasterGro had reported increased yields to Spreaders, that Spreaders had no formal approval as suppliers of MasterGro, and that it had not previously supplied MasterGro for cabbage growing. Spreaders was aware, however, that other suppliers had reported that MasterGro produced poor quality cabbages and low yields.

Advise Fred as to whether he can take action in relation to any of the statements made to him by Growers plc and Spreaders, so as to recover compensation for his poor crop of cabbages, and the fact that he is unable to sell them to his usual outlets.

Answer plan

This problem is concerned solely with liability for statements made prior to a contract. Any other possible action (eg under the **Sale of Goods Act 1979**) is precluded by the instructions.

Statements made prior to a contract can give rise to liability in four ways:

- as terms incorporated into the contract;
- as misrepresentations;
- as collateral contracts; and
- in the tort of negligent misstatement.

As indicated in the introduction to this chapter the fourth of these possibilities is not considered here. The other three will need to be discussed in relation to the statements made to Fred by Graham and Spreaders. Collateral contract is the most likely basis for liability based on Graham's statement as to the BOFA approval. Spreaders statements may be either incorporated into the contract, or be misrepresentations.

Answer

When there have been discussions between the parties prior to a contract questions can arise as to whether any of these pre-contractual negotiations were intended to be incorporated into any subsequent contract. If they were not, then there may still be liability based on misrepresentation or a collateral contract. These possibilities are raised by Fred's dealings with Growers and Spreaders.

Fred's cabbage crop has been disappointing, and he is looking for compensation. The first statement to be considered is that by Graham, when he claimed that MasterGro was approved by the BOFA. The problem for Fred in relation to this statement is that, although it was untrue, he did not enter into any contract with Growers for the supply of the fertiliser, and so he cannot argue that this statement was part of such a contract. Nor can he use the remedies for misrepresentation since these are also only available when the statement is made by one contracting party to the other. The only remaining possibility is to argue that there was a collateral contract with Growers plc.

The collateral contract device is well illustrated by the case of *Shanklin Pier v Detel Products* (1951). The plaintiff pier owners wished to repaint their pier. The defendants, who were paint manufacturers, told them that their paint would last for seven years, and on this basis the plaintiffs specified the defendants' paint for use in the painting contract. It began to peel off after three months. The plaintiffs did not appear to have any remedy, since they had specified the paint to be used but had not themselves bought it. It was found, however, that the defendants could be liable on a 'collateral' contract. This took the form of a promise that if the plaintiffs specified their paint for the main contract, the defendants would guarantee that it would last for seven years.

In our case, Fred would need to argue that Graham's statement about the BOFA was a 'promise', the consideration for which was his ordering MasterGro from Spreaders. In other words, this was a unilateral contract, in the form 'if you promise that MasterGro is approved by the BOFA, then I will order it for use on my cabbages'. The difficulty for Fred would be that he would have to prove that the statement by Graham was made with the contract to order the fertiliser in prospect. In the similar case of *Wells (Merstham) Ltd v Buckland Sand & Silica Co Ltd* (1965), the plaintiff ordered from a third party a specific type of sand produced by the defendants, on the basis of the defendants' assurance as to its composition. It was held that although it was not necessary for a specific contract to be in contemplation, the statement had to be made *animo contrahendi* – that is, with a view to a contract being made shortly.

This means that, at least, Fred will need to show that Graham was aware that he was a farmer, and interested in purchasing MasterGro, rather than say, a journalist writing an article about organic fertilisers, or a member of a pressure group interested in organic farming methods. Provided that Fred can show that Graham was aware that he, Fred, was a potential customer for MasterGro, then this may well be enough for him to establish a collateral contract, and so recover some compensation from Growers.

The other potential defendant is Spreaders. In relation to that company, Fred will be trying to argue either that the statements made were incorporated into the contract for the purchase of the fertiliser, or that they were misrepresentations. He might also consider arguing that some of the statements form a collateral contract with Spreaders.

Looking first at the possibility of incorporation, this can occur if the courts regard a pre-contractual statement as being sufficiently important that it must have been intended to be part of the contract. This was the case in *Bannerman v White* (1861), in which a buyer of hops had been assured that sulphur had not been used in their production. He had made it clear that he would not be interested in buying them if it had. When it turned out that sulphur had been used, he was entitled to reject them for breach of contract. In considering whether the statement is of sufficient importance to be incorporated, the courts will also look at the lapse of time between the statement and the contract (*Routledge v McKay* (1954)) and whether the party making the statement has held himself out as having special knowledge. In *Oscar Chess v Williams* (1957), a private seller of a car was held to have no special knowledge as to its year of manufacture. In contrast, in *Dick Bentley v Harold Smith* (1965), a car dealer was taken to have special knowledge as regards the mileage of a second-hand car, so that his statement became part of the contract. Applying this approach to Fred's case, the statement about Spreaders being an 'approved supplier' is unlikely to be regarded as being of sufficient importance to make it a part of the contract. The other two matters – the increased yield and the effectiveness with cabbages – are clearly important to Fred, and Spreaders is in the position of having 'special knowledge' of these issues. On the other hand, Fred waits five days, and does some more research of his own before placing his order for the fertiliser. In *Routledge v McKay*, a gap of a week was held to be sufficient to suggest that the statement should not be regarded as being incorporated. The same conclusion may well be arrived at here.

This brings us to the possibility of 'misrepresentation'. A misrepresentation is a false statement of fact or law, made by one party to a contract to the other, which induces the contract. In other words, it provides a reason (not necessarily the only or most important reason: *Edgington v Fitzmaurice* (1885)) for the contract being made. In Fred's case, all of the statements made by Spreaders are statements of fact, and the first two – that it is an approved supplier, and that all of the customers have reported increased yields – are clearly untrue. The third statement, about not having reports of problems with cabbages, is more difficult. Technically it is true, but it conceals the fact that Spreaders has not supplied MasterGro for cabbage growing before. In some circumstances, 'half-truths' have been held to constitute misrepresentations. In

Dimmock v Hallett (1866), for example, the statement that certain flats were fully let when, in fact, as the maker of the statement knew, the tenants had given notice to quite was capable of being a misrepresentation. On this basis, it would seem that Spreaders' statement about the lack of reported problems with cabbages would be treated as a false statement of fact.

Did these statements of fact induce the contract? There is a similar problem here as there was with the issue of incorporation, in that Fred not only waited five days before making the contract, but carried out his own research on the Internet. Spreaders would no doubt suggest that this indicates that Fred did not rely on its statements when he made the contract. If this argument is accepted, Fred will have no remedy for misrepresentation.

If, however, Fred can convince the court that he did rely on one or more of Spreaders' statements, he will be best advised to base his action on **s 2(1)** of the **Misrepresentation Act 1967**. The primary common law remedy for misrepresentation is rescission of the contract, but that is of no use to Fred. He will want damages. **Section 2(1)** provides the same damages as are available for the tort of deceit,[1] but with the advantage that it would be up to Spreaders to prove that the maker of the statement had reasonable grounds to believe it was true – which seems unlikely on the facts.

A final possibility would be to recast Spreaders' statements as promises – eg 'we promise that we are approved suppliers of MasterGro' – and use the collateral contract device outlined above. It is possible to use a collateral contract between two contracting parties (*Esso v Mardon* (1976)). On the facts, however, this would seem rather artificial, and it would be better for Fred to rely on the action for misrepresentation under the **1967 Act**.

In conclusion, Fred has possible actions against both Growers and Spreaders, but neither is without its problems. In relation to Growers, there is the need to prove that the statement was made with a contract in mind, and in relation to Spreaders, Fred needs to prove that the statements had a role in inducing him to make the contract, despite the fact that he had carried out some of his own research.

Think point

1 Should negligence attract the same remedies as fraud? This was the view taken by the Court of Appeal in *Royscot Trust Ltd v Rogerson* (1991), but the House of Lords in *Smith New Court Securities Ltd v Scrimgeour Vickers (Asset Management) Ltd* (1994) expressed some scepticism as to whether this was the correct approach. It did not go so far as to overrule *Royscot v Rogerson*, however, so the case must still be regarded as good law.

Question 19

In June, Samira bought a collection of valuable pictures and furniture from a sale at a manor house in Leicester. She needed to arrange for these items to be moved from Leicester to Petworth in Sussex, to sell in her antiques shop. She approached Speedy Deliveries. During discussions that took place on 3 June, Samira made it clear that, because of the requirements of her insurers, the pictures must be transported vertically, and that items should not be stacked on top of each other unless separated by packing material of a thickness at least 10 cm. These points were accepted by the representative of Speedy Deliveries. On 10 June, Speedy Deliveries provided a written confirmation of the contract, on the back of which were its terms and conditions of carriage. Clause 7 stated that 'items will be packed to make most efficient use of the space in the carrier's lorry and at the discretion of the carrier's employees'. Later that day, Samira telephoned Speedy Deliveries and arranged for the transport of her items to take place on 12 June. On 12 June, the items were loaded into Speedy Deliveries' lorry. During the journey, the lorry was involved in a crash, which was not the fault of Speedy Deliveries' driver. Many of Samira's items were badly damaged. She has learnt that a number of the paintings were being carried horizontally, that the packing material used was only of 5 cm thickness, and that these factors have aggravated the damage to her goods.

Samira's insurance company are now refusing to compensate her, because the goods were not packed in the specified manner. Speedy Deliveries has, on the other hand, evidence that the way in which the goods were packed met the standards generally applicable in the transport industry.

Advise Samira.

Answer plan

This question is concerned with whether pre-contractual oral agreements can form part of a subsequent contract. Note that it is not concerned with misrepresentations, since the specification of the way in which the goods were to be carried did not involve statements of fact, but promises as to future behaviour. That is, Speedy Deliveries' representative, in accepting Samira's requirements, was impliedly promising that the goods would be carried in the way she had stipulated. The question is then whether this promise was part of the contract of carriage – or was, perhaps, a collateral contract.

The following approach is suggested:

- identify the factors at which the courts look in deciding whether pre-contractual statements have formed part of the subsequent contract, that is:

- ○ intention of the parties (*Bannerman v White* (1861));
- ○ lapse of time (*Routledge v McKay* (1954));
- ○ imbalance in skill and knowledge (*Dick Bentley Productions Ltd v Harold Smith (Motors) Ltd* (1965); *Oscar Chess Ltd v Williams* (1957));
- ○ where the contract has been put into writing, whether the oral promise was included (the so-called 'parol evidence' rule);
- note that the last of these factors may be the most difficult for Samira, but that it is not an absolute rule – *Evans & Son Ltd v Andrea Merzario Ltd* (1976) (a case with similar facts to Samira's); and
- consideration of the possibility that Samira may be able to take action under a collateral contract (*City of Westminster Properties v Mudd* (1959)).

Answer

In this problem, Samira will seek to argue that Speedy Deliveries (SD) is in breach of contract, because it has failed to transport her goods in the way specified. Speedy Deliveries' response is likely to be that its terms of carriage allow the goods to be packed at the discretion of its employees, and that the evidence that it had followed the general practice in the industry means that it has not been negligent.

The first issue to consider is whether Samira's statements made during part of the discussions form part of the contract between her and SD. It is assumed for the purposes of this answer that the contract was formed by Samira's phone call to SD on 10 June, in which she must be taken to have accepted the offer made in its quotation.

The courts look at a number of factors when trying to decide whether pre-contractual promises do in fact form a part of the subsequent contract. The most important of these is the intention of the parties. This may be difficult to determine, however, so the courts look to certain external factors, which may help to identify the intention. If, for example, the alleged term relates to something that was clearly of fundamental importance to one of the parties, then the courts will be likely to conclude that it should be part of the contract. In *Bannerman v White* (1861), the buyer's insistence that sulphur should not have been used in the production of hops fell into this category. This may be helpful to Samira; the other factors that the courts consider may be less so. For example, they will look at any significant lapse of time between the making of the pre-contractual statement and the contract. In *Routledge v McKay* (1954), a gap of a week was held to indicate that the statement was not part of the contract. Here, Samira makes the contract a week after the statement – but this should not be conclusive, as the courts are in this area exercising a flexible rule rather than a hard-and-fast time limit.

A further factor that has been important in some cases is any imbalance between the skill and judgment of the two parties. Statements made by a party with greater knowledge are more likely to be held to be incorporated into the contract. Compare, for example, *Oscar Chess Ltd v Williams* (1949), in which a statement by a private individual to a garage as to the age of a car was not incorporated, with *Dick Bentley Productions Ltd v Harold Smith (Motors) Ltd* (1965), in which a statement of mileage made by a garage to a private individual was incorporated. This test does not seem to help particularly as between Samira and SD, where there does not seem to be any significant imbalance between the parties.

The final test may be the most important in these circumstances. This is that where a contract is put into writing, then generally evidence as to previously agreed oral terms that do not appear in, or contradict, the written agreement is not allowed. This is sometimes referred to as the 'parol evidence rule'. SD will argue that this should apply here. The terms and conditions that it supplied, and which Samira must be deemed to have accepted on 10 June, allowed SD to pack the lorry as it wished (as long as it did not do so negligently). There are, however, some exceptions to the parol evidence rule. The one that is relevant here is exemplified by *Evans & Son Ltd v Andrea Merzario Ltd* (1976), a case in which the facts are similar to those of the problem. It concerned the carriage of goods by sea. The owner had been given an oral assurance that they would be carried in the hold. The written conditions of the carrier, however, allowed them to be carried on deck, and this is what happened. The goods were swept overboard in a storm. The Court of Appeal held that because the owner had made it clear that it was of the utmost importance that the goods should not be carried on deck, and this had been accepted by the carrier, the oral promise should be taken to override the terms stated in the written agreement.

Samira will obviously seek to rely on this authority. She had made it clear to SD's representative that, because of the requirements of her insurance company, it was of the utmost importance that her goods were packed in the way in which she had specified. Against this, SD will no doubt argue that she should have made this clear again when she arranged for the transport on 10 June. On balance, taking into account that Samira had made it clear that her conditions arose from the need to ensure that her insurance policy would cover the transport of the goods, a matter of considerable importance when valuable items were being carried, it is suggested that a court might well follow *Evans v Merzario* and hold that Samira's conditions as to the packing of the goods were part of the contract. If that is so, SD will be in breach of contract, and Samira will be able to recover damages resulting from this breach, which will amount to the sum she would otherwise have been able to claim from her insurance company.

A further possibility for Samira, even if the pre-contractual promise is not incorporated, is to argue that there was a collateral contract. This type of contract sits alongside the main contract and can operate to provide a remedy in relation to pre-contractual promises. It will generally be in the form of a unilateral contract, taking the form: 'If you will promise X, then I will enter into the main contract.' Entering into the main contract then becomes the consideration to make X enforceable. In the problem, Samira would be taken to be saying to SD on 3 June: 'If you promise that the goods will be carried in the way in which I have specified, then I will give you the contract to carry them.'

An example from the cases of the way in which this can operate is *City of Westminster Properties v Mudd* (1959). This concerned the renewal of a tenancy agreement in relation to a shop. The new agreement contained a clause forbidding the tenant from sleeping on the premises – something that he had been in the habit of doing. He objected to the new clause, but was assured orally that if he signed the new agreement, he would still be allowed to sleep on the premises. The landlord subsequently tried to rely on the tenant's 'breach' of the new clause as a basis for terminating the tenancy. It was held that, in the circumstances, the oral assurance formed a collateral contract, which the tenant was entitled to enforce. Samira's situation is not quite identical. To be so, she would have had to have objected on 10 June to clause 7 of SD's standard terms, and received an oral assurance that this would not be relied upon. Nevertheless, it is still possible for Samira to argue that she did have a collateral contract with SD, made through the agency of its representative on 3 June, relating to the way in which the pictures were to be carried and the thickness of the packing material, and that this should take precedence over the written terms. If that is the case, then she ought to be able to claim damages for breach of this contract – to be assessed in the same way as if the term had been a part of the main contract.

In conclusion, then, Samira has two main arguments that she can use against SD. First, she can argue, using *Evans v Merzario* as precedent, that the statements made on 3 June were incorporated into the contract of carriage and overrode SD's standard terms. Second, she can argue that there was a collateral contract, under which she only agreed to enter into the main contract of carriage, on the basis of the promises as to the way in which her goods would be packed. If either argument is successful, then she will be able to recover damages, which should be equivalent to the amount she would otherwise have been able to recover from her insurance company.

CHAPTER 6

EXCLUSION CLAUSES

INTRODUCTION

The questions in this chapter, like those in Chapter 5, are concerned with the contents of the contract. In this chapter, however, the focus is on a particular type of clause – the exclusion or exemption clause.

To answer questions on this topic, it is necessary to have a good grasp of the common law rules, the provisions of the **Unfair Contract Terms Act 1977 (UCTA)** and the **Unfair Terms in Consumer Contracts Regulations 1999 (UTCCR)**. Although the interrelation of common law and statute causes some complications, the rules themselves are relatively well established and clear. Provided that a systematic approach is adopted, then writing a good answer should not prove too difficult.

In answering a problem question, for example, the following issues should normally be considered in the following order.

- Is the clause incorporated?

- Does it cover the breach?

- Does **UCTA** apply? For example: (a) is it business liability – **s 1(3)**; (b) is it a clause of the type covered by the **UCTA**? See **s 13** and, for example, *Smith v Bush* (1989).

- Is it a negligence case? If so, look at **s 2** of the **UCTA**.

- Is it a consumer contract or a standard term contract? If so, look at **s 3** of the **UCTA**.

- Does the test of reasonableness apply and, if so, is it satisfied? See **s 11** of and **Sched 2** to the **UCTA**.

- Is the situation affected by the provisions of the **UTCCR** (see Question 21)?

Two other issues may need consideration.

- Is there a privity problem? That is, does the clause try to exclude the liability of someone who is not a party to the contract?

- Is it a sale of goods contract? If so, then look at **s 6** of the **UCTA**. (An example of this type of case is to be found in Question 23.)

Essay questions will frequently require you to compare the common law and the statutory approach to exclusion clauses. Much of the above material will still be relevant. In addition, however, you may need to deal with the proposals for reform of the **UCTA** and the **UTCCR** recently put forward by the Law Commission in Law Com No 292, *Unfair Terms in Contracts*, Cm 6464, 2005. This area is dealt with by Question 21.

Checklist

You should be familiar with the following areas:

- the rules of incorporation;
- the rules of construction;
- the doctrine of fundamental breach (at least in outline);
- general provisions of the **UCTA** 1977 – **ss** 1, 2, 3 and 11;
- special provisions of the **UCTA** relating to sale of goods contracts – **s** 6 and **Sched 2**;
- the meaning of 'reasonableness' under the **UCTA**;
- the provisions of the **UTCCR** 1999; and
- the Law Commission's proposals for reform of the legislation.

Question 20

Pamina owns a washing machine that has needed regular repair over the past two years. On the latest occasion on which it breaks down, she phones David, who has mended the machine on previous occasions. He agrees to come out on the basis of an 'all inclusive' charge of £50. When he has repaired the machine, he asks Pamina to sign a form stating that all work has been completed satisfactorily, that David will replace any parts that break down within three months, but that otherwise David accepts no liability for loss or damage caused by his work. Pamina signs the form.

The next time that Pamina uses the washing machine, it floods, causing £500 worth of damage to Pamina's carpets. When Pamina tries to switch it off, she receives a powerful electric shock from the casing, which severely burns her arm.

Advise Pamina.

Answer plan

This is a straightforward exclusion clause problem. As with most such problems, the issues to be considered are:

- was the exclusion clause incorporated?
- if so, does the clause cover the breach (rule of construction)?
- if so, does the **UCTA** apply?
- if so, is the clause void? Or, if applicable, does it satisfy the requirement of reasonableness?
- what is the effect of the **UTCCR**?

An answer of 'no' to either of the first two questions strictly speaking concludes the answer. In practice, however, even if you think that the clause was not incorporated or does not cover the breach, you should go on to deal with the applicability of the **UCTA** and the **UTCCR**.

Note that the issue of incorporation, which generally turns on the time and extent of notice, is here further complicated by the fact of previous dealings between the parties.

Answer

This question concerns the issue of whether David can rely on the exemption clause contained in the document that Pamina signed.

To start with, it is assumed that the problems of the flooding and the electric shock result from work that David has done. If he has done the work with reasonable care, and the subsequent problems arise from some other cause, then he will not be in breach of contract, nor liable in tort for negligence, and Pamina will have no remedy. If, on the other hand, the problems are a consequence of the work, then Pamina may have an action in contract or tort, or both.

If Pamina tries to sue David, and can establish causation and negligence on his part, he will no doubt try to rely on the exemption clause in the document that Pamina signed as protecting him from liability. For an exemption clause to be valid, it must be incorporated, and must on its true construction cover the breach that has occurred. If it satisfies both these tests, then it will be necessary to consider whether it is affected by the **Unfair Contract Terms Act 1977 (UCTA)** or the **Unfair Terms in Consumer Contracts Regulations 1999 (UTCCR)**.

To start with incorporation, the first rule is that the clause must have been put forward before, or at the time, the contract was made. If it is introduced later, then it cannot be part of the contract. This is illustrated by *Olley v Marlborough Court* (1949), in which an exemption clause displayed in a hotel bedroom was held not to be incorporated, since the contract had been made at the reception desk. How does this apply here? Pamina might well argue that she made her contract with David over the phone. He agreed to do the work; she agreed to pay £50. All of the essential elements of a contract seem to be present. If that is the case, then the document containing the exemption clause can be said to have come too late, and so not be part of the contract.[1] On the other hand, David might well be able to rely on the fact that he has dealt with Pamina in the past. Assuming that she has always had to sign a form of the kind used in this case, he might argue that she had sufficient notice of the clause from previous dealings. This was the approach taken by the court in *Spurling v Bradshaw* (1956), in which the clause was in a document delivered several days after the contract was made. It was, nevertheless, held to be effective because a similar document had been supplied in previous contracts between the parties. The course of dealing must be consistent, however. If David has sometimes used this document in his dealings with Pamina, but has not always done so, he may not be able to rely on it: *McCutcheon v McBrayne* (1964). Provided that the point as to timing is satisfied, Pamina will have difficulty arguing against incorporation of the term on the basis of lack of reasonable notice, which was the test established by *Parker v South Eastern Railway* (1877). Since she signed the document containing it, she will be deemed to have notice of its terms: *L'Estrange v Graucob* (1934).

The next issue to consider, assuming that the clause is incorporated, is whether it covers the breach which occurred. The basic approach to construction is the *contra proferentem* rule, which means that any doubt or ambiguity will be interpreted against the person trying to rely on the clause. The particular issue that may be relevant here is liability for negligence. In *White v John Warwick* (1953), it was held that the phrase 'nothing shall render the owners liable' referred only to strict liability under the contract, not to liability for negligence. Pamina might argue here that David's clause only refers to his liability to supply materials of satisfactory quality, and not to his negligent repairs. In recent cases, however, the appellate courts have emphasised the undesirability of seeking strained construction of clauses in order to strike them down: for example, *George Mitchell v Finney Lock Seeds* (1983). Parliamentary intervention in the area by means of the **UCTA** to protect the claimant, and in particular the consumer claimant, means that the courts should simply give the words of the clause their natural meaning. It is by no means clear that the simple lack of an all-encompassing phrase such as 'howsoever caused' will prevent David claiming that the clause does cover the breach.

If he succeeds on the incorporation and construction arguments, David will then face the restrictions of the **UCTA**. The **UCTA** applies mainly to attempts to exclude liabilities arising in the course of a business: s 1(3). The main provision that is relevant here is **s 2**, which deals with 'negligence'. This covers both tortious negligence and the negligent performance of a contract. It is assumed here that the cause of the problems with Pamina's washing machine is David's negligent workmanship.

Section 2(1) says that in relation to personal injuries caused by negligence there can be no exclusion of liability. As far as Pamina's injury to her arm is concerned, therefore, David will not be able to rely on the clause at all. The same approach to exclusion of liability for personal injury is taken in the **UTCCR**. In relation to other loss and damage caused by negligence, s 2(2) says that an exclusion clause will only be liable insofar as it satisfies the requirement of reasonableness. This is set out in **s 11**, and states that a clause must be a fair and reasonable one to have been included in the contract. The test relates to the time at which the contract was made, not the time when it was broken. There is little guidance from the case law as to how exactly the test should be applied. The appeal courts clearly feel that it is a matter best decided by the trial judge, who has heard all of the evidence, and they have indicated a reluctance to lay down guidelines: *Mitchell v Finney Lock Seeds* (1983). The Act itself contains, in **Sched 2**, some guidelines to be applied in relation to sale of goods cases. The Court of Appeal has confirmed that it is appropriate to consider these guidelines whenever the test of reasonableness is in issue: *Overseas Medical Supplies Ltd v Orient Transport Services Ltd* (1999). They include strength of bargaining power as a matter to be considered.

The court may also be influenced by the practice in other parts of the industry: *Mitchell v Finney Lock Seeds*. In the end, the court has simply to decide whether the level of exemption was reasonable in all of the circumstances. In this case, was it fair and reasonable for David to exclude his entire liability for any property damage caused by his negligently defective workmanship? It might well have been reasonable for him to limit his liability to a specified sum, but it is submitted that the attempt to reduce liability to zero goes too far, and that the court ought to hold this clause unreasonable. Again, the application of the provisions of the **UTCCR** is likely to result in a similar outcome.

In conclusion, then, it seems that Pamina has a good chance of success. David's strongest ground probably relates to the construction of the clause. It does seem to cover the situation that has arisen. However, even if David can show that the clause was a part of the contract with Pamina, and this is by no means certain, the effect of the **UCTA** and the **UTCCR** will be that he will certainly be unable to avoid liability for Pamina's injury to her arm, and may well also be liable for the damage to her carpets.

Think point

1 Could it be argued that there is a separate contract relating to the guarantee, which is given in exchange for the exemption of other liability? If so, the timing problem disappears.

Question 21

What potential problems are caused by the fact that some contracts are governed by both the **Unfair Contract Terms Act 1977** and the **Unfair Terms in Consumer Contract Regulations 1999**? Evaluate the extent to which the recent Law Commission proposals for amalgamating the legislation (Law Com No 292, *Unfair Terms in Contracts*, Cm 6464) would resolve these.

Answer plan

This question requires you to know your way around the **UCTA 1977**, the **UTCCR 1999** and the Law Commission's proposals. There is no need for a full description of both pieces of legislation, however. Since the **UTCCR** are only concerned with consumer contracts, you do not need to deal with the parts of the **UCTA** that relate solely to transactions between businesses. The following order of treatment is suggested:

- an outline of the relevant provisions of the **UCTA 1977**;
- an outline of the effect of the **UTCCR 1999**;
- identification of the problem areas;
- an outline of the Law Commission's proposals; and
- an evaluation of whether the proposals will solve the problems.

Answer

There are two pieces of legislation that control exemption and exclusion clauses under English law. These are the **Unfair Contract Terms Act 1977 (UCTA)** and the **Unfair Terms in Consumer Contracts Regulations 1999 (UTCCR)**. The potential for problems arises from the fact that in relation to some contracts, and some terms, both pieces of legislation will apply, but the controls that they contain are not identical.

The **UCTA 1977** is concerned with 'business liability' (as defined in **s 1**), but its provisions are not only concerned with contracts between businesses and consumers. Exclusion clauses in contracts between two businesses are subject to the controls in the Act if they deal with negligence (**s 2**), are contained in written standard terms (**s 3**), or relate to the statutorily implied terms in contracts for the supply of goods (**ss 6 and 7**). Since the area of overlap with the **UTCCR** relates solely to contracts between businesses and consumers, however, it is this type of contract on which attention will be focused here.

As between businesses and consumers, the **UCTA** has the following effects. If a contractual term purports to exclude liability for death or personal injury arising from negligence, it will be void (**s 2(1)**); in relation to other types of loss or damage the term will be subject to the 'requirement of reasonableness' (which is discussed further below). If the term purports to exclude liability for one of the statutorily implied terms in a contract for the supply of goods, it will be void (**ss 6 and 7**). If it relates to any other situation, not falling within **ss 2, 6** or **7**, then the terms will be subject to the requirement of reasonableness (**s 3**).

From this it will be clear that the concept of the 'consumer' is important to the scope of the UCTA. **Section 12** of the Act states that a person 'deals as a consumer' when they do not make the contract in the course of a business. The phrase 'dealing as a consumer' under the **UCTA** received judicial consideration in the case of *R & B Customs Brokers v UDT* (1988). The plaintiff in this case was a private company, which had bought a car for the business and personal use of one of the directors. The company was in the export business, and had no connection with the motor trade. The Court of Appeal held that the company, in buying the car, was not buying in the course of business for the purposes of **s 12** of the **UCTA**. This meant that the company could be treated as dealing as a consumer, and therefore gain the protection against exemption clauses provided by **s 6** of the **UCTA**, noted above.

This was regarded as a somewhat surprising decision, and was viewed with some scepticism by the Court of Appeal in *Stevenson v Rogers* (1999), which was concerned with the phrase 'in the course of business' as used in **s 14** of the **Sale of Goods Act 1979**. In *Feldarol Foundry plc v Hermes Leasing (London) Ltd* (2004), however, the Court of Appeal felt bound by *R & B Customs Brokers*, and confirmed its effect in relation to **s 12** of the **UCTA**. As far as the definition of 'dealing as a consumer' under this section is concerned, the *R & B Customs Brokers* decision is still good law.

So the **UCTA** uses a broad definition of 'consumer', and provides that all exclusion clauses in a contract with a consumer are either void, or subject to the requirement of reasonableness.

The **UTCCR** deal only with contracts made with consumers, but they apply to most terms in such contracts, not only exclusion clauses. The discussion here, however, will relate only to the effect of the Regulations on exclusion clauses, because this is the area of overlap with the **UCTA**.

It is first important to note that the **UTCCR** uses a narrower definition of 'consumer' than the **UCTA**. Under the Regulations a consumer must be a 'natural person' acting outside his trade, business or profession. This means that the claimants in *R & B Customs Brokers v UDT* and *Feldarol v Hermes Leasing* could not be treated as consumers under the Regulations. This, then, is one area of potential confusion between the **UCTA** and the **UTCCR**. On the same facts a claimant may be treated as a consumer by one, but not the other.

The **UTCCR** does not make any specific categories of term automatically void, in the way that we have seen the **UCTA** does in certain circumstances. It simply requires clauses to be 'fair' (**reg 8(1)**). The test in the **UTCCR**, contained in **reg 5(1)**, is whether the term 'contrary to the requirement of good faith . . . causes a significant imbalance in the parties' rights and obligations under the contract, to the detriment of the consumer'. The corresponding aspect of the **UCTA** is the 'requirement of reasonableness'. This is defined by **s 11** of the **UCTA** as meaning that the clause must have been a fair and reasonable one to include in the contract.

Although 'fairness' is the test in both pieces of legislation, it is defined in different ways. The focus in the **UTCCR** is on good faith and the balance between the parties. In *Director General of Fair Trading v First National Bank plc* (2002), the House of Lords held that good faith related to procedural fairness, while 'imbalance' related to the substance of the clause. In the **UCTA**, the test of reasonableness can draw on a range of factors, as set out in **Sched 2** to the Act. The list in **Sched 2** is stated to apply where **ss 6** and **7** are under consideration, but has been held to have more general application (for example, by the Court of Appeal in *Overseas Medical Supplies Ltd v Orient Transport Services Ltd* (1999)). The list includes the bargaining balance between the parties, but also refers to such matters as whether the claimant had any choice about contracting with the defendant, or received an inducement to agree to the clause, the claimant's knowledge of the clause, and, as regards goods, whether they were manufactured, processed or adapted to the special needs of the claimant.

It is therefore conceivable that a clause could be held to be fair under the **UTCCR** but unreasonable under the **UCTA**, or vice versa. This is clearly unsatisfactory, although in practice it does not seem to have caused problems to date.

The Law Commission's reform proposals do address some of the issues. The main change, in itself an improvement, is that there would be only one piece of legislation, rather than two. As far as consumer contracts are concerned, it would impose a test of reasonableness on all terms, other than 'core' terms (for example, relating to the price, or defining the subject matter), not only exclusion clauses. To this extent the proposals follow the **UTCCR**. They also adopt the **UTCCR** approach to who is a consumer. Only private individuals acting for non-business purposes would be covered; the effect of *R & B Customs Brokers v UDT* would be reversed. There would therefore be less confusion on this issue.

As to what clauses would be struck down, the proposals would leave in place the **UCTA** prohibition on clauses that are automatically ineffective (for example, under **s 2(1)** or **ss 6** and **7**). Other clauses would need to satisfy a test of reasonableness – based on the test of whether the clause was a fair and reasonable one to include in the contract. The **UTCCR** references to 'good faith' and 'significant imbalance' would not be part of the new test. The new Act would, however, set out a list of factors that would be relevant to the new test, including the need for 'transparency'. Otherwise, the factors will be similar to those set out in **Sched** 2 to the **UCTA**.

The conclusion must be that the reforms proposed by the Law Commission would go a long way to deal with the issues that currently arise from the dual system of controls that exist in relation to consumer contracts. The definition of who is a consumer would be clarified, and there would be only one test of what is 'reasonable'. The fact that the controls extend to all terms, as under the **UTCCR**, rather than only exclusion clauses, is also a desirable development. Unfortunately, at the moment there is no indication that the government is prepared to find time to enact these proposals, and the confusions that potentially arise from the current situation are likely to continue for some time to come.

Question 22

HeatSafe Ltd cleans and services ovens for the catering trade. Glutton is caterer, who supplies ready-cooked meals, using the five gas ovens that he has on his premises. HeatSafe and Glutton entered into an agreement by exchange of emails whereby HeatSafe contracted to clean and service Glutton's ovens every 12 weeks. HeatSafe then sent Glutton copy of its 'Terms and Conditions of Business'. Clause 5 of these read:

> HeatSafe Ltd shall not be responsible under any circumstances for any loss, damage or injury suffered by the client [ie Glutton], except to the extent that such loss or damage is attributable to the negligence of any employee of HeatSafe Ltd. In any case, HeatSafe's liability is limited to a maximum of £500.

Four services were carried out satisfactorily. At the next service, HeatSafe's engineer Tom, did not arrive as scheduled, because of a mix-up in relation to his work rota. The following week, as a result of a fault in a part in one of the ovens, which would have been discovered as part of the service, the oven exploded, causing burns to Glutton, and extensive damage to the kitchen. The kitchen was out of action for a week, and Glutton lost business to the value of £5,000.

Advise HeatSafe Ltd as to any liability it may have towards Glutton, and as to its defences.

Answer plan

This is a question primarily on exclusion clauses. You will need to deal first with the issue of liability, but this should be done fairly briefly. There are two bases for liability:

- the failure to carry out a service is a breach of the primary obligations under the contract – Heatsafe will be strictly liable for the breach of this obligation;
- possible negligence of Tom in failing to turn up for the service, or of other employees in messing up the rota – HeatSafe will be vicariously liable for any such negligence.

As with any exclusion clause questions you need to consider the common law first, that is:

- has the clause been incorporated? In this case it might be argued that the contract has been concluded before HeatSafe sends its terms and conditions containing the exclusion clause;
- does the clause cover the breach? The clause is widely drawn, and specifically mentions negligence, so it seems likely that it will be found to cover the situations that have arisen.

Once the common law has been dealt with, it is necessary to consider the statutory controls. Since this is not a consumer contracts, the **UTCCR 1999** will not be relevant, so only the **UCTA 1977** needs to be considered. The two main provisions to be considered will be:

- **s 2** – which will be relevant if the liability is based on negligence;
- **s 3** – which will be relevant in relation to strict contractual liability. Since HeatSafe's written standard terms are being used, **s 3** will apply.

There may well be issues relating to the reasonableness of the clause, under the **UCTA** provisions, which will need to be discussed, alongside the relevant case law.

Answer

The failure of HeatSafe to carry out a service under its contract with Glutton has resulted in injury to Glutton, damage to his premises, and loss to his business. The main issue is whether and to what extent HeatSafe may be able to avoid or restrict its liability by reliance on the exclusion clause contained in its standard terms and conditions. Before that issue is discussed, however, the basis of HeatSafe's potential liability must be clarified. This is important because the exclusion clause has different consequences depending on the type of liability.

The contract requires regular services to be carried out. HeatSafe has failed to perform one of the scheduled services. This is clearly a breach of contract, and Glutton should, subject to the effect of the exclusion clause, be able to recover damages for any losses caused by it, provided that they are not too remote. The alternative basis of liability is that HeatSafe or its employees have been negligent in the performance of the contract. There is an implied obligation in **s 13** of the **Supply of Goods and Services Act 1982** that services will be supplied with reasonable care and skill. Does mixing up the rota, so that Tom does not turn up when he should, constitute a failure of reasonable care and skill? It is at least arguable that it does, and it will be assumed for the purposes of this answer that Glutton has the possibility of basing his action on negligent performance, as well as strict liability.

What, then, is the effect of the exclusion clause, contained in clause 5 of Heat-Safe's standard terms and conditions? The first questions to ask relate to the common law rules in relation to exclusion clauses, which are that the clause must be incorporated into the contract, and that the clause must cover the type of breach that has occurred.

Looking first at incorporation, a clause can become incorporated in two ways. First, it could be contained in a document that is signed by the contracting parties (*L'Estrange v Graucob* (1934)). Alternatively, reasonable notice of the clause could be given (*Parker v South Eastern Railway* (1877)) before or at the time of the contract (*Thornton v Shoe Lane Parking* (1971)). Since HeatSafe did not sign a document containing the clause, there are two issues here. First, when was the contract made? Second, was reasonable notice of the clause given before or at that time? Glutton will no doubt wish to argue that the contract was formed as soon as the initial exchange of emails was complete, assuming that they contained a clear offer and acceptance, establishing the main terms. On this basis, HeatSafe's standard terms and conditions would come too late to be a part of the contract. If that were the case, then HeatSafe would not be able to rely on its clause 5 at all, and would be fully liable for its breach of contract. It may well be, however, that HeatSafe's emails will have made reference to its terms and conditions. If that is the case, then a court would probably say that as long as Glutton was aware of the existence of the conditions and had the possibility of finding out what they contain, they will be part of the contract: *Thompson v London, Midland and Scottish Railway* (1930).

If the issue of incorporation is decided in favour of HeatSafe, there is then the question of construction. Does the language of clause 5 cover the type of breach that actually occurred? The courts will interpret any ambiguity in favour of the claimant – that is, Glutton in this problem.[1] The language of the clause 5 is quite comprehensive. It refers to 'any circumstances' and would certainly seem to cover the 'strict liability' breach involved in the failure of HeatSafe to carry out the scheduled service. As regards liability based on negligence, the courts require very clear language if an exclusion of liability on this basis is to be upheld: *Canada Steamship Lines Ltd v The King* (1952). Clause 5 refers specifically to 'negligence' by its employees, and since the only way in which a company can be negligent is via the actions of its employees, it would seem that this is sufficient to find that the clause cover negligence liability.

If the common law rules are determined in HeatSafe's favour, the statutory controls over exclusion clauses must be considered. The only set of controls that need to be considered are those contained in the **Unfair Contract Terms Act 1977**, since it is clear that Glutton does not contract as a consumer within the meaning of the **Unfair Terms in Consumer Contracts Regulations 1999**.

The section of the **UCTA** that will be most relevant will depend on the basis of HeatSafe's liability. If it is strict liability based simply on the failure to perform, then it is **s 3** that needs to be considered. **Section 3** applies where either, the claimant is a consumer (which is not the case here), or the contract is made on the defendant's written standard terms (which is the case here). Where **s 3** applies, the exclusion clause will only be enforceable if it satisfies the 'requirement of reasonableness' under the statute. The application of this test will be considered later in this answer.

If, on the other hand, the basis for liability is negligence in the performance of the contract, then **s 2** must be considered. This section has two subsections. **Section 2(1)** deals with death or personal injury resulting from negligence. It provides that a party cannot exclude liability for such consequences. If HeatSafe's liability is based on negligence, therefore, it cannot avoid liability for the injuries that Glutton has suffered when the oven exploded. Clause 5 will be ineffective to restrict its liability for this. As regards the damage to his Glutton's property and his business losses, it is **s 2(2)** that is relevant. This says that any exclusion for such damage or loss resulting for negligence is only valid insofar as it satisfies the statute's requirement of reasonableness.

The test of reasonableness is therefore important whether liability is strict or based on negligence. It is partially defined by **s 11** of the **UCTA**, which says that the clause must have been a fair and reasonable one to include in the contract. It also states that where a clause limits liability to a specific sum, the court should take account the defendant's resources and the availability of insurance: **s 11(4)**. This is relevant to the part of HeatSafe's clause that purports to limit its liability for negligence to £500. The only other guidance in the statute appears in **Sched 2**. This states that it is relevant to contracts for the supply of goods, but the courts have found that it can have wider relevance: *Overseas Medical Supplies Ltd v Orient Transport Services Ltd* (1999). **Schedule 2** directs the court to take into account such matters as the relative bargaining strength of the parties, whether it would have been possible to contract elsewhere without the exclusion, and the claimant's knowledge of the clause.

The question of whether a clause is reasonable under this test is essentially one of fact, and the appeal courts have shown a reluctance to set out rules as to how it should be applied, or to overturn the view of the trial judge who has considered all the evidence, including that of witnesses: see, for example, *Phillips Products Ltd v Hyland* (1987). On the other hand, the appeal courts have also suggested that where a clause is contained in a contract between two businesses, the trial judge should not rush to find it unreasonable. Business people should be allowed to organise the division of risks and responsibilities between themselves, and it is not generally sensible for the courts to intervene after the event to undo what has been agreed: *Watford Electronics Ltd v Sanderson CFL Ltd* (2001).

Applying all of this to the consideration of clause 5, it should be noted that the clause is very wide in its scope. In *Balmoral Group Ltd v Borealis (UK) Ltd* (2006), it was held that a blanket exclusion of liability, judged at the time that it was included in the contract when the outcome of any breach would be uncertain, was unreasonable. This would count in Glutton's favour. On the other hand, it may be that HeatSafe was not in a position to insure against extensive losses – in which case it becomes more reasonable for it to limit is liability. £500 seems a very low limit, however.

On balance, although this is a contract between two businesses, there was no negotiation over these terms, and Glutton appears to have been presented with them on a 'take it or leave it' basis, which makes it easier to treat them as unreasonable. It is clear that the exclusion of liability for Glutton's injuries cannot be excluded if liability is based on negligence; it is submitted that it should be found to be unreasonable even if liability is strict (and the test of reasonableness under **s 3** applies). As to the other loss and damage, although it might be reasonable for HeatSafe to restrict its liability in these areas, a limit of £500 seems very low. It is hard to believe that it could not obtain insurance for a much larger sum.

In conclusion, it is likely that Glutton will be able to enforce his actions for breach of contract against HeatSafe without the restrictions imposed by clause 5.

Think point

1 This principle is often referred to as the *contra proferentem* rule.

Question 23

Fiona is the managing director and main shareholder of Fiona's Fashions Ltd, which runs a clothes shop. In May, she approached Williams Motors Ltd with a view to buying a used van, which was on display at its premises. Fiona intended to use the van for her business, and also to transport the double bass that she plays in an amateur orchestra. The salesman told her that the van had just been serviced (which was true), and that the exhaust pipe had recently been replaced (which was not). In fact, the salesman was confusing this van with another, but would have realised his mistake if he had checked the garage's documentation. Fiona bought the van on behalf of Fiona's Fashions Ltd for £9,000 on 1 June. At the time of the sale, Williams Motors Ltd gave Fiona a document headed 'Terms and Conditions of Sale'. It stated in clause 4 that Williams Motors Ltd accepted no responsibility for any pre-contractual statements as to the quality of vehicles, and in clause 15 that it would only be liable for defects notified to it within 14 days of delivery. The van was delivered on 3 June.

On 20 June, Fiona was using the van when the engine started stalling whenever she stopped at a junction. Fiona has been told by her garage that all of the valves in the engine need replacing, which will cost £750. She has also been told that the exhaust pipe will need replacing within the next six months, at a cost of a further £200.

Williams Motors claims that it is protected from any liability for these defects by virtue of clauses 4 and 15 of the contract.

Advise Fiona.

Answer plan

This is a straightforward problem about the effectiveness of exclusion clauses. The issues that will need discussion are:

- were the exclusion clauses incorporated into the contract? The answer is almost certainly 'yes', by virtue of the document given to Fiona at the time of the contract;
- do the clauses cover the alleged breach? The relevant breaches relate to the **Sale of Goods Act 1979** implied terms, and misrepresentation. Clause 15 may be said to cover both; clause 4 purports to deal with misrepresentations, but is the statement that the exhaust pipe has been replaced a statement as to 'quality'?
- what is the effect of the **Unfair Contract Terms Act 1977**? This requires consideration of whether Fiona Fashions Ltd buys the van 'as a consumer'. The cases of *R & B Customs Brokers v UDT* (1988) and *Feldarol Foundry plc v Hermes Leasing (London) Ltd* (2004) will need to be considered; and
- the possibility of excluding liability for misrepresentation, and the effect of s 3 of the **Misrepresentation Act 1967**.

Note that the **Unfair Terms in Consumer Contract Regulations 1999** will not be relevant, because the purchaser is a company, not a private individual.

Answer

Fiona will be seeking to take action on behalf of Fiona's Fashions Ltd, who bought the van that has turned out to be defective. There are three possible bases for action:

(a) breach of the implied term as to satisfactory quality under s 14 of the **Sale of Goods Act 1979**, in relation to the valves (and possibly the exhaust pipe);

(b) breach of the implied term as to description under s 13 of the **Sale of Goods Act 1979**, as regards the statement that the van had a new exhaust pipe; and

(c) negligent misrepresentation under s 2(1) of the **Misrepresentation Act 1967**, again in relation to the statement about the exhaust pipe.

In relation to each of these, Williams Motors is arguing that it is protected from liability by clauses 4 and 15 of its Terms and Conditions.

The first issue to consider whenever a party seeks to rely on an exclusion clause is whether the clause forms part of the contract. Has it been incorporated? Here, the contract appears to have been made orally between Fiona and the representative of Williams Motors. At the time of the contract, however, Fiona is given a document headed 'Terms and Conditions'. Although Fiona might try to argue that by the time she saw this the contract of sale had been made, so that it came too late (as in *Olley v Marlborough Court Hotel* (1949)), in general, provided that terms are given around the time of the contract, the likelihood is that it will be held that sufficient notice has been given. It will be assumed, therefore, that clauses 4 and 15 do form part of the contract between Fiona's Fashions and Williams Motors. The second issue is whether the clauses on their proper construction cover the breaches that have occurred. There seems to be no doubt that clause 15 satisfies this test. It is in general terms, and is wide enough to apply to any of the breaches that Fiona might allege. Clause 4 is slightly more contentious. If Fiona argues that the statement about the exhaust pipe is a statement as to description rather than quality, then she can say that clause 4, which refers only to statements as to quality, is not applicable. A similar argument can be run by Fiona if she is basing her action in relation to the false statement on misrepresentation. She can argue that a misrepresentation of this kind is not a 'statement as to quality'. On the other hand, the courts have in recent years shown a reluctance to be as strict as they used to be in relation to the construction of exclusion clauses (see, for example, *Photo Production Ltd v Securicor Ltd* (1980) and *Ailsa Craig Fishing Co Ltd v Malvern Fishing Co Ltd* (1983)). This change of approach is a result of the statutory intervention in this area, as a result of the **Unfair Contract Terms Act 1977 (UCTA)**. Since Parliament has not provided a scheme of protection in relation to exclusion clauses, especially when they apply to consumers, there is less need for the courts to impose strict controls on the construction clauses. Instead, they should give effect to what appears to have been the intention of the clause. This is particularly the case where the contract is between two businesses. Here, therefore,

Williams Motors might well be successful in arguing that clause 4 should be interpreted as covering the statement about the exhaust pipe, since this is in general terms concerned with the 'quality' of what is being supplied. Assuming that the clauses are found to be part of the contract, and to cover the alleged breaches, so that the common law tests of incorporation and construction are satisfied, the effect of the **UCTA** must be considered.

If Fiona is alleging breaches of the implied terms under **ss 13** or **14** of the **Sale of Goods Act 1977**, the relevant provision of the **UCTA** is **s 6**. This states that where the buyer deals as a consumer, as defined by **s 12** of the **UCTA**, there can be no exclusion of liability for these implied terms. If the buyer buys in the course of a business, on the other hand, exclusion can be allowed, provided that the clause meets the 'requirement of reasonableness' set out in **s 11** of the **UCTA**. It is crucial, therefore, to determine whether Fiona's Fashions Ltd buys the van 'as a consumer' or in the course of business. At first sight it seems obvious that the contract is made 'in the course of business', since it is made by a company, but that phrase has been given a restrictive interpretation in two Court of Appeal decisions: *R & B Customs Brokers Ltd v UDT* (1988) and *Feldarol Foundry plc v Hermes Leasing (London) Ltd* (2004). In both cases, a company had bought a car for the use of one of its directors. The car turned out to be defective and the buyer took action under the **Sale of Goods Act 1979** implied terms. The seller sought to rely on an exclusion clause. In *R & B Customs Brokers*, the Court took the view that the company that had bought the car was not dealing 'in the course of business' for the purposes of **s 12**. The business of the company was import/export, and it did not regularly deal in the purchase and sale of cars. The purchase of the car was therefore to be treated as a consumer contract, and the seller could not rely on the exclusion clause. Some doubts as to whether this was the correct approach were raised by the subsequent Court of Appeal decision in *Stevenson v Rogers* (1999), which gave a broader meaning to the phrase 'in the course of business' in **s 14** of the **Sale of Goods Act 1979**. It held that a sale of a fishing boat by a fisherman was 'in the course of business'. In *Feldarol v Hermes*, however, the Court of Appeal felt bound to follow the approach taken in *R & B Customs Brokers* as to the interpretation of **s 12** of the **UCTA**. In *Feldarol v Hermes*, the buyer's business was that of an aluminium foundry, and so had nothing to do with dealing in cars. The Court held that the purchase of the car was not in the course of business, and so again the seller was unable to rely on the exclusion clause.

This might suggest that Fiona's Fashions Ltd is buying the van as a consumer, since dealing in vans is not part of what it normally does. There is, however, an additional requirement to **s 12**, where the purchaser is not a private individual. This is that the goods bought must be of a type 'ordinarily supplied for private use or consumption'. In *R & B Customs Brokers* and *Feldarol v Hermes*, this was satisfied by the fact that the item was a car. In Fiona's case, however, we are dealing with a van. Although vans can be used by private individuals, as indicated by Fiona's plan to use the van to transport her double bass, it may be arguable whether they are 'ordinarily supplied for private use or consumption'. If they are not, then Williams Motors will be able to rely on its exclusion clauses, provided that the clause satisfies the requirement of reasonableness. This is set out in s 11 of the UCTA, and requires the clause to be a 'fair and reasonable' one to have been included in the contract. This is supplemented by Sched 2 to the UCTA, which sets out a list of guidelines for deciding on reasonableness – including the relative bargaining power of the parties, and whether it was reasonable to expect that compliance with any condition for avoiding the restriction of liability would be practicable. The appeal courts have shown reluctance to lay down anything further by way of guidelines on reasonableness, generally taking the view that it is an issue best decided at trial by the judge who has heard all of the evidence. Moreover, the courts have tended to take the view that in relation to contracts between businesses, they should normally be allowed to reach their own agreements as to the distribution of liability, so that courts should not rush to find clauses unreasonable: for example, *Granville Oil & Chemicals v Davis Turner & Co Ltd* (2003).

If the reasonableness test is to be applied to Fiona's situation, she will presumably seek to argue that Williams Motors was in a stronger bargaining position and could impose terms on her. We have no evidence in relation to this.

She will also argue that 14 days is an unreasonably short period for the discovery of defects in a vehicle, which may take some time to manifest. It is difficult to predict how this would be resolved. It may well be, however, that if the courts decided that Fiona's Fashions Ltd was not dealing as a consumer, they will also hold that the exclusions of liability were reasonable.

To the extent that Fiona is relying on the action based on misrepresentation, the reasonableness of clause 4 will be in issue. Section 3 of the Misrepresentation Act 1967, as inserted by the UCTA, requires that any attempt to exclude liability for misrepresentation should satisfy the requirement of reasonableness. There is no difference in approach as between business and consumer contracts in this case. The test of reasonableness will be the same as outlined above. Although, again, there is no clear authority on the issue, there are suggestions in *Inntrepreneur Estates (CPC) Ltd v Worth* (1996) and *Thomas Witter Ltd v TBP Industries Ltd* (1996) that clauses like clause 4, which attempt to avoid all liability for pre-contractual statements, should be treated as unreasonable.

It may well be, therefore, that Fiona's Fashions Ltd, assuming that it is treated as contracting in the course of business, rather than as a consumer, will be caught by clause 15 in relation to the potential action under the Sale of Goods Act 1979, but will be able to take action for the salesman's misrepresentation in relation to the exhaust pipe.

CHAPTER 7

MISTAKE AND MISREPRESENTATION

INTRODUCTION

This chapter is the first of several that look at various arguments which may be used by the parties to a contract to say that the agreement should be regarded as 'void' or 'voidable'. These arguments are often grouped under the general heading of 'vitiating factors'. The two that are considered in this chapter are 'mistake' and 'misrepresentation'.

The reason for linking these two topics is that it will often be the case that a particular set of circumstances gives rise to the possibility of argument in either mistake or misrepresentation. It is useful, therefore, to consider the advantages of one against the other. This issue is dealt with specifically in Question 24. It should not be forgotten, however, that although it is not uncommon to find a contract question that requires an answer covering both mistake and misrepresentation, the issues are not necessarily linked. Indeed, certain aspects of misrepresentation have already been discussed in Chapter 5. Some of those aspects are explored further in Question 27. Question 25, on the other hand, is an example of a question raising mistake issues, but not misrepresentation.

Neither of these areas is particularly easy to deal with. In relation to misrepresentation, the problems arise from the fact that there are remedies under both the common law and statute. In mistake, the complications arise from the fact that the case law on what amounts to an operative mistake is not very clear (particularly the implications of the decision in *Bell v Lever Bros* (1932)), and the fact that equity has in some situations stepped in to mitigate the rather strict common law rules. The scope for such intervention has, however, been significantly reduced by the recent decision in *Great Peace Shipping Ltd v Tsavliris Salvage (International) Ltd* (2002), in which the Court of Appeal held that there is no power to rescind a contract in equity as distinct from the common law power to hold it void.

There is no easy way to simplify these areas. The advice must be simply to take each question step by step, perhaps in the following order (assuming that it is a problem question):

- is there a misrepresentation?
- if so, what remedy would the claimant want – that is, rescission or damages?

- if damages are enough, can the **Misrepresentation Act 1967** be used?
- if rescission is required, are there any bars, such as the involvement of third parties?
- if misrepresentation cannot provide an adequate remedy, is there an operative common law mistake? Remember that if there is, this will inter alia override any third-party rights, and allow the recovery of property transferred as a consequence of the mistake;
- if there is no common law mistake, can equity assist? Equity may take account of less serious mistakes, but can only provide limited remedies (for example, refusal of specific performance), which will not override third-party rights.

Note that, for the reasons given in the introduction to Chapter 5, the action in tort of negligent misstatement under *Hedley Byrne v Heller* (1964) is not discussed in any detail in this chapter.

Checklist

You should be familiar with the following areas:

- the difference between various types of mistake – for example, common, mutual, unilateral;
- the effects of an operative mistake, both in common law and equity;
- the definition of a misrepresentation;
- common law remedies for misrepresentation, including the bars on rescission; and
- remedies for misrepresentation under the **Misrepresentation Act 1967**.

Question 24

'Most situations where either or both parties enter into a contract on the basis of a mistake of fact can nowadays be dealt with quite satisfactorily by the remedies for misrepresentation. There are very few situations where the doctrine of mistake has any practical role to play.'

Discuss.

Answer plan

This question requires you to think about two areas: mistake and misrepresentation. It is not a question that be attempted unless you have a firm grasp of both. Two particular areas that you will need to consider are as follows:

- are there situations involving a contract being made on the basis of a mistake that do not also involve a misrepresentation?

- are there situations in which the remedies for misrepresentation are inadequate, and the remedies for mistake more satisfactory?

The essay will need to start with a description, supported by examples from the case law, of the basic principles operating in relation to misrepresentation and mistake, before going on to discuss the two issues set out above.

Answer

It is certainly true that there are situations in which a contract made on the basis of a mistake of fact also involves a misrepresentation. A clear example would be where one of the contracting parties deliberately pretends to be someone other than who they really are, as in, for example, *Lewis v Averay* (1971).[1] The statement 'I am Richard Greene' was a misrepresentation. The subsequent contract was also made on the basis of a unilateral mistake. Even where the mistake is mutual, if one of the parties has been misled by the other's mistake, this may well have involved a misrepresentation. An example might be *McRae v Commonwealth Disposals Commission* (1951), in which the invitation for tenders could be said to have amounted to a misrepresentation as to the existence of the oil tanker. Before looking in more detail at the degree of overlap between mistake and misrepresentation, the basic principles of the two areas will be outlined.

A misrepresentation is a false statement of existing fact or, probably, law, made by one party to a contract to another, which induces the other party to enter into the contract. It may be made innocently, negligently or fraudulently. The state of mind of the misrepresentor is irrelevant to the issue of whether there is an operative misrepresentation, although it is of considerable importance as regards remedies.

A statement of opinion (*Bisset v Wilkinson* (1927)) will not generally be a misrepresentation.[2] A statement of intention may be a misrepresentation if the intention is falsely stated – *Edgington v Fitzmaurice* (1885): 'The state of a man's mind is as much a fact as the state of his digestion.'

The statement must, at least to some extent, induce the contract. It does not have to be the only reason for making the contract, but it must be an operative factor:

Edgington v Fitzmaurice. The *reliance does not, it seems, have to be reasonable*. In *Museprime v Adhill* (1990), the unreasonableness of reliance was said to be simply evidence that might suggest that there had been no actual reliance. Once it has been established that there is an operative misrepresentation, the remedies will depend on whether it was made innocently, negligently or fraudulently. For all three types of misrepresentation, rescission of the contract will be available unless one of the bars to this equitable remedy exists. If there has been an undue lapse of time, or if it is impossible to restore the parties to their original positions (because, for example, goods have been consumed), or, perhaps most importantly for this essay, if third-party rights have become involved, then no rescission is possible. If the misrepresentation is entirely innocent, then the claimant will be left without any remedy. If it was negligent or fraudulent, however, a remedy in damages will still be available. For negligent misrepresentation, this is provided for by **s 2(1)** of the **Misrepresentation Act 1967**, which applies where the person making the statement is unable to show that they had reasonable grounds for believing it to be true. Fraudulent misrepresentation is governed by the tort of deceit. In *Royscot v Rogerson* (1991), the Court of Appeal ruled that the assessment of damages is the same under **s 2(1)** as for fraud. In particular, the wide remoteness rule applicable to the tort of deceit (*Doyle v Olby* (1969)) applies equally to **s 2(1)**. The House of Lords in *Smith New Court Securities Ltd v Scrimgeour Vickers (Asset Management) Ltd* (1996), in confirming *Doyle v Olby*, expressed some scepticism as to whether the same rule should apply to **s 2(1)**. The issue was not directly before the House, however, so *Royscot v Rogerson* must still be regarded as good law.

Turning now to the doctrine of mistake, this is a complex area, and only a brief outline can be given. There are basically three types of mistake, often categorised as common, mutual and unilateral.[3] Common mistake arises where the parties are in agreement, but that agreement assumes some fact to be true when it is not. For example, the parties contract about a cargo, in ignorance of the fact that the ship on which it is being carried has sunk (cf *Couturier v Hastie* (1852), in which the cargo had been disposed of by the master of the ship). Following the Court of Appeal decision in *Brennan v Bolt Burdon* (2004), common mistake can also arise in relation to a mistake of *law*. On the facts of that case, however, the law was in an uncertain state at the time the agreement was made – a common mistake could only arise where the law was clear, and the agreement was based on an incorrect understanding of it. Mutual mistake arises where the parties are at cross-purposes, but neither is aware of this, as in *Raffles v Wichelhaus* (1864), in which there was confusion resulting from two ships of the same name sailing from the same port at about the same time. A unilateral mistake exists where one party is aware of the other's mistake. Many of the cases of mistaken identity, such as *King's Norton Metal Co Ltd v Edridge* (1897), involve unilateral mistake.

In relation to mutual and unilateral mistake, there is no contract because there never was in fact an agreement. The parties were at cross-purposes, or one party was aware that the other party was agreeing on the basis of something that was untrue. In relation to common mistake, there may be an agreement but, if the mistake is operative, then the contract will be declared void from the beginning at common law. In all cases, the mistake, to be operative, must be about something that is fundamental to the contract. The existence of the subject matter is clearly fundamental. The quality of the subject matter (*Bell v Lever Bros* (1932)), or the identity of the person with whom you are contracting, may or may not be fundamental (compare *Ingram v Little* (1961) – identity fundamental – with *Lewis v Averay* – not fundamental), depending on all of the surrounding circumstances. If a contract is found never to have existed, or is declared void for common mistake, then the whole transaction must be unscrambled. None of the bars to rescission noted in relation to misrepresentation operates, and even third-party rights can be overridden. If, on the other hand, there has been a mistake that, while significant, is not so fundamental as to require that the contract be regarded as non-existent or void, the equitable remedies of refusal of specific performance or rectification may be available. The power to rescind a contract in equity, derived from *Solle v Butcher* (1950), has, however, now been firmly rejected by the Court of Appeal in *Great Peace Shipping Ltd v Tsavliris Salvage (International) Ltd* (2002). Where equitable remedies are available, however, they will be subject to third-party rights.

What, then, is the relationship between mistake and misrepresentation? Would it be possible, as the question suggests, for misrepresentation effectively to replace the doctrine of mistake in virtually all cases? In answering this, there are two questions to consider:

- are there situations involving a contract being made on the basis of a mistake that do not also involve a misrepresentation?
- are there situations in which the remedies for misrepresentation are inadequate, and the remedies for mistake more satisfactory?

We have seen at the beginning of this essay that there are clearly examples of situations in which mistake and misrepresentation overlap. This overlap is not, however, complete. It is quite possible to envisage situations involving either common or mutual mistake that did not involve a misrepresentation by either party. In *Bell v Lever Bros*, for example, the validity of the employment contracts was assumed, without there being any representation. Cases of unilateral mistake are much more likely to involve a misrepresentation, but even here it is not inevitable. One party assumes that the painting he is buying is by Constable; the other party knows that the buyer is making this assumption, and knows that it is false. No representation needs to have taken place, but the contract is made on the basis of a mistake that, even if not operative at common law, may well provide a remedy in equity.

Turning to remedies, the problem with misrepresentation is that, although it now provides damages in the majority of cases, rescission is not always available, because of the equitable bars to it. In cases such as *Ingram v Little*, although there had been a clear misrepresentation of identity, which had induced the contract, there could have been no rescission for misrepresentation because the car had been sold on to an innocent third party. The remedy of damages was also of little use, because the misrepresenting purchaser had disappeared. Making the contract void for mistake was the only way of providing an effective remedy. Whether the drastic effects on the third party are justifiable may be questionable, but that is a fault of the absence of any remedy allowing losses to be shared, rather than an argument for the abolition of the doctrine of mistake.

The conclusion must be that although in many situations misrepresentation can provide a very satisfactory and in some ways more flexible alternative to the doctrine of mistake, there are still a small number of cases in which mistake provides the only possible remedy. The number may be small, but it is not so small as to justify being ignored altogether. The doctrine of mistake should be retained to deal with these situations, although there may well be a case for revising the remedies that it provides.

Think points

1 What other cases could have been used here? *Phillips v Brooks* (1919) is another example of this situation.

2 When will a statement of opinion amount to a representation? This will occur when the maker of the statement is aware of facts that make the opinion untenable, as in *Smith v Land and House Property Corp* (1884) – tenant said to be 'desirable' when in fact in arrears with the rent.

3 What other way of categorising mistakes do the courts use? In *Bell v Lever Bros* (1932), Lord Atkin referred to 'mistakes nullifying consent' and 'mistakes negativing consent': see Stone, *The Modern Law of Contract*, 7th edn, 2008, pp 374–5.

Question 25

Bernard owns an oil painting and a smaller pencil sketch, which are both thought to be by Daniel, an artist who has recently died, and whose work is fetching increasingly large amounts at auction. Bernard writes to his friend Edwina, offering to sell her 'my little Daniel picture' (meaning the sketch) for £2,000. Edwina, who knows little about modern art, accepts, saying: 'I am pleased to accept your offer. As you may know, I am hoping to build up a collection of modern paintings.' Bernard delivers the Daniel sketch while Edwina is out. Edwina in fact wanted the oil painting, not the sketch. Before she can return it, however, another friend, who is an expert on Daniel's work, tells her that the sketch is of poor quality and not worth more than £50. A good quality sketch would have been worth £700 to £1,000. Bernard, however, who had himself bought the sketch for £1,500, refuses to take it back, and insists that Edwina must pay him £2,000. The oil painting is valued at £7,000.

Advise Bernard and Edwina.

Answer plan

This question raises two issues in relation to the doctrine of mistake. The first relates to the question of what happens when parties are at cross-purposes as to the subject matter of the contract. This is the kind of mistake that is often referred to as a 'mutual mistake', or a 'mistake negativing agreement'. The cases of *Raffles v Wichelhaus* (1864) and *Smith v Hughes* (1871) are relevant here. The second issue concerns the position when both parties make a mistake as to the value of what they are contracting about. This may be a 'common mistake' or a 'mistake nullifying agreement'. The case of *Bell v Lever Bros* (1932) is the leading authority on this issue as far as the common law rules are concerned, although it may also be necessary to consider the role of equity in this area.

The order of treatment here will be:

- mutual mistake:
  - ○ has there been a 'mutual mistake'?
  - ○ if so, is the mistake operative?
  - ○ if so, what is its effect?
- common mistake:
  - ○ has there been a 'common mistake'?
  - ○ if so, is the mistake operative?
  - ○ if so, what is its effect?
  - ○ if the mistake is not operative at common law, what is the position in equity?

Answer

In certain situations, in which the parties to a contract have made their agreement on the basis of a mistake of fact, the courts will be prepared to say either that the mistake means that there never really was an agreement (and, therefore, there was no contract), or that the mistake is so fundamental that the contract should be set aside.

We have the possibility of both types of mistake operating in this question. The first mistake that we need to consider arises from the fact that Bernard and Edwina seem to be at cross-purposes over the subject matter of the contract. Bernard intends to sell the sketch; Edwina intends to buy the oil painting. Is there a contract here? It is clear that, in some cases of this kind, the courts will say 'no'. In *Raffles v Wichelhaus* (1864), for example, the contract referred to a ship of the name *Peerless* sailing out of Bombay. Unfortunately, there were two ships that matched this description. The court held that the contract could not be enforced. It was impossible to determine which ship was intended.

A misunderstanding of this kind will not, however, always lead to the decision that there is no contract. The approach taken by the courts is an objective one. They will ask not what did these parties intend, but what would a reasonable third party think that they intended, or what would a reasonable offeror think was being offered? In *Raffles v Wichelhaus*, it was not felt possible to give a clear answer even to the objectively stated question, and so no contract existed.[1] In *Smith v Hughes* (1871), however, a different view was taken. The plaintiff had offered to sell oats to the defendant. The defendant thought that he was buying 'old' oats. When delivered, they turned out to be 'new', and of no use to the defendant. The defendant argued that the contract was void for mistake. The court disagreed. Applying an objective test, there was no ambiguity about the contract. The plaintiff had offered to sell, and the defendant had agreed to buy, a specific consignment of 'oats'. The fact that the defendant had mistakenly thought that the oats were of a different type was his own fault, and not a reason for excusing him from the contract.

How should these principles apply to the dealings between Bernard and Edwina? On a subjective approach, it is clear that there was no agreement. Edwina never intended to buy the sketch. Looked at objectively, however, things are not so clear. Although Edwina's reference to building up a collection of 'paintings' might be taken as indicating her mistake, this is fairly vague, and there are a number of things that point in Bernard's favour. First, he refers in his offer to 'my little Daniel picture'. We are told that the sketch is smaller than the painting, and so it can be argued that the objective bystander would assume that the sketch is what Bernard is offering to sell. Second, it is clear that an offer to sell the painting at £2,000 would be to undervalue it considerably, given that we are told that its market value is £7,000. But should Edwina have known this? We can probably only hold this point against her if a reasonable person with Edwina's knowledge would have realised that the price was so low that Bernard was very unlikely to have been intending it to apply to the painting as opposed to the sketch.

On balance, it would seem that this is not a case to which *Raffles v Wichelhaus* should apply. Looked at objectively, there was not sufficient ambiguity to mean that there was no contract at all. Edwina cannot therefore escape from the disadvantageous bargain on this basis. The possibility that equity might afford her some relief is considered further below.

Turning to the issue of the mistake as to the value of the sketch, the leading case is *Bell v Lever Bros* (1932). Here, an employee was paid £30,000 compensation on the termination of his contract. It later transpired that the employer would have been entitled to dismiss him without compensation, because of certain previous breaches of contract by the employee. The employer tried to argue that the contract for compensation was void for mistake. The House of Lords, while recognising the possibility of a contract being void where there is a fundamental mistake as to the subject matter, nevertheless held that on the facts the contract was not void. This has led some to argue that virtually the only common mistake that the courts will regard as operative is a mistake as to the existence of the subject matter.[2] This interpretation was not accepted by Steyn J in *Associated Japanese Bank (International) v Credit du Nord SA* (1988). He held that a mistake could make a contract void provided that it rendered the contract 'essentially and radically' different from the one that the parties thought they were making. However, even applying this broader doctrine to the facts of the problem, it seems unlikely that Edwina will have any remedy. The contract was for the sale of a Daniel picture, and that is what she got. The fact that it is a less valuable picture than she thought does not make the contract 'essentially and radically' different.

At common law, then, it seems that Edwina will not be able to escape from this contract. In some situations, however, equity will provide relief in relation to both mutual and common mistakes that are not sufficiently serious to render the contract void. This will only apply where the courts feel that it is just that it should do so in all the circumstances, and where there will be no effect on third parties' rights. The scope for equitable intervention was, however, significantly reduced by the Court of Appeal's decision in *Great Peace Shipping Ltd v Tsavliris Salvage (International) Ltd* (2002), in which it rejected the possibility of the remedy of rescission being used in a situation in which under the common law the mistake was not sufficiently serious to render the contract void. This approach had previously been adopted in cases such as *Solle v Butcher* (1950) and *Grist v Bailey* (1967). The position now is that where it may be appropriate for equity to intervene, the only remedies that are available are the rectification of a document, or the refusal to grant an order of specific perform-ance. These remedies may also be available as regards mutual mistakes, as shown by *Malins v Freeman* (1837), in which a bidder at an auction by mistake bid for one lot thinking that he was bidding for another. The court refused to order specific performance of the contract.[3]

In relation to the facts of this problem, although both Edwina's mistake as to which picture she was buying and the common mistake as to its value might be sufficiently serious to give rise to the possibility of equitable relief, neither rectifica-tion nor the refusal of specific performance is of any help to her. Rescission would have been the most useful remedy, but that is no longer available following the *Great Peace* decision. It seems, therefore, that Edwina will be obliged to pay the £2,000 (since Bernard will be able to recover this in an action for debt, rather than through an order for specific performance) for the picture that she did not want, despite the fact that it is only worth £50 at most.

Think points

1 Are there any other cases that might be cited here? One possibility is *Scriven Bros v Hindley* (1913). In this case, a person bidding at an auction mistakenly thought that two lots (which carried the same shipping mark) were both of hemp, whereas one was of less valuable tow. As a result, he bid well over the market price for the tow. He was allowed to escape from the contract on the basis of his mistake.

2 This situation is sometimes known by the Latin *res extincta*. Note also *res sua* – that is, the unusual situation in which a purchaser attempts to buy property that he or she already owns.

3 Would the position be the same if the bidder made a mistake as to what property was included in the lot? It would seem not – in *Tamplin v James* (1879), the mistake was of this kind, but the court held the bidder to the contract, and ordered specific performance.

Question 26

'The House of Lords' decision in *Shogun Finance Ltd v Hudson* (2004) has done nothing to clarify the law relating to the effect of mistaken identity on a contract. It must be regarded as a missed opportunity to remove the anomalies that plague this area of the law.'

Discuss.

Answer plan

As the statement that you are asked to discuss makes clear, this question is concerned with the law relating to mistakes as to the identity of one of the contracting parties. Can the party who has made the mistake set the contract aside for that reason? Since the question asks directly about the House of Lords' decision in *Shogun*, you should not attempt it unless you are fully familiar with this case. You will also need to show, however, that you understand the previous case law, and can identify what the question refers to as the 'anomalies' that have arisen. The following approach is suggested:

- set out the basic principles relating to mistaken identity, as they stood prior to *Shogun*, referring to cases such as *Cundy v Lindsay* (1878) and *Phillips v Brooks* (1919);
- identify the 'anomalies', which the setter of the question presumably intends to mean:
  - the distinction between face-to-face contracts and those conducted by correspondence; and
  - the fact that even within face-to-face contracts there are inconsistencies of approach (cf *Ingram v Little* (1960) with *Lewis v Averay* (1971));
- explain how the case of *Shogun Finance Ltd v Hudson* (2004) relates to the previous principles; and
- conclude by considering whether the criticisms of the majority's decision in *Shogun* contained in the question are justifiable.

Answer

The law relating to contracts made on the basis of mistaken identity is not straightforward – as was acknowledged by several members of the House of Lords in *Shogun Finance Ltd v Hudson* (2004). This arises in part from the fact that the court often has to decide which of two 'innocent' parties should bear the loss caused by the fraud of a third party, who is no longer available to be sued.

Typically, the difficulty arises where A contracts with B, thinking, on the basis of false representations by B, that B is in fact C. A allows B to take property without paying for it, or paying by an uncleared cheque, thinking that B is the creditworthy C. B then sells the property to T, who is innocent of the fraud, and disappears. Can A recover the property from T? The original contract is of course likely to be voidable on the basis of B's fraudulent misrepresentation, but a voidable contract needs to be rescinded before an innocent third party acquires rights, because this will mean that the right of rescission is lost. A's only hope in that situation is to argue that the original contract was void, rather than voidable, on the basis of an operative mistake. In other words, there never was any contract between A and B, and therefore B was not in a position to pass on any rights over the property to T.

English law has traditionally dealt with this situation by drawing a distinction between contracts made face-to-face (or *inter praesentes*) and those made through correspondence. The leading authority on the latter type of contract is the House of Lords' decision in *Cundy v Lindsay* (1878). In this case, a fraudulent individual named Blenkarn tricked the plaintiffs into thinking that they were dealing with a respectable firm of the name 'Blenkiron', and by this means obtained possession of a large quantity of handkerchiefs on credit. Blenkarn sold the handkerchiefs on to the defendant, who was an innocent third party. The House of Lords held that the plaintiffs were entitled to recover the handkerchiefs from the defendant, because the original contract with Blenkarn was a nullity. The plaintiffs had never intended to deal with anyone other than Blenkiron, and so there was no real agreement to sell to Blenkarn.

By contrast, where the parties dealt face-to-face, the tendency has been to treat the contract as simply voidable for fraud, even if one party has been misled about the identity of the other. A leading example of this approach is *Phillips v Brooks* (1919). In this case, the contract was formed in a jeweller's shop, where a customer claimed to be 'Sir George Bullough' of a certain address. The shopkeeper checked in a directory that Sir George lived at the stated address, and then allowed the customer to take a ring with him (a cheque having been given in payment). The customer was not Sir George, the cheque was dishonoured, and the ring was sold to an innocent third party. In this case, in contrast to *Cundy v Lindsay*, it was held that the jeweller could not recover the ring. The jeweller had intended to contract with the person in front of him, and the contract was not void for mistake. This line has been adopted in most later cases concerned with face-to-face contracts.

This highlights what might be described as the first 'anomaly' in this area of the law – the different approach taken to contracts made by correspondence and face-to-face. Is there any real justification for the distinction? In *Phillips v Brooks*, it is arguable that the identity of the customer was of importance to the jeweller, as evidenced by his checking in the directory. Alternatively, in *Cundy v Lindsay*, would the plaintiffs have complained if Blenkarn had paid for the handkerchiefs? It was his character as a fraudulent party rather than his identity that was arguably the important factor, just as it was in *Phillips v Brooks*. Moreover, in a society where contracts may be made by a variety of more or less personal dealings – post, telephone, fax, email, video-conference – is it sensible to try to draw a hard-and-fast line between contracts made through correspondence and those made face-to-face?

A further 'anomaly' may be said to exist within the case law on face-to-face contracts. This appears in relation to the two Court of Appeal decisions in *Ingram v Little* (1960) and *Lewis v Averay* (1971). Both cases concerned the private sale of a car, paid for by a cheque, where the seller had allowed the buyer to take the car away before the cheque had cleared, because the seller had been convinced that the buyer was creditworthy as a result of his (fraudulent) representations as to his identity. In *Ingram v Little*, the plaintiffs were three elderly women who had been duped by a 'Mr Hutchinson', whose supposed identity they had checked in a telephone directory. The Court of Appeal held that the contract was void for mistake, and allowed them to recover their car. The plaintiff in *Lewis v Averay* was a student who had been fooled by a false studio pass into thinking that the buyer was a well-known actor. In this case, the Court of Appeal held that the contract was merely voidable, and that since the car had been sold on before the fraud was discovered, the plaintiff could not recover it.

There have been attempts to explain how these two apparently contradictory decisions can stand, but none that is convincing. In general, *Lewis v Averay* is thought to be the better decision, but the conflict simply highlights the difficulty of finding the characteristic of a mistake as to identity that is sufficient to make any contract based on it totally void, rather than just voidable.

The chance for the House of Lords to review and rationalise the law came in *Shogun Finance Ltd v Hudson*. The situation in this case again involved a car, but was a little more complex. The fraudulent buyer had approached a dealer about buying a car on hire purchase terms. The dealer put the buyer in touch with Shogun Finance. The buyer, through the dealer, provided Shogun with false details in order to obtain the contract, pretending to be a Mr Patel of a certain address. Later the car was sold to the defendant, an innocent third party. Under special provisions of the hire purchase legislation, the defendant would have been able to retain the car, provided that it had been held under a genuine hire purchase contract. The House of Lords held that it had not been so held. The majority took the view that the decision in *Cundy v Lindsay* still governed this situation. The case was not a face-to-face contract, since the dealer could not be regarded as the agent of the finance company for these purposes, and all dealings between the purchaser and the finance company took place 'at a distance' and on paper. The company had offered the contract to Mr Patel, whose creditworthiness it had checked, and did not intend to contract with anyone else. Therefore, the hire purchase agreement was void for mistake. Consequently, the protective legislation could not assist the defendant.

This decision therefore effectively leaves the law as it was. The House was invited to reconsider *Cundy v Lindsay*, and the minority was prepared to do so. They would have taken the view that all contracts based on a mistake as to identity induced by fraud should be treated as voidable rather than void. This would apply whatever the method by which the contract was made. Doubts were also expressed about the correctness of the decision in *Ingram v Little*. The effect of the minority decision would thus have been that the rule applied in *Phillips v Brooks* and *Lewis v Averay* to face-to-face contracts would become of general application. This would have removed the 'anomaly' of having different rules depending on the method of contracting, and would also have dispatched *Ingram v Little* to the status of an historical footnote in the development of the law. It is hard not to agree that this would have constituted an improvement in the law. The statements in the question are therefore probably true: the law has not been clarified by the House of Lords, and an opportunity to get rid of the anomalies has been missed.

Question 27

David has run a kitchen-fitting business in Narchester for some years. In March, he decides to sell up, as he has had some health problems, and wants to retire. Philip, who lives in the neighbouring town of Lightville, where he works as a carpenter, is interested in buying the business. David tells him that the turnover is around £150,000 per annum, and the profit about £30,000. He also says that there is clear room for expansion in the market, and that there are few serious competitors in Narchester. Philip asks if the two employees that David has working for him are reliable, and David confirms that they are. Philip says that he will need time to think it over, and to see if he can raise the money to buy the business. David says that he can have until the beginning of May. He also gives Philip some accounts relating to the last two years. Philip looks at these, but does not really understand them, as he has no experience of dealing with accounts. At the beginning of May, Philip decides to buy the business as a going concern, and takes on David's employees. At the end of the first six months, the business is operating at a loss, partly because a large DIY chain opened in Narchester in April, operating a free fitting service for kitchens purchased from it. Philip has also discovered that, although the turnover has been as high as £150,000, in the last year it was only £100,000; this would have been apparent from the accounts supplied by David. Moreover, it turns out that one of David's employees has had a record of frequent absence on health grounds over the past 12 months.

Philip is seeking advice as to whether he can rescind the contract for the purchase of the business, or claim compensation from David.

Answer plan

This problem raises various issues relating to misrepresentation. The main basis for Philip being able to rescind the contract, or claim compensation will be that David's statements made prior to the contract amount to misrepresentations. The statements that need discussion are:

- that the turnover is around £150,000 – this has been true but is not any longer. Does it matter that Philip could have discovered this from the accounts? *Redgrave v Hurd* (1881) will be relevant;

- that there is room for expansion in the market – is this a statement of fact or opinion? See *Bisset v Wilkinson* (1927);

- that there are few serious competitors – this may have been true at the time, but perhaps becomes false. Should David have told Philip about the opening of the DIY store? See *With v O'Flanagan* (1936);

- that David's two employees are reliable – is this a statement of fact or opinion? Should David have told Philip about the frequent absence of one of the employees? Consider *Smith v Land and House Property Corp* (1884).

The suggested order of treatment is:

- a general statement of the requirements of misrepresentation;
- consideration of the statements listed above, and whether they are actionable;
- consideration of the remedies available under the common law and the **Misrepresentation Act 1967**.

Answer

Philip's possible actions against David will be based on misrepresentation. The general requirements for misrepresentation will be noted first, before considering the effect of the statements that David made to Philip prior to their making the contract.

For a pre-contractual statement to amount to a misrepresentation, it must be a false statement of fact or law (not opinion), which induced the other party to enter into the contract. If a misrepresentation has induced the contract, then the other party may be able to rescind the contract or claim damages (or, in some situations, both). There are three statements that are possible misrepresentations by David to Philip, and these need to be considered in turn.

The first statement relates to the turnover of the business. David says that this is 'around' £150,000 per annum. This appears to be a statement of existing fact, so potentially a misrepresentation. The accounts that David has produced show that the turnover is now lower than David has stated, although in the past it has been £150,000. There are two issues that need to be considered. Is the decline to £100,000 still within the scope of David's statement that it is 'around' £150,000? The answer should probably be 'no': a figure that is only two-thirds of the stated amount cannot really be said to be 'around' that amount. More importantly, what of the fact that David gave Philip some sets of accounts that it seems should have enabled him to discover the true picture? Will this mean that Philip will not be able to take action on any misrepresentation? The answer seems to be 'no'. A similar situation occurred in *Redgrave v Hurd* (1881), relating to the sale of a solicitor's practice. The seller had overstated the income from the practice. The fact that the plaintiff had had the opportunity to examine documents that would have shown the true position, but had declined to do so, did not prevent him from taking action on the misrepresentation. Applying this to David and Philip, the fact that Philip had been given the accounts, but had not understood them, should not prevent his taking action for misrepresentation. On the other hand, if Philip had sought professional help to understand the accounts, then this would prevent him from taking action. He would be held not to have relied on David's statement. This is shown by the decision in *Attwood v Small* (1838), in which the plaintiff purchaser of a mine sought to confirm the seller's statements as to its potential by commissioning his own report. The purchaser did not rely on the seller's statement, and so could not take action for misrepresentation.[1] There is no evidence on the facts that Philip did seek professional help, so he can probably treat the statement as to turnover as a misrepresentation.

The second statement is that there is room for expansion in the market. By itself this is probably not a statement of fact – it is a statement of opinion. In *Bisset v Wilkinson* (1927), a statement as to the number of sheep that a piece of land would support was held to be only a statement of opinion, because the maker of the statement had never kept sheep on the land. David's view of the future, provided that it is honestly held, would also not be likely to be actionable. This statement is, however, linked to the one that says that there are few competitors. This may well have been true at the time that it was made. Is the position changed by the opening of the DIY store, and if so, should David have told Philip about this? Generally, there is no obligation to volunteer information – silence does not amount to a misrepresentation. There are some exceptions to this, however, including where the situation changes in a significant way between the making of a representation and the creation of the contract. In *With v O'Flanagan* (1936), for example, a doctor made a true statement about the financial state of the practice he was selling. Between the statement and the contract, however, his health deteriorated, and the practice with it. The failure to notify the prospective purchaser of this was held to constitute a misrepresentation.

How would this apply to David and Philip? David might argue that the addition of one more competitor – the DIY store – does not really change the fact that there are 'few' competitors. On the other hand, a national chain, with the resources to offer special offers and 'loss leader' deals, is obviously a very significant player. On balance it is suggested that Philip would be able to argue that the opening of the store, and the offers it was making about fitted kitchens, was new information that David should have supplied to him.[2]

The final statement to consider is the one about the reliability of David's employees. Again, this looks at first sight like a statement of opinion, rather than fact. What, precisely, constitutes 'reliability'? The case of *Smith v Land and House Property Corp* (1884) is relevant here. In this case, a landlord who was selling the property described a tenant as 'desirable' when he knew that the tenant was in arrears with the rent. It was held that the statement by the landlord, although on its face a statement of opinion, was an actionable misrepresentation, because the landlord was aware of facts that made the opinion untenable. Another line of argument would be to use *Edgington v Fitzmaurice* (1885), in which it was held that to state an opinion that you do not genuinely hold is a misrepresentation of your state of mind (a fact), and therefore potentially an actionable misrepresentation (if the statement has induced a contract).

Applying this to David and Philip, David's statement about his employee is likely to be regarded as a misrepresentation either because it is untenable to call an employee who is frequently absent 'reliable', or because David did not genuinely hold that opinion.

It seems then, that Philip may well be able to claim that he entered into the contract following one or more misrepresentations from David. He will need to show that one or more of these statements were at least part of the reason why he agreed to contract. They do not have to be the sole, or main, reason: *Edgington v Fitzmaurice*. It is apparently not necessary that his reliance on the statement was 'reasonable': *Museprime Properties Ltd v Adhill Properties Ltd* (1990). The time between the making of the statements and the contract should not be a problem here – this type of period would be quite reasonable in relation to contract of this sort, and does not indicate that the pre-contractual statements were unimportant, or not an influence on Philip.

What remedies will be available to Philip? The main non-statutory remedy is rescission of the contract. This can be lost, however, by affirmation of the contract, lapse of time, impossibility of restitution, or affect on third parties' rights. Of these, the one that might be relevant here would be lapse of time. It is six months since the contract was entered into and this might be considered too long to allow rescission. It is difficult to predict the attitude of the courts to this, however. One of the few reported cases on this principle, *Leaf v International Galleries* (1950), involved a delay of five years, but it is likely that a much shorter period could be regarded as sufficient for the claimant to lose the right to rescind. The other remedy available would be damages. Assuming that David has not been fraudulent, the best remedy to pursue is that available under s 2(1) of the **Misrepresentation Act 1967**. Indeed, since the damages available under s 2(1) have been held to be the same as those for the tort of deceit (*Royscot Trust Ltd v Rogerson* (1991)), there would seem to be little point in Philip trying to prove fraud. By using s 2(1), he will put the burden on David to prove that he had reasonable grounds to believe, and did believe, in the truth of his statements up until the time of the contract. Since David is referring to things that should all be within his personal knowledge, he will find it difficult to do this.

In terms of the amount of damages, the object will be to put Philip into the position he would have been in had the contract not been made. If the case of *East v Maurer* (1991) is followed, this would mean that if Philip could show that he would have bought another, more profitable business, if he had not bought David's, he will be able to recover for the lost profits he might have obtained from such a business.

Overall, then, it seems that Philip has a good chance of taking an action for misrepresentation against David. Although he may have lost the opportunity to rescind the contract, he should be able to recover substantial damages under s 2(1) of the **Misrepresentation Act 1967**.

Think points

1 Doesn't this mean that it is better to be careless, and not to look at or try to understand information supplied, rather than to seek help and lose the right of action for misrepresentation?

2 Might David argue that since Philip lived in a nearby town, and the DIY store would presumably have publicised its opening and offers widely, Philip should have known about it anyway? There is no case law on this point.

CHAPTER 8

DURESS AND UNDUE INFLUENCE

INTRODUCTION

The vitiating factors covered in this chapter are the related concepts of duress and undue influence. Duress is a common law concept, based on threats made to a contracting party. Undue influence developed in equity to deal with situations in which there was improper pressure, without necessarily any specific threats. Because the two concepts are closely related, questions raising one will often require discussion of the other. The fact that both areas have widened in scope in recent years also raises the issue of a general principle attacking 'unconscionability' in contracts, and this not infrequently appears in questions on these topics.

In dealing with a problem question on duress, the following questions should be considered:

- was there a threat to carry out an unlawful (not necessarily criminal) act?
- was the threat 'operative' – that is, did it cause the person threatened to enter into the contract?
- did the threat involve, or itself constitute, a criminal offence?
- if not, did the person threatened have any reasonable alternative to compliance?

In relation to undue influence, the questions should be:

- was the relationship between the parties one of those that automatically raises a presumption of influence?
- if not, had the particular relationship developed in such a way that influence should be presumed?
- if 'yes' to either of the above, was entering into the contract disadvantageous to the person influenced?
- if influence cannot be presumed, do the circumstances surrounding the contract suggest that undue influence was in fact operating?

In relation to both concepts, if either is found to be operative, the question of remedies will then have to be discussed. The most likely remedy to be sought in both cases will be rescission of the contract. However, as with misrepresentation, the right to rescind may be lost, by lapse of time, affirmation of the contract, etc.

Question 28

What are the differences between 'duress' and 'undue influence'? Do the two concepts together constitute a law against unconscionable contracts?

Answer plan

There are three parts to this answer:

- a description of the concepts of 'duress' and 'undue influence';
- an indication of the differences between them; and
- consideration of whether the two concepts preclude unconscionable contracts in general, or whether they amount to only a partial prohibition.

The third part is obviously the most difficult, but it is an issue that is quite often raised. The issue of substantive versus procedural fairness will need discussion. The views of Lord Denning in *Lloyds Bank v Bundy* (1974) will need to be noted, along with the adverse reaction to them in later cases. The cases involving allegations of undue influence are probably more relevant to this issue than the cases on duress.

Answer

The concepts of duress and undue influence are related, in that they both deal with the situation in which a person enters into a contract when, if left to his or her own devices, he or she probably would not have done so. In other words, the contract is made as the result of some external pressure or interference. On the other hand, there are significant differences between them, and it is probably not accurate to regard them as simply aspects of a more general principle attacking unconscionable bargains.

Duress involves a threat: for example, 'if you do not make this contract, I will hit you'. A contract made in such circumstances will be voidable. There is no true agreement, and so the person subject to the threat should not be held to the contract.[1] Unlawful threats of physical violence are clearly going to have this effect, but in recent years the courts have extended the concept far beyond this. Any threat of criminal behaviour will apparently amount to duress, but the courts have also recognised the category of so-called 'economic duress'. One of the earliest examples of this was in *Universe Tankships Inc v International Transport Workers Federation* (1983), in which industrial action was threatened to force the owners of the ship to improve the working conditions of the crew. To escape the action, the owners made a payment to the union's welfare fund. They then brought an action to recover this as a payment made under duress.

The court held that the threatened industrial action was unlawful under English law, and the payment was held to have been made under duress. From this and subsequent decisions, it seems that any threat of an unlawful act, such as a tort or breach of contract, can amount to duress. Where the threat is not of a crime, however, there is an additional requirement, which is that the person threatened has no reasonable alternative but to agree. This derives from Lord Scarman's speech in *Pao On v Lau Yiu Long* (1979), in which he was attempting to distinguish between duress and legitimate commercial pressure. Where the person threatened with a breach of contract, for example, can expect to be fully compensated by damages or specific performance, then there is no reason to bring in duress. If, however, as was the case in *Atlas Express v Kafco* (1989), the carrying out of the threatened breach of contract would effectively put the other party out of business, there may be no reasonable alternative to compliance. In this situation, the courts will be prepared to intervene on the basis of duress. The Court of Appeal, in *CTN Cash and Carry v Gallaher* (1994), suggested that in certain circumstances a threat to carry out a lawful act (for example, to withdraw credit facilities) could amount to economic duress.

Similarly, in *Attorney General v R* (2003), the Privy Council confirmed that in some circumstances a lawful threat could be illegitimate, drawing the analogy with blackmail – in which the illegitimacy does not derive from the unlawful nature of the threat but the nature of the demand that the pressure is applied to support (that is, the payment of money in exchange for silence). These statements were in both cases obiter, but if followed they make it difficult to see exactly where the boundaries between legitimate and illegitimate pressure should be drawn. Turning to undue influence, it is important to note that here there are two categories: presumed undue influence and actual undue influence. In both cases, the essence of the defence is that one of the parties to a contract has been in such a position of influence over the other that there is a danger that the person subject to the influence has been led into making a disadvantageous agreement. The difference between the two categories is that there are certain relationships in which it is presumed that such influence will exist. Where no such presumed influence arises, the party seeking to escape from the agreement will have to prove that as a matter of fact he or she was acting under the influence of the other party.

The relationships in which influence is presumed include parent/child, doctor/patient, solicitor/client, religious adviser/disciple, but not, it should be noted, husband/wife. The relationships are ones in which one person places trust and confidence in another, and so is liable to act on their suggestions without seeking independent advice. Outside these general categories, a particular relationship may develop in such a way over a period of time that influence will be presumed. In *Lloyds Bank v Bundy* (1974), the relationship was that of banker and customer. Mr Bundy had placed great reliance on the bank over a number of years. When the bank was relied on to provide advice on a business transaction, there was held to be a presumption of influence.

The category of actual undue influence covers situations falling outside the presumption. Here, the burden of proof is on the person alleging influence. It can apply between husband and wife, as recognised in *Bank of Credit and Commerce International SA v Aboody* (1989). The nature of the influence is, however, the same as for presumed influence. In other words, the person influenced must have acted out of their trust in the influencer, without seeking or obtaining advice from elsewhere.

In relation to presumed influence, whether such influence is to be regarded as undue will turn in part on whether the transaction was disadvantageous to the person influenced. This test derives from the case of *National Westminster Bank v Morgan* (1985) and was at one time applied in a fairly rigid manner as a test of 'manifest disadvantage'. The House of Lords in *Royal Bank of Scotland v Etridge (No 2)* (2001), however, adopted a rather more flexible approach. If a transaction is disadvantageous, then it will raise suspicions that undue influence has been used, which it will be up to the alleged influencer to dispel. In relation to situations of actual undue influence, however, the question of the disadvantageous nature of the transaction has no relevance: *CIBC Mortgages v Pitt* (1993). What, then, are the differences between these two related concepts of duress and undue influence? One is that duress is a common law concept, whereas undue influence originates in equity. This does not seem to result in any great practical distinction between the two. In both cases, the consequence of a successful argument for the existence of the concept is that the resulting contract is regarded as voidable.

It is also clear from the above descriptions that duress results from a specific threat, made on a particular occasion, whereas undue influence is more likely to arise from a continuing relationship. What has happened in the past between the two parties may be just as important as the events surrounding the making of the particular contract about which there is a dispute.

More significant is the difference between the position of the party who has benefited from the contract in each case. In relation to duress, it is clear that he or she must have acted improperly.[2] Subject to the statements in *CTN Cash and Carry v Gallaher* and *Attorney General v R* mentioned above, the threat must generally be to carry out some unlawful act, either a crime or a civil wrong. Where undue influence is concerned, however, there is no need for the influencer to have acted with an improper motive. Particularly in the category of presumed influence, it may be that he or she was simply overenthusiastic, and did not realise the effect of his or her influence. Provided that the resulting agreement is disadvantageous, however, the other party will be able to escape from it.

A further difference is that the contract which results from duress does not have to be disadvantageous to the person who is persuaded to enter into it. The court is here concerned with the procedural impropriety rather than the issue of substantive fairness. In relation to presumed (although not actual) undue influence, as we have seen, the unfairness of the transaction is a prerequisite for a successful plea. This difference is clearer when the duress results from a criminal threat, for, again as we have seen, where a civil wrong is threatened there is the additional requirement of 'no reasonable alternative'. This perhaps comes close to saying that the contract must be disadvantageous.

Finally, the relationship of the two concepts to a general rule of 'unconscionability' must be considered. This would require a general ban on 'unfair' contracts, whenever the unfairness was such that a court could not in all conscience allow it to stand. Duress and undue influence do not equal unconscionability for a number of reasons. First, both concepts place more stress on procedural fairness than substantive fairness. Unconscionability would require the courts to focus more directly on the nature of the contract itself, rather than the events that led to it being formed. To that extent, the concepts are clearly narrower than an approach based on unconscionability.

Second, in relation to duress, it is clear that this concept can be looked at as being wider than unconscionability, in the sense that a contract which is substantively fair can be struck down simply because it was made under duress. It is also significant that attempts by some judges, most notably Lord Denning in *Lloyds Bank v Bundy*, to argue for a general rule against unconscionable contracts have not gained favour, and indeed have been specifically disapproved in later cases, such as *National Westminster Bank plc v Morgan*. This ties in with an indication of reluctance to allow the concept of economic duress to expand too rapidly, and to overlap into the area of legitimate commercial pressure. This reluctance probably results in part from a desire for certainty. The occurrence and consequences of procedural unfairness are relatively easy to predict. If the courts had to look at the substance of contracts in every case to see if they were 'fair', then there would be great increases in uncertainty in the commercial world, and far more litigation. The current approach of the English courts may at times seem cautious, but it is probably the right one.

Think points

1 This concept is often expressed in the cases by a reference to the threatened person's 'will' being 'overborne', or that they acted 'involuntarily'. Is this accurate? Some commentators suggest that it is not, in that the person has decided to make the contract, and in doing so has exercised a choice. This is not the same as the involuntary act of an automaton.

2 Is it necessary to show that the party guilty of the duress was aware that the other party was acting under it? The decision in *Universe Tankships Inc of Monrovia v International Transport Workers Federation* (1983) suggests not.

Question 29

Answer both parts.

Part (a)

Apex plc has a contract with Nadir Ltd. Apex tells Nadir that unless Nadir enters into a five-year contract with Apex's subsidiary, Crux Ltd, on terms that are particularly advantageous to Crux, Apex will 'terminate its agreement' with Nadir. Despite the fact that the terms suggested mean that Nadir will make a loss on the deal with Crux, it agrees because of the value that it places on its contract with Apex. Two years later, Apex goes out of business. Nadir now wants to escape from the contract with Crux.

Advise Nadir.

Would it make any difference if Apex's threat, rather than being to terminate its agreement, was not to renew its contract with Nadir?

Part (b)

Maria, an orphan, married Harold four years ago when she was aged 17 and he was aged 30. She has a valuable collection of jewellery that she inherited from her mother. Harold, whose business is in debt, asks her to guarantee a loan of £20,000. Maria refuses. Later, Harold brings his bank manager home, and presents Maria with papers to sign, guaranteeing the loan of £20,000 and using Maria's jewellery as security. The bank manager tells her that she may consult her solicitor if she wishes, but that there is little danger of her losing her jewellery. Maria signs the guarantee. Harold's business collapses, and the bank wants to enforce the guarantee.

Advise Maria.

Answer plan

Part (a) of this question deals with duress, and part (b) with undue influence. The issues raised are quite distinct, and so the two parts should be looked at separately.

Part (a)

We are dealing here with 'economic' duress. The threat by Apex plc is to break its contract with Nadir. In looking at the cases on economic duress, of which *Atlas Express Ltd v Kafco (Importers and Distributors) Ltd* (1989) is perhaps the most relevant, the issue of whether Nadir had any reasonable alternative to compliance will need to be considered. A further issue is the question of the two-year delay before Nadir attempts to avoid the contract. The alternative scenario will not need lengthy consideration. The threat here appears not to be to do anything unlawful, and so, subject to the obiter comments of the Court of Appeal in *CTN Cash and Carry v Gallaher* (1994) and of the Privy Council in *Attorney General v R* (2003), there will be little possibility of pleading duress.

Part (b)

The two types of undue influence, presumed and actual, will both need discussion. The issues are as follows.

• Has the relationship between Harold and Maria developed in a way that creates a presumption of undue influence? (Remember that there is no automatic presumption of influence between husband and wife.)

• If not, has Harold exercised actual undue influence (as in *Bank of Credit and Commerce International SA v Aboody* (1989))?

• If Harold has influenced Maria, is the bank affected by this on the basis of the tests laid down in *Barclays Bank v O'Brien* (1993) and *Royal Bank of Scotland v Etridge (No 2)* (2001)?

• Has the bank itself used undue influence over Maria (as in *Lloyds Bank v Bundy* (1974))?

Answer

Part (a)

If Nadir wishes to escape from the contract with Crux, the only possibility would seem to be a plea of duress. There may be problems for Nadir, however, as to whether the threat was sufficiently serious, and as to the delay of two years before it attempted to avoid the agreement.

Duress is a common law concept, which enables a person who has entered into a contract as a result of threats to treat the contract as voidable. Not all threats will have this effect, however, and the right to rescind the contract may in any case be lost in certain circumstances.

Originally, the concept of duress was based on threats of criminal activity – for example, if you do not make this contract, you will get beaten up (see *Barton v Armstrong* (1976) for a modern example). Over the past 25 years, however, it has been recognised that in certain situations commercial pressure can go beyond what is legitimate between businesses, and itself amount to duress. For this to be the case, there are two main requirements:

- the threat, although not of a crime, must be of some action that is improper. This has generally been taken to mean an act that is unlawful, involving at least a civil wrong, such as a tort or breach of contract. There are obiter statements by the Court of Appeal in *CTN Cash and Carry v Gallaher* (1994) and the Privy Council in *Attorney General v R* (2003) which suggest that in certain circumstances a threat of a lawful act can amount to duress, but this has not as yet been developed in subsequent cases; and

- the person threatened must have no practical alternative to compliance (*Pao On v Lau Yiu Long* (1979)).

In the problem, the first requirement seems clearly to be satisfied. Apex plc is threatening to break its contract with Nadir, which is sufficiently unlawful to give rise to the possibility of duress. The difficulty arises with the second requirement. When can it be said that the person threatened has no real alternative but to comply? The cases talk of the person's will being 'overborne', but this is not particularly helpful, since they are still in fact making a choice of compliance, even if they do so to avoid some other consequences. An example in which this requirement was satisfied was *Atlas Express v Kafco* (1989). The defendant, Kafco, was a small manufacturing company that had a very valuable contract with Woolworths, a store with branches nationwide. Kafco employed Atlas, a national firm of carriers, to make deliveries to Woolworths. Atlas found that it had, through its own mistake, entered into the contract with Kafco on uneconomic terms. Atlas told Kafco that it must agree to an increase in the charge for carriage, or otherwise Atlas would not make the deliveries. Kafco could not risk being in breach of its contract with Woolworths, and so agreed to the change under protest. When Atlas brought an action to recover the increased charges, Kafco resisted on the grounds of duress. It was held that losing the contract with Woolworths, or being sued by that company, would be so disastrous for Kafco that it had no real alternative but to go along with Atlas' suggestion. Kafco was not obliged to pay the additional carriage costs.

Does the same argument apply here? The alternative to making the contract with Crux is for Nadir to lose the contract with Apex. We are told that Nadir places great value on this contract, but it is not clear just how vital it is to its business.[1] If it was felt that Nadir could be adequately compensated for the loss of the contract by suing Apex for damages for breach, then Nadir would not be able to rely on duress to escape the agreement with Crux.

A final problem for Nadir is that it is now two years since the contract with Crux was made. Duress renders a contract voidable at the option of the person subject to the duress, but it is also clear that the right to rescind can be lost. In *The Atlantic Baron* (1978), this occurred when the party threatened was held to have affirmed the contract, and failed to raise their claim until over six months after the ship that was the subject of the contract had been delivered. Here, there is a delay of two years between the threat and the attempt to avoid the contract. It is likely that, because of this, Nadir will not be allowed to rescind the contract. The alternative scenario, where the threat is of non-renewal rather than termination, does not involve any threat to do something unlawful, and so is unlikely to constitute duress. Although the Court of Appeal in *CTN Cash and Carry v Gallaher* (1994) and the Privy Council in *Attorney General v R* (2003) have indicated, obiter, that the illegitimacy of a threat does not necessarily depend on its unlawfulness, it would seem likely that the courts would be looking for behaviour that was more outrageous than that of Apex in this problem in order to find duress. Nadir is therefore unlikely to have a remedy as a result of this threat.

Part (b)

Maria has not entered into the guarantee agreement as a result of any threats made to her, so her claim to be able to escape from it will have to be based on undue influence. There are two possible arguments for this to exist on these facts. The first will be based on the fact that her husband may be in such a dominant position over her that she is unduly influenced by him. The second will relate to the relationship between banker and client, since she signs the agreement as a result of the involvement of the bank manager.

Looking first at Harold's influence over Maria, the relationship of husband and wife does not automatically raise a presumption of influence. The particular relationship, however, may have developed in a way that gives rise to a presumption. There is little evidence of this from the facts. Although Harold is much older than Maria, there is no evidence of any regular pattern of Maria signing documents presented to her by Harold. Indeed, in relation to the guarantee, she at first refuses to sign. This might well indicate that she is taking an independent decision, and does not simply fall within her husband's wishes. Could Maria prove actual undue influence? A case that illustrates the principles operating in this area, and which bears a close factual resemblance to the problem, is *BCCI SA v Aboody* (1989). Mrs Aboody married her husband when she was quite young. He was 20 years older than her. For many years, she signed documents relating to her husband's business, of which she was nominally a director, without reading them or questioning her husband about them. She signed guarantees and charges relating to the matrimonial home, to support loans by the bank to the business. She had taken no independent advice, although she had on one occasion been encouraged to do so by the bank's solicitor. It was found that, although Mr Aboody had not acted with any improper motive, he had unduly influenced his wife. Will the same argument apply here?

There are significant differences between Maria's case and that of Mrs Aboody. Although, as has been noted above, there is a similar age difference between husband and wife in the two cases, there is no clear evidence that Maria was on this occasion intimidated by Harold. Moreover, there is no evidence that Harold was present at the signing of the document, whereas Mr Aboody was. If he had been, this might well have strengthened Maria's claim. As it is, without further evidence of the way in which Harold may have exercised influence over Maria, it seems unlikely that she will succeed on this ground.

If Harold has not influenced Maria, then the bank cannot be affected by Harold's actions. If Harold is found to have influenced her, however, the question is whether the bank had notice (actual or constructive) of this: *Barclays Bank v O'Brien* (1993). The bank should be put on inquiry if the transaction is not to Maria's financial advantage, and it is a transaction of a type in relation to which there is a substantial risk that a husband will have committed a legal wrong in getting the wife to agree. Since the transaction provides no direct financial assistance to Maria, and being a guarantee or surety is regarded as falling within the second condition, it seems that these requirements are satisfied. The bank can only protect itself by taking reasonable steps to ensure that the wife is fully aware of the nature of the transaction, and has had every opportunity to take legal advice.

Recent case law has been fairly lenient to the lender in relation to the issue of legal advice. The leading authority is *Royal Bank of Scotland v Etridge (No 2)* (2001), in which it was said that in this type of situation the bank must insist on the wife receiving independent legal advice, with the solicitor confirming to the bank that the documentation and its implications have been explained to her. On the facts given here, it appears that the bank has not satisfied these requirements, since Maria has simply been told that she may consult a solicitor if she wishes. Nor does there even seem to have been much of an attempt to explain the transaction by the bank. Assuming, therefore, that Harold has unduly influenced Maria (which is not very likely), the bank would not be allowed to enforce the guarantee.

A further possible argument for Maria is based on what the bank manager said to her. It is clear that in some cases the relationship between banker and customer will be such as to give rise to a presumption of undue influence: *Lloyds Bank v Bundy* (1974). But this will not always be the case,[2] as was illustrated by *National Westminster Bank v Morgan* (1985). Here, a wife had again signed a charge relating to the matrimonial home, in order to obtain a loan to avoid the house being repossessed by the building society to which it was mortgaged. The bank manager who called at the house to obtain the wife's signature had innocently misrepresented the scope of the charge. The House of Lords, however, took the view that the wife knew what she was doing, and there was no undue influence. Is Maria's situation best regarded as being like that of Mr Bundy or Mrs Morgan? As was the case with Harold's influence, there is no indication here that she has relied on the bank manager over a period of time, which had been the case with Mr Bundy.[3] It is a one-off event, apparently, as with Mrs Morgan. There is perhaps slightly more influence being used here than in Morgan, but it must be doubtful whether it is sufficient to raise the presumption.

Even if it does, there is a further problem. Where presumed influence is being alleged, the courts will only be likely to find the influence 'undue' where the transaction is disadvantageous to the person influenced: *National Westminster Bank v Morgan*, as reinterpreted in *Royal Bank of Scotland v Etridge (No 2)*. So, even if Maria can establish that she was influenced by the bank manager to sign the guarantee, she will not be able to avoid it unless it is to her clear disadvantage. In one sense, this is so, in that she puts her jewellery, which is probably of sentimental as well as commercial value to her, at risk. On the other hand, the survival of her husband's business is to her benefit, and if this is the only way it is likely to be achieved, then it cannot be said to be a totally disadvantageous arrangement. For this to be so it would probably have to be shown that there never was a real chance of Harold's business being saved by the extra money from the bank.

In conclusion, then, it seems that on the basis of the facts given, and in particular in the absence of any long-term influence exercised by either Harold or the bank, Maria must be advised that she has little chance of avoiding the guarantee on the basis of undue influence.

Think points

1 Is it significant that Apex is a 'plc' (that is, a public limited company), whereas Nadir is simply 'Ltd'? This almost certainly indicates that Apex is a much larger company than Nadir, which may mean, as in *Atlas Express v Kafco*, that Nadir is very dependent on this one contract.

2 What relationships do result in an automatic presumption of influence? Examples include parent/child, doctor/patient and solicitor/client: *Goldsworthy v Brickell* (1987). Husband/wife does not give rise to such a presumption.

3 What period of time might be necessary to establish a relationship of influence? In *Goldsworthy v Brickell*, a matter of months rather than years was sufficient.

Question 30

Harry, who is 25, lives in a large house that was left to him by his parents. Harry is gay, and in 2000, his friend Tom, aged 40, comes to live with him. Harry allows Tom to take all of the decisions about the organisation of the household, and most of the time they live together happily. At times, however, Tom becomes violent, and Harry knows that in the past he has served a prison sentence for assault. When, therefore, Tom tells Harry that he thinks that Harry should sell him a half-share of the house for £20,000, Harry agrees, even though the house is worth about £400,000, as he fears what Tom's reaction would be if he refused. The transfer takes place. One year later, Tom's business is running into difficulties, and he suggests that the house should be used as security for a loan that he is negotiating from the bank. Tom tells Harry that the limit of the security will be £75,000. This is untrue, as the security is in fact unlimited. Harry goes to the bank with Tom, where the papers are presented to him for signature. As he is about to sign, the bank's employee says: 'Are you sure you don't want to think about this a bit longer, or take legal advice?' Harry says: 'No thank you, I am happy to trust Tom.'

Tom's business has now, a year after the loan was made, collapsed with debts of £500,000, and the bank is seeking to enforce the security by taking possession of the house.

Harry wishes to avoid: (a) the transfer of the half share in the house to Tom; and (b) the security transaction with the bank. Advise Harry.

Answer plan

This question is clearly designed to raise the issues dealt with by *Barclays Bank v O'Brien* (1993), in which a debtor tries to escape liability by arguing undue influence or misrepresentation by a third party. Note, however, that this only arises in relation to part (b). The first part requires a consideration of duress (because of the possibility of Tom's violence) and undue influence as between Tom and Harry.

You will need to discuss the following.

Part (a)

• The requirements for duress
• The requirements for actual and presumed undue influence

Part (b)

- The effect of Tom's influence, or misrepresentation, on Harry's liability to the bank
- In that context, the doctrine of 'notice', as explained in *Barclays Bank v O'Brien*
- The requirements for legal advice set out in *Royal Bank of Scotland v Etridge (No 2)* (2001)
- The possibility of the bank itself having unduly influenced Tom.

In other words, part (a) requires the discussion of the basic principles of duress and undue influence, and part (b) the application of the latter in the particular context of three-party relationships.

Answer

Harry is seeking to escape from contractual obligations that he has undertaken in respect of Tom and his bank. One way of persuading a court to set aside an agreement is to show that it was made as a result of duress or undue influence. Duress is a common law concept, whereas undue influence has developed in equity. Can Harry use either of these to avoid his contractual obligations?

Let us consider first the transfer of the half-share in the house at a gross undervalue (approximately one-twentieth). It is well established that, if a contract is made as a result of threats of physical violence, it will be vitiated (for example, *Barton v Armstrong* (1975)). The reason is said to be that the threatened party is not truly consenting to the agreement, and that therefore one of the essential elements of a binding contract is missing. If, therefore, Tom had said to Harry, 'Sell me your share for £10,000, or I will break your legs,' there is no doubt that Harry would not be bound to the agreement. This is not what happened, however. We do not have any indication of specific threats by Tom. Harry complies simply because he is frightened by the possibility of a violent reaction following his refusal. There is nothing in the cases to suggest that this is sufficient to found a plea of 'duress'.

Unless there has been something more specific in the way of a threat, therefore, it seems that any argument based on duress must fail.

Can Harry argue that he has been unduly influenced by Tom into entering into this agreement? Undue influence is divided into two categories in English law: actual and presumed. The difference is primarily concerned with the burden of proof. In relation to actual undue influence, the party alleging that he or she has been influenced must prove this on the balance of probabilities. If the influence is presumed, however, it is the alleged influencer who must prove (again, on the balance of probabilities) that no undue influence was used. Whether there is a presumption of influence depends on the relationship between the parties. Certain types of relationship – for example, solicitor/client, parent/child, doctor/patient – will automatically be presumed to involve influence. Tom and Harry do not fall into any of these categories. If, however, there is a clear dominant party in any relationship, and the other party regularly acts in accordance with that person's wishes, then again, influence may be presumed (for example, *Lloyds Bank v Bundy* (1975)). Whether the relationship has developed in this way is of course a question of fact. Here, it seems that Harry is very much the subservient partner in the relationship. We are told that he 'allows Tom to take all the decisions about the organisation of the household', which might well indicate that he has become accustomed to doing what Tom says. It is likely, therefore, that a court would be prepared to presume influence. Moreover, since the sale is clearly at a gross undervalue and thus disadvantageous to Harry, it will be presumed that Tom used his influence in an improper way, and it will be up to him to prove that Harry acted entirely freely in entering into the agreement. There is a difficulty for Harry, however, in that the remedy that he is seeking will be 'rescission'. This equitable remedy is subject to certain bars, one of which is lapse of time. Thus, in *Allcard v Skinner* (1887), a woman who had given much of her property to a religious order while under the influence of that order was not able to recover, because she did not start her action until six years later. The position is not quite so clear-cut here, in that it is only two years since the transfer took place. It still seems likely, however, that a court would have expected Harry to act more quickly to avoid this transaction.

In conclusion on this part of the problem, then, it seems that although there is some evidence that Harry entered into the contract on the basis of undue influence, it is unlikely that he will be able to get it rescinded.

Turning to the second transaction from which Harry wishes to escape, it may again be argued that he has been influenced by Tom. What is even more clear, however, is that Tom has misrepresented the extent of the liability, in that he has told Harry that the limit of the security is £75,000, whereas in fact it is unlimited. As against Tom, therefore, any agreement would be rescindable on the basis of misrepresentation. The contract that Harry has made, however, is not with Tom, but with the bank. Can he avoid this transaction on the basis of Tom's influence or misrepresentation?

The normal answer would be 'no', in that the actions of a third party (Tom) will not normally operate to vitiate a contract between two other people (Harry and the bank). This area is, however, one in which the courts have developed some special rules. The basis of the current approach is to be found in the case of *Barclays Bank v O'Brien* (1993). This concerned a wife who had been misled by her husband as regards an agreement to use the matrimonial home as security for a loan. The House of Lords ruled that the same principles applied whether the surety had entered into the agreement on the basis of undue influence or misrepresentation. The approach of the courts should be based on the doctrine of notice, which is very important in equity. In other words, the question of whether the creditor was affected by the misrepresentation or undue influence of the third party should depend on whether he or she had actual or constructive notice of it. Actual notice will arise where the creditor has witnessed, or has become aware of, specific instances of influence or misrepresentation. This is largely a question of fact. More difficulty exists in identifying constructive notice. In the House of Lords' view in *Royal Bank of Scotland v Etridge (No 2)* (2001), wherever the relationship between a surety and a debtor is 'non-commercial', the lender should be put on inquiry. This is not limited to, but clearly includes, relationships between cohabitees (married or unmarried, heterosexual or homosexual). If the creditor is aware of the relationship, and the transaction is one that is not, on its face, to the financial advantage of the surety, the creditor should be put on inquiry, and will be 'infected' by any misrepresentation or undue influence of the debtor, unless certain steps are taken. These are that the creditor must warn the surety (not in the presence of the debtor) of the risks involved in the transaction, and advise him or her to take independent legal advice.

Applying these principles to the facts of the case, does the bank have constructive notice of the risk of misrepresentation or undue influence by Tom? It appears that Harry and Tom are a cohabiting homosexual couple, but even if their relationship is simply one of friendship, it is clearly personal and not 'commercial'. If the bank is aware of this, then one element of the constructive notice is satisfied. The transaction is not to Harry's financial advantage, so this requirement would also be satisfied. The bank's position therefore seems to turn on its knowledge of the relationship between Harry and Tom. Since the bank must almost certainly be aware that Tom and Harry live at the same address, then this will be a clear indication that their relationship is a personal one, and that Harry's role in acting as a surety is not part of a business transaction. They will, therefore, be put on inquiry. If this is so, then the rather tentative suggestion of 'more time' or 'legal advice', made in Tom's presence, would almost certainly be insufficient to satisfy the requirements as to the steps that creditors should take to protect themselves. These requirements were reviewed and restated by the House of Lords in *Royal Bank of Scotland v Etridge (No 2)*. They said that in this type of situation, in which there is a 'non-commercial' surety, the bank must insist on the surety receiving independent legal advice. The solicitor giving the advice must confirm to the bank that the documentation and its implications have been explained to the surety. On the facts given here, it appears that the bank has not satisfied these requirements. The bank's employee has simply asked Harry: 'Are you sure you don't want to take legal advice?' This is clearly inadequate, and Harry may well be able to resist the enforcement of the security against him.

One final possibility that must be considered is whether the bank itself is guilty of using undue influence on Harry. This possibility was recognised in *Lloyds Bank v Bundy* (1975), in which an elderly farmer was held to have been unduly influenced by a representative of a bank with which the farmer had had a long relationship, and in which he placed his trust and confidence. There is no evidence here, however, that Harry's relationship with the bank is of this kind. It seems unlikely, therefore, that he would be able to escape from the security transaction on this basis.

In conclusion, then, it appears that there is little Harry can do about the transfer of the half-share of the house. He may, however, be able to resist the enforcement of the security by the bank, if it can be shown that the bank should have had constructive notice of the likelihood of Harry's being unduly influenced by Tom, or being affected by Tom's misrepresentation.

Question 31

'It is not clear that the House of Lords has yet managed to find a satisfactory balance between the need to protect those vulnerable to undue influence, and the need to ensure that banks and other financial institutions remain willing to lend money to small businesses in situations where domestic property may provide the only realistic security.' (Stone, *The Modern Law of Contract*, 7th edn, 2008, p 449)

Discuss.

Answer plan

This essay focuses on one particular aspect of the law on undue influence – that is, the extent to which those lending money on the security of domestic property (probably the matrimonial home) can be prevented from enforcing the debt because of undue influence (by the creditor or a third party) over the person providing the security. Two decisions of the House of Lords dominate this area: namely, *Barclays Bank v O'Brien* (1993) and *Royal Bank of Scotland v Etridge (No 2)* (2001). You should not attempt the question unless you are confident that you have a firm grasp of both cases. Note that the question does not merely require an exposition of the law derived from these cases, but also requires you to adopt a critical perspective, addressing the issue of whether the balance of rights between the various parties is being struck correctly.

The suggested order of treatment is:

- outline the problem;
- explain the principles to be derived from *Barclays Bank v O'Brien*;
- explain how those principles have been modified by subsequent case law, and in particular *Royal Bank of Scotland v Etridge (No 2)*; and

- consider critically the question of whether the balance between the rights of creditors and the rights of those providing security has been struck satisfactorily – that is, protecting the vulnerable while not 'scaring off' prospective lenders.

Answer

Over the past 15 years, the English courts have been grappling with a difficult problem involving the interaction of the law of contract with an area of social and economic sensitivity. It is important for the economy that small businesses flourish. Such businesses often cannot do so without significant and substantial borrowing. Creditors will only be willing to lend the sums concerned on the basis of some appropriate security. The only available security will often be the house in which the borrower is living with his or her partner. The danger is that the partner, having a legal interest in the house, may be persuaded by undue influence or misrepresentation to allow it to be used for security without a full appreciation of the risks involved. The courts may then be asked to prevent the creditor from enforcing the security, in order to protect the rights of the partner. The situation most commonly arising is that in which the borrower is a man and the person supplying the security is his wife, although as the House of Lords has now made clear, care needs to be taken wherever the relationship between borrower and surety is 'non-commercial'.

The starting point for discussion of the modern law applying to this area is the House of Lords' decision in *Barclays Bank v O'Brien* (1993). In this case, Mrs O'Brien had been misled by her husband as to the extent of the security being supplied to support his business overdraft with the bank. The jointly owned matrimonial home was used as security for the debt. The relevant documents were presented for her signature by an employee of the bank, who did not explain the transaction or suggest that she should take independent legal advice. When the bank subsequently tried to enforce its security, the question arose as to whether it was prevented from doing so by Mr O'Brien's misrepresentation to his wife. While the case was thus primarily concerned with misrepresentation, the House of Lords made it clear that the same principles should apply where the allegation was that the borrower had used undue influence on the surety.

There was no suggestion in the *O'Brien* case that the bank itself had been guilty of undue influence or misrepresentation (unlike, for example, *Lloyds Bank Ltd v Bundy* (1975), in which the bank itself was at fault). The question was rather whether the bank was 'infected' by Mr O'Brien's wrongdoing in the form of the misrepresentation. The House of Lords rejected arguments that this type of situation was best analysed in terms of agency (with the husband acting as agent for the bank), or on the basis of some kind of 'special equity' protecting wives. Instead, it held that the governing principle should be that of actual or constructive notice. Was the bank aware ('actual notice') of any wrongdoing by Mr O'Brien that would have entitled Mrs O'Brien to set aside any transaction as against her husband? If not, should it have been aware ('constructive notice') of the risk of such wrongdoing, and taken steps to negate its effect? On the facts, the House found that although Mrs O'Brien had not been unduly influenced by her husband, she had been materially misled by his misrepresentation, so that she would have had a right to set aside the transaction vis-à-vis her husband. The bank was obviously aware of their relationship, and aware that the transaction was one that was risky from Mrs O'Brien's point of view. The bank should, therefore, have taken steps to advise Mrs O'Brien separately and to ensure that she was fully aware of the nature and extent of the security being provided. As it had not done so, Mrs O'Brien was entitled to set aside the security transaction vis-à-vis the bank.

Cases subsequent to *O'Brien* accepted the general approach laid out there, but became somewhat confused over when exactly the creditor should be put on notice, and what steps needed to be taken to protect its position. In particular, there were queries as to what the position was when the surety received legal advice, but from the same lawyer as was acting for the borrower. These issues were thoroughly reviewed by the House of Lords in *Royal Bank of Scotland v Etridge (No 2)* (2001).

The first question concerns when the creditor is put on notice. The House of Lords decided that this could not be limited to transactions involving husband and wife, cohabitees and sexual partners (as had been suggested in some of the earlier cases). The case of *Credit Lyonnais Bank Nederland NV v Burch* (1997) indicated that this was too narrow an approach, since here the 'victim' of the undue influence was a junior employee in the borrower's firm. In *Etridge*, therefore, the view was taken that the creditor should be put on notice wherever the relationship between the borrower and the surety was 'non-commercial'. To this extent, the House has extended the protection given by the law, by requiring that all non-commercial sureties should receive proper independent advice.

As regards the steps that should be taken by the creditor to ensure that proper advice is given, the House moved away from the position in *O'Brien*, which put the emphasis on the creditor itself providing advice. The House recognised, as had been shown by many of the cases post-*O'Brien*, that it was often preferable and more practical for the advice to be given by a solicitor. In relation to this, the creditor should communicate directly with the surety to determine whom he or she wishes to use as a legal adviser. This can be the same solicitor that is acting for the borrower, as long as the surety is happy with this. The legal adviser must be provided with all of the relevant information, including any confidential financial information provided by the borrower to the creditor, and any suspicions that the creditor may have that the surety may have been misled or unduly influenced. The surety must then have the transaction fully explained by the legal adviser. The surety should also be asked to sign a document indicating that the transaction and its implications have been fully explained and understood. Once it has been confirmed to the creditor by the legal adviser that all of these steps have been taken, then the creditor will be fully protected from any subsequent claim that the surety was misled or unduly influenced.

What is the position if these steps are not taken? This will mean that the validity of the security transaction is vulnerable to challenge, but it does not necessarily mean that the transaction will be set aside. The surety will still need to show that there was some misrepresentation or influence from the borrower (or from the creditor) that justifies the court treating the transaction as voidable. It is in this area that *Etridge*, while extending the situations in which the creditor needs to take steps to protect itself, has probably narrowed the situations in which undue influence will be found. One of the factors that will be relevant to a finding of such influence is whether the transaction is disadvantageous to the surety. The House was clear that it did not regard the most common situation that arises in this area – that is, one where the wife provides security for her husband's business debts – as being one that as a matter of course would give rise to a presumption that the husband's influence was undue. Wives may well be willing to support their husbands' businesses in this type of situation, not least because the business may provide the main family income, and so be prepared to take risks to achieve this. This does not in itself mean that they have been unduly influenced. It may be questioned whether, in taking this line, the House of Lords has in fact given appropriate weight to the pressures that will be placed on a wife in this type of situation. If she is asked by her husband to support his business, it may be very difficult for her to say no. A refusal would be likely to put a severe strain on their relationship, which she will presumably wish to continue. Her ability to resist would be assisted if she were to receive independent legal advice that emphasises the risks involved. The focus in *Etridge* is on the importance of such advice in protecting the position of the creditor. It is just as important that sureties in this situation should receive such advice, both for their own protection and to provide support for a decision not to proceed with the transaction. It is likely to be easier to say, 'I am not going ahead because the solicitor advised me of the risks involved,' as opposed to, 'I am not going ahead because I don't trust you to make a success of the business'. Even with such support, however, the decision to refuse to provide the necessary security is likely to be a difficult one.

At the moment, the law in this area seems to be weighted in favour of the creditor, despite the fact that *O'Brien* was seen as a 'victory' for wives who act as sureties. This is indicated by the fact that a significant majority of the cases that have subsequently come before the appeal courts have resulted in a decision against the surety. The House of Lords in *Etridge*, while providing welcome clarification of various issues, and in particular the steps that a creditor needs to take to protect itself, has done nothing to change this imbalance. The risk of shifting it too far in favour of the surety is, of course, that creditors will become reluctant to lend money when the security is domestic property in which someone other than the borrower has an interest. It is submitted, however, that there is scope for more protection to be provided to sureties in this type of situation, without the risk of scaring off the majority of potential lenders.

CHAPTER 9

ILLEGALITY

INTRODUCTION

The vitiating factor that is considered in this chapter is 'illegality'. There is a variety of ways in which a contract can be deemed to be 'illegal' and thus unenforceable. In this chapter, Question 32 deals with the illegal performance of employment contracts, and the first part of Question 33 with the effects of illegality. The second parts of Question 33 and Question 34 both deal with aspects of the restraint of trade doctrine.

The rules that apply in this area are reasonably well settled, and questions on restraint of trade, in particular, should not provide too much difficulty. One problem in answering such questions, however, arises from the fact that whether a restraint is enforceable or not will depend on whether it is regarded as 'reasonable' in all of the circumstances. This means that it is difficult to give a firm and definite answer. What must be done, however, is to give some answer, albeit qualified, and to back it up with reasons drawn from past decisions, or the facts of the problem itself, or both.

The main points to be remembered in relation to restraint of trade are that:

- restraints are prima facie void;
- they will, however, be valid if:
  - there is a legitimate interest to protect;
  - the restraint goes no further than is reasonable to protect that interest; and
  - the restraint is not otherwise against the public interest

One aspect of restraint of trade that is of growing importance, but is beyond the scope of most contract courses, is the effect of **Art 81** of the **EC Treaty**. This applies where the restraint has an effect on cross-border trade within the European Union. All of the questions in this chapter, as is usual in most undergraduate contract examinations, relate to restraints that affect only domestic UK trade. Nor is there any attempt here to deal with the legislative regime contained in the **Competition Act 1998**. This area, like the European element, is more commonly part of a specialist course on competition law.

Question 32

Peter came to England from Serbia in July 2006, joining his cousin, Velma, who had lived in London since 1982. Peter had very poor English, but Velma helped him make an application for asylum, on the basis of the persecution that he claimed to have suffered in Serbia. Peter was sent a letter in August 2006 stating that he could remain in England while his application was considered, but that he could not work in the meantime without permission from the Home Office.

In January 2007, Peter moved away from London, and found a job in Leicester, working for Dave, a friend of Velma's, who ran a garage there. Peter, who had some mechanical skills, did basic servicing jobs, and was paid in cash, without deduction of tax or National Insurance. In May 2008, Peter, whose English was still very poor, misunderstood Dave's instructions, and put the wrong type of oil into an engine. Dave told Peter not to bother coming in to work any more. Peter, with Velma's help, has now brought an action for unfair dismissal against Dave. Dave is defending the action on the basis that he has now discovered that Peter had not obtained the required permission from the Home Office, and that his contract of employment was therefore void for illegality.

Advise Peter.

Would your answer be different if Peter *had* received permission to work from the Home Office?

Answer plan

This question concerns the extent to which an action based on a contract, here a claim for unfair dismissal, is affected by the fact that its performance involves some illegality. This is not a contract in which the activity is illegal – as it would be, for example, in a contract to pay someone to beat up a third party. But there are two areas of illegality in performance:

- Peter does not have permission to work, as required by the Home Office;
- Peter is being paid without deductions of tax or National Insurance.

The principles to be applied in this area were restated in *Hall v Woolston Hall Leisure Ltd* (2000); the facts of this problem have similarities with the subsequent cases of *Vakante v Addey & Stanhope School* (2004) and *Wheeler v Quality Deep Trading Ltd* (2005). The following order of treatment is suggested:

- state the general principles applying to illegality;
- note that there are two possible areas of illegality on the facts – the lack of permission from the Home Office, and the payment without deductions;
- state the principles set out in *Hall v Woolston Hall Leisure Ltd* (2000), and their application in the two recent cases noted above;
- apply these principles to the first set of facts – where the focus will be on the lack of permission, together with Peter's understanding of his situation;
- consider the alternative set of facts – where the focus will be on the lack of deductions.

Answer

This problem involves a situation in which aspects of the contract – in this case, a contract of employment – involve illegality. There are two types of situation in which English contract law will find that illegality makes a contract void and unenforceable. The first is where the contract involves an agreement to commit a crime or tort – for example, where A agrees to kill C in return for a payment of £5,000 from B. An example from the cases is *Parkinson v College of Ambulance* (1925), which involved an alleged promise to obtain a knighthood for the claimant in return for a payment to charity.[1] The second type of situation is that in which the object of the contract is lawful, but the way it is performed involves illegality. This is the situation that arises in this problem. It is not illegal in itself for someone to work as a car mechanic, but it may become so if the employee is working in breach of immigration controls, or is being paid in a way that defrauds HM Revenue & Customs. Where a contract is found to be illegal on one of these grounds, it will generally be treated as void and unenforceable by either party. For Peter, unless he has a valid contract of employment, he will be unable to sustain an action for unfair dismissal. In relation to Peter's situation, there are two possible types of illegality. First, there is the fact that he had not obtained permission to work, as required by the Home Office. This will constitute an offence under immigration law. Second, he is being paid without deductions of tax or National Insurance. This is also an offence. It is only the first of these two areas of illegality that Dave has raised – presumably because he can claim that he was unaware of the problem, and can argue that the illegality was all Peter's fault.[2] The approach to be taken in cases of this kind has been set out by the Court of Appeal in *Hall v Woolston Hall Leisure Ltd* (2000). This was an employment case, in which the employee had been paid in a way that, as she knew, involved an attempt to defraud HM Revenue & Customs. She sued for sex discrimination, in relation to the reasons for her dismissal (that is, pregnancy). She was allowed to recover, despite the illegality in relation to the method of payment. The approach suggested by the Court of Appeal in that case required a consideration of whether the claim was so closely connected to the illegality that the Court could not provide a remedy without appearing to condone the illegal conduct. On the facts of *Hall v Woolston*, the Court felt able to allow the claimant to recover compensation.

The approach taken in *Hall v Woolston* has been applied in two more recent cases, but with differing consequences. The two cases have similarities to the facts of the problem involving Peter and Dave. In *Vakante v Addey & Stanhope School* (2004), the applicant had been employed as a teacher at a school, while not having permission to work in the UK (although he had acquired a National Insurance number). The school was unaware of his immigration status. He brought a claim for racial discrimination and victimisation, as part of which he alleged that he had never been given a written contract of employment. The Court of Appeal, applying the *Hall v Woolston* test, held that the contract was void for illegality. The applicant was committing a criminal offence by working without permission, and the illegality went to the root of the employment relationship. By contrast, in *Wheeler v Quality Deep Trading Ltd* (2005), the applicant was a woman of Thai origin with limited knowledge of English. She had been employed as a cook, but was paid without deductions of tax or National Insurance, although her payslips were inaccurate in relation to this. She brought a claim for unfair dismissal. The tribunal noted that the applicant's husband had good English and must have been aware that something was wrong in the way in which she had been paid. It held that the employment contract, was illegal, so that she could not claim. The Court of Appeal disagreed. The test to be applied, where the illegality was in relation to the manner of performance of the contract, was that set out in *Hall v Woolston*. This meant, the Court of Appeal held, that the employee would only be precluded from claiming if the tribunal was satisfied that she knew the facts that made the performance illegal, and had actively participated in it. The applicant's husband had not, apparently, been aware of what was on the payslips until shortly before the hearing. On that basis, the Court of

Appeal held that the claim should not be ruled out on the basis of illegality, but should be assessed on its merits.

How does this apply to the dispute between Peter and Dave? The decision in *Vakante v Addey & Stanhope School* would suggest that Peter will be unable to claim. As with the applicant in that case, Peter is working in breach of his immigration status. Are there any points of distinction? One might be whether Peter was aware that he was acting illegally. We are told that he still has poor English, so it is possible that he may not have understood the restriction on his employment. On the other hand, his cousin Velma, who was involved in his asylum application and has been continuing to help him, would surely have explained to him that he was not allowed to work without permission. The second difference might be if it could be shown that Dave was aware that he was employing someone who did not have permission to work, whereas in *Vakante* the school was ignorant of the situation. However, the Court of Appeal in *Vakante* put the emphasis on the fact that the employee had acted criminally, and the guilt or innocence of the employer did not seem to be a relevant factor. On balance, therefore, it would seem that, if Peter is working in breach of his immigration status he will not be able to sustain his claim for unfair dismissal.

If Peter did have permission to work, would this make any difference to the outcome? There would still be illegality in relation to the contract of employment, in that he was being paid without deductions of tax or National Insurance. The case would be much closer to the situation in *Wheeler v Quality Deep Trading Ltd*. In that case, the fact that the employer was paying wages in an illegal manner was held not to prevent the employee from claiming unfair dismissal. It was important, however, in *Wheeler* that it appeared that the employee was unaware of the employer's wrongful action. Was Peter similarly unaware? We have no clear evidence in relation to this, but it may be significant that Peter's English is poor, like the applicant in *Wheeler*. Moreover, it may well be that Velma, who might be thought to have been able to pick up the fact that Dave was acting illegally, is in London rather than Leicester, and so probably unaware of the situation. It seems that if Peter has permission to work, then the manner in which he was being paid will not prevent him bringing his claim for unfair dismissal.

In conclusion, then, on the initial facts, Peter's claim against Dave is likely to be dismissed, because of the fact that he is committing an offence by working without permission. On the alternative facts, however, the illegality relating to his wages will probably not be sufficient to bar his claim.

Think points

1 Would this also apply to a contract that involved a breach of professional rules, amounting to a disciplinary offence, rather than a crime or tort? It was

held that it did in *Mohammed v Alaga* (1999), a case involving a breach of the **Solicitors' Practice Rules**.

2 Is this true? Shouldn't Dave have made inquiries about Peter's immigration status? Would this make a difference to the contract action? The case law suggests it may depend on who is suing. In some cases only the innocent party has been allowed to enforce the contract – see Stone, *The Modern Law of Contract*, 7th edn, 2008, pp 468–70.

Question 33

Answer both parts.

(a) What is the general rule about recovery of money or property transferred under an illegal contract? What are the exceptions?

(b) Sid owns a shop in Westbridge, a large town. His business mainly consists of selling and repairing Easifly lawnmowers. His is the only shop in Westbridge that deals in this type of lawnmower. Sid is now considering opening another shop in Eastchester, where he lives. Eastchester is a small town some five miles from Westbridge. Sid plans to sell his shop in Westbridge. The prospective purchaser is Greengrass plc, a national firm that owns a chain of garden centres, and which specialises in Easifly lawnmowers. This firm wants Sid to agree not to open another shop selling 'Easifly lawnmowers, or any other make of lawnmower, or any other garden equipment, anywhere in the United Kingdom', for the next ten years.

Advise Sid.

Answer plan

Part (a)

The answer to this part of the question will be largely descriptive. The general rule of non-recovery can be stated quite briefly, although at least one example should be given from the cases. The main part of the answer will be concerned with the exceptions, that is:

- illegal purpose not carried out;
- oppression;
- fraud;
- no reliance on illegal transaction; and
- class-protecting statutes.

Part (b)

The problem is concerned with the enforceability of restraints on the seller of a business. These will be permissible, provided that the restraint:

* protects a legitimate interest;
* is reasonable in its scope; and
* is not contrary to the public interest.

An additional factor that will need to be considered is whether the restraining clause, if unreasonable as it stands, can be cut down, using the 'blue pencil' test, to make it reasonable.

Answer

Part (a)

If the courts have found that a contract is unenforceable because it is illegal, they are reluctant to allow it to be used in any way as the basis of a legal action. The basic rule, therefore, is that money or property transferred under an illegal contract cannot be recovered.

A good example of this principle in operation is *Parkinson v College of Ambulance* (1925). The plaintiff had made a contribution to a charity on the basis that he would get a knighthood in return. When no such honour was forthcoming, the plaintiff brought an action to recover his contribution. It was held that a contract to purchase a title is illegal and the plaintiff knew this. He could not therefore recover his money.

There are, however, a number of exceptions to this general principle. The first is where the contract is still executory, and the claimant is allowed to withdraw from his illegal purpose. This derives from *Taylor v Bowers* (1876), in which the plaintiff had transferred goods as part of a scheme designed to defraud his creditors. At the point at which he sought to recover the goods, however, no creditors had been defrauded, and so he was allowed to recover. For this argument to succeed there must be a genuine withdrawal, not only a frustration of the claimant's purpose through inaction on the other side (as in *Parkinson v College of Ambulance*). Nor must there be any substantial performance of the contract (*Kearley v Thomson* (1890)).

A second exception arises where the illegal contract has been made as a result of 'oppression'. In *Atkinson v Denby* (1862), for example, a creditor refused to accept a composition agreement unless he was paid an additional £50. The debtor paid the money, but then sought to recover it. It was held that, although the agreement to pay the money was a fraud on the other creditors, and therefore illegal, the debtor could recover because he had virtually been forced to agree because of his weak bargaining position. The rationale of this exception is that the parties are not equally at fault.[1] This will also be the case where the contract is made as a result of a fraudulent misrepresentation that it is lawful (*Hughes v Liverpool Victoria Legal Friendly Society* (1916)).

If a claimant can establish a right to possession of the property concerned without relying on the illegal transaction, recovery will be allowed. For example, in *Bowmakers v Barnet Instruments* (1945), the plaintiff was allowed to recover possession of machines transferred under illegal hire purchase transactions. Since the hire purchase agreements had not transferred ownership of the goods, the plaintiff was held to be allowed to recover on the basis of his basic rights of ownership, without relying on the agreement.

A similar approach was taken by the House of Lords in *Tinsley v Milligan* (1993), in which a resulting trust in relation to a house was held to be unaffected by the illegal purpose that had led to the house being put into the name of the trustee alone.

The final exception is to be found in the area of so-called 'class-protecting statutes'. This concerns the situation in which a statute making an agreement illegal was passed to protect the members of a particular class (for example, tenants under the **Rent Acts**). A member of that class may be able to recover property given under the agreement notwithstanding the illegality. If, for example, a tenant paid a premium in order to obtain a tenancy, and such an agreement was unlawful under the **Rent Acts**, the tenant would be allowed to recover the premium (*Kiriri Cotton Co Ltd v Dewani* (1960)).

Here, again, the basis of the exception is that there is not equal fault between the parties. The statute indicates a recognition by Parliament that some contractors may be taken advantage of by others who are in a stronger position. It would be wrong to then apply the statute in a way that penalised the weaker party. In fact, all of the exceptions, apart from the first (illegal purpose not carried out), appear to be based on the application of this principle, which therefore provides a unifying theme to most of the rules operating in this area.

Part (b)

This scenario is concerned with an attempt to impose a restriction on the vendor of a business. Such a restriction will be regarded as being 'in restraint of trade' and therefore prima facie illegal. Sid will only be bound by it, therefore, if Greengrass can overturn the presumption of illegality by showing that the restraint is reasonable to protect a legitimate interest. Even if it is unreasonable as worded, the court may be prepared to enforce it if the scope can be narrowed by cutting out some part of the restriction.

The starting point for this kind of restraint is the decision of the House of Lords in *Nordenfelt v Maxim Nordenfelt* (1894), which held that all covenants in restraint of trade are prima facie contrary to public policy and therefore void. It was recognised, however, that the presumption could be rebutted if the restraint could be shown to be reasonable with reference to both the interests of the parties and the public interest. For the restraint to be reasonable, Greengrass will have to show that it has a legitimate interest to protect, that the scope of the restraint does not extend further than is reasonable to protect that interest, and that there is no more general public interest in preventing the restriction.

Looking at these requirements in turn, the first – the requirement of a legitimate interest – is easily satisfied. Where a person sells a shop as a going concern, an important element in the sale is likely to be the 'goodwill'. This means the fact that people know of the existence of the shop dealing with a particular type of goods, and the fact that there may well be a regular clientele. Reputation and established customers are both commercially valuable assets. It is almost certain that Sid will wish to increase the price of his business by including these elements in its valuation. It is well established that the protection of the goodwill in a business being bought is a legitimate interest that can be protected by a reasonable restrictive covenant. This indeed was the situation in *Nordenfelt v Maxim Nordenfelt* itself. The approach benefits the vendor as well as the purchaser, in that if the vendor were not able to accept a binding obligation not to compete, then he might have difficulty selling the business at all, and would certainly have to do so at a much lower price than would otherwise be the case.[2]

So, it would seem that Greengrass does have an interest to protect. Is the restraint reasonable to protect that interest? It covers the sale of any make of lawnmower and other garden equipment, anywhere in the UK, for ten years. It will have to be considered reasonable in respect of scope, area and time if it is to stand. On the face of it, the clause seems likely to fail on each count. Sid's business has been mainly concerned with Easifly lawnmowers, whereas the restraint extends to other lawnmowers and other garden equipment. It will be a matter of fact as to the extent to which Sid's existing business deals in these other items but, on the facts given, the suggestion would seem to be that the business relating to Easifly lawnmowers is by far the most important element. A restraint that extends, as this one does, far beyond this area is likely to be regarded as unreasonable. The purchasers must tailor the restraint to the scope of the business that they are acquiring, not the scope of their own business (*British Reinforced Concrete Engineering Co Ltd v Schelff* (1921)).

As to area, it must be noted that in *Nordenfelt* a worldwide restriction was held to be reasonable. Here, the restriction applies simply to the UK. However, as with the scope, the area must relate to the interest being protected. It seems unlikely that Sid could do serious harm to Greengrass by opening up a shop in an area in which he was unknown. Moreover, there are very likely to be some areas of the UK where Greengrass does not have any existing shops that might be affected by Sid's competition. In the circumstances, the area, like the scope, would appear too wide.

Finally, the length of the restriction must be considered. It is stated to last for ten years. This is a period that could rarely be regarded as reasonable in relation to a restriction on employment, but different considerations will apply in relation to a business. The question to be asked is presumably whether, if at any point within the next ten years Sid were to open a shop in competition to Greengrass, he would be likely to recover any of his previous customers, so as to reduce the value of the goodwill sold to Greengrass. It is difficult to provide a clear answer to this, but it may well be that this aspect of the restraint is reasonable.

It has been suggested above that the restraint is probably unreasonable as regards scope and area. This is not the end of the story, however. The courts may be prepared to sever unreasonable parts of the restraint, and give effect to what is reasonable. Thus, in *Goldsoll v Goldman* (1915), a restraint that listed a number of countries where the vendor of a business was not to compete was held to be unreasonable as to area. It was, however, made reasonable by cutting out those countries where there was no real risk of competition and letting the rest stand. The test is sometimes called the 'blue pencil' test, in that what the courts are supposed to do is simply strike out the offending words. What is left should still make sense, without the need to add anything or rewrite anything. The excision must also not change the whole nature of the restraint: *Attwood v Lamont* (1920). In this case, a list of activities in an employment contract could not be cut down to the one in which the defendant had been engaged, since it was held that the whole point of the restraint had been to protect the entire range of the plaintiffs' business.

Applying this to the facts of the problem, it would seem relatively easy to narrow the scope of this clause by cutting out the phrases 'any other make of lawnmower, or any other garden equipment'. The question of area (or time, if this is thought unreasonable) is more difficult, in that no list of places is included that can be cut down. Excising 'anywhere in the United Kingdom' would not narrow the area, but leave it entirely open. The courts might be prepared to do this, however, if they were to combine it with another approach, used in *Littlewoods v Harris* (1977) and *Clarke v Newland* (1991), in which it was held that a wide restraining clause has to be interpreted in the context in which it was put forward. In *Littlewoods*, this meant the area of the business in which Harris had been employed, and, in *Clarke v Newland*, the type of medical practice concerned. The area of operation would then be related to the area in which Sid had been carrying on his business.[3] If this approach can be combined with the 'blue pencil' test, it may be possible for the clause to become reasonable.

The final possibility is that the restraint, while reasonable between the parties, is contrary to the general public interest. There does not seem to be any reason why this should operate on these facts.

In the light of the above discussion, the advice to Sid should be that if he agrees to the suggested clause, it is unlikely to be enforced as it stands. If, however, by the methods outlined above, it is found to be reasonable to a limited extent, it almost certainly would prevent him opening an 'Easifly' shop in Eastchester. His repair business, however, would not seem to be affected, and it is unlikely that he would be prevented from dealing in other lawnmowers or other garden equipment. To that extent, Sid may have a viable business prospect, even if his range of activities is slightly restricted by the covenant.

Think points

1 Reference could be made here to the principle of *in pari delicto potior est conditio defendentis*, or *in pari delicto* for short. This Latin tag translates roughly as 'if both parties are equally at fault, the defendant is in the stronger position'. Although the Latin is not so much in general use nowadays, the underlying principle remains the same.

2 Would the position be different if Sid were happy to sell the premises without the goodwill? It almost certainly would be. The purchaser would then have no interest to protect, and the restraint could not be allowed to stand.

3 Could this approach also be applied to the time restraint, should that be regarded as unreasonable? It would seem difficult to do so.

Question 34

Max has a talent for the development of interactive video games. When he was 19 years old, he entered into a contract with BadGames plc. The contract was stated to last five years, and under it Max agreed to supply ideas and scenarios for video games exclusively to BadGames during this period. In return, the contract provided that BadGames would pay Max a royalty of 1 per cent on the net proceeds of sales of any of his proposals that went into production. Over the past two years, Max has provided over twenty proposals to BadGames, but only one of these has been taken forward, and Max has yet to receive any royalties. He has now been given the opportunity of a full-time job as an associate programme developer with VidDev plc, a competitor to BadGames. He notices that the contract that he has been shown contains a clause stating that if he leaves the employment of VidDev he must not work for any other video game company, in any capacity, anywhere in the world, for a period of two years.

Max now seeks your advice as to whether:

(a) he can escape from the 'exclusivity' provision in his contract with BadGames, since part of the job with VidDev will involve Max in providing ideas for new video games;

(b) if he takes the post with VidDev, the clause in the employment contract restricting for whom he may work in the future would be binding on him.

Answer plan

This is a question on 'restraint of trade'. There are two parts to it: one concerned with a contract for 'exclusive dealing' and the other a restriction on future employment. The best way to tackle this will be to deal first with the general principles applying to contracts in restraint of trade, that is:

- they are prima facie unenforceable; but
- they may be enforced if they protect a legitimate interest, and go no further than is reasonable in protecting that interest; and
- they are not contrary to the public interest.

You should then move on to consider these principles in the light of the two contracts.

(a) The contract with BadGames is one of 'exclusive dealing'. Max is promising to provide all of his ideas for video games to BadGames and no one else. Comparisons can be drawn with cases on similar arrangements in the music industry – in particular, *Schroeder Music Publishing Co Ltd v Macaulay* (1974). The courts have tended to find such arrangements unenforceable in this context, but the detail of the provisions needs to be considered.

(b) This is a straightforward restraint on employment of a common type. You will need to consider whether VidDev has a legitimate interest to protect. If it does, is the restraint reasonable as regards:
   (i)   time;
   (ii) geographical area;
   (iii) scope;
   (iv) public interest?

Answer

This question is concerned with provisions of contracts that may be argued to be 'in restraint of trade' – that is, they restrict the freedom of a person to conduct business or take employment. The contract with BadGames is one of 'exclusive dealing', in that Max is to provide all of his games ideas to BadGames for a period of five years. The employment contract with VidDev contains a restriction on future employment, if Max leaves VidDev.

The general approach of English law to contracts in restraint of trade derives from the House of Lords' decision in *Nordenfelt v Maxim Nordenfelt* (1894), which held that all agreements in restraint of trace are prima facie contrary to public policy and so unenforceable. The presumption of unenforceability can be overturned, however, if the person seeking to rely on the restraint can prove that he or she has a legitimate interest to protect, and that the restraint goes no further than is reasonably necessary to protect that interest.

The two agreements need to be considered in turn.

(a) Max's contract with BadGames is one of 'exclusive dealing'. Such arrangements are common in contracts for the supply of petrol to petrol stations, and the supply of alcoholic drinks to pubs. In that context, they are often referred to as 'solus agreements'. The situation here is different, but there are examples from the cases of similar arrangements in the music industry, with writers and performers tying themselves to a particular company, and agreeing that all of their output for the duration of the contract will be channelled through that company. The courts have held that such agreements fall within the general principles applying to contracts in restraint of trade: *Schroeder Music Publishing Co Ltd v Macaulay* (1974).

Assuming that Max's contract with BadGames is in restraint of trade, because of the fact that he is unable to submit his ideas to any other company, the first question is whether BadGames has any legitimate interest to protect. The consideration for Max's agreement seems simply to be the promise of a royalty on any games that are developed from his proposals. If so, there is very little risk here for BadGames. It would be otherwise, perhaps, if BadGames were obliged to provide Max with new computer equipment each year, or were to be committed to making some payment to him even if his ideas did not reach the stage of full development. In that situation, it would be making an investment in Max, and taking the risk that his talent would produce some usable proposals.

The case seems very similar to that of *Schroeder v Macaulay*. In that case, a music publisher entered into a contract with a young songwriter, under which the songwriter agreed to assign the copyright in all of his songs to the publisher for a five-year period, in return for a royalty on those that were published. There was no obligation on the publisher to publish any of the songwriter's songs. Moreover, the agreement could be assigned to someone else by the publisher, and the agreement could be terminated by one month's notice. Neither of these rights was available to the songwriter. The House of Lords upheld the decision of the lower courts that the agreement was unenforceable against the songwriter. The publishing company had been in a dominant position in making the contract with the songwriter, and in that context the restrictions on the songwriter's freedom to publish his work were unreasonable. The same approach was taken in relation to an agreement in similar terms involving a pop group (Fleetwood Mac): *Clifford Davis Management Ltd v WEA Records Ltd* (1975).

Applying this approach to Max's case, it would appear that BadGames was in a strong bargaining position in making this contract with a teenager. Given that element of inequality, the overall fairness of the agreement needs to be assessed. There is little in the way of an interest for BadGames to protect, as outlined above, and the terms of the agreement would seem to beyond what might be reasonable to protect such interest as the company does have (that is, the investment in new and unproved games developer).

Overall, Max can be advised that it is unlikely that a court would enforce BadGames contract against him, and he should feel free to enter into the contract with VidDev.

(b) The issue in the contract with VidDev is different. Here, we are concerned with a restraint of a more common type – attempting to control for whom an employee works after he has left a particular job. The first question to consider, again, is whether VidDev would have a legitimate interest to protect. There are two general categories of interest that have been found to be worthy of protection – that is, contacts with customers, and trade secrets or other confidential information. There is no evidence in this case that Max will have any relationship with customers, so there does not appear to be a legitimate interest under this heading. As regards confidential information, this would depend on exactly what Max's job involves. If he is involved with programming, for example, it may be that he would have knowledge of particular programming techniques created or developed by VidDev that could come into the category of trade secrets. The simple fact that Max had developed his skills as a programmer while working for VidDev would not be enough: *Herbert Morris Ltd v Saxelby* (1916). He would have had to have had access to processes that his employer could reasonably regard as 'secret'.

The other type of confidential information that might be relevant here would be information about the products that VidDev had under development. Knowledge of games that were being produced, and likely to come on the market in the future, might well be valuable to VidDev's competitors. An analogy can be drawn here with *Littlewoods Organisation v Harris* (1978), in which an employee had knowledge of the contents of his employer's forthcoming mail order catalogue, and this was held to be information that the employer was entitled to protect.

It appears that VidDev may well have an interest to protect on one of these bases. The question is then whether the restraint that it is imposing is reasonable in relation to that interest. The courts will look at three aspects of the restraint in reaching a decision, namely:

(i)   its length;

(ii) its geographical area;

(iii) its scope, in relation to the types of activity covered.

Looking at these in turn, the period for which the restraint is imposed is two years. If the interest relates solely to what games are being produced this looks like rather a long restriction. Given the fast-moving market in video games, it would seem likely that, unless VidDev could produce evidence to the contrary, anything more than a year would be unreasonable. If the interest relates to programming techniques, it may be that a longer restraint could be justified, but even here it seems unlikely that as much as two years would be needed.

Turning to the geographical area, the restraint is stated to be worldwide. At first sight, this might seem unduly broad, but the nature of the video games business must be taken into account. It is global in its scope, and work can be done in any country. In that context, a ban covering the whole world is probably reasonable.

Finally, as regards scope, the clause refers to working 'in any capacity'. Again, this is very broad. VidDev may argue that if what it is trying to protect is confidential information, then it does not matter what role Max is nominally playing within a rival organisation; he will be able to pass on information that may be valuable, and contrary to VidDev's interests.

There is, therefore, potential for the restraint to be unreasonable in relation to both time and scope. There is the possibility, however, of 'severance' whereby the unreasonable part of a restraint can be excised, and the rest enforced. This must generally be achieved, however, by simply cutting words out, and not by inserting alternative, more reasonable, provisions: *Mason v Provident Clothing Co* (1913). Moreover, it is said that the excision must retain the 'nature of the contract' (*Attwood v Lamont* (1920)), although this requirement does not seem to have been enforced strictly in recent years.

In Max's case, although it would be difficult to reduce the scope of activities by simply excising words, an approach adopted in *Littlewoods v Harris* might well be used. In this case, a very broad clause was interpreted as being intended only to apply to the area of business in which the defendant had been directly involved – ie the mail order catalogue. Similarly, in *Clarke v Newland* (1991), a restraint on a doctor 'not to practise' was interpreted to mean practise as a GP, rather than in a hospital, since that was the work that the doctor had been doing. In Max's case, the restraint could be interpreted as only being intended to apply to working in the same area of business as that in which he has been engaged with VidDev.

The time of the restraint is more difficult. There is no scope for reinterpretation here, and the excision of the phrase would leave the restraint unlimited as to time. If it is decided that two years is unreasonable, it seems that for this reason the whole restraint clause will fail. This indicates the importance for those wishing to use such restraints to make sure that they are appropriately limited. From Max's point of view, it means that he can be advised that the restraint in the VidDev contract is unlikely to be binding on him, because it would last for an unreasonable time.

CHAPTER 10

FRUSTRATION

▋ INTRODUCTION

The doctrine of frustration is one of the more straightforward areas of the law of contract. Although it involves a mixture of common law rules and statute (in the form of the **Law Reform (Frustrated Contracts) Act 1943**), which might have the potential to cause difficulties, in this case, the two fit together fairly comfortably. This is probably because the Act is primarily concerned with the effects of frustration, whereas the question of what amounts to a frustrating event is left to the common law. Both common law and statute must be understood, however, before attempting questions on this topic.

Of the questions in this chapter, Question 35 is primarily concerned with what amounts to a frustrating event, whereas Question 36 concentrates more on the consequences of frustration. Question 37 brings the two aspects together. In dealing with the meaning of 'frustration', the following issues are likely to be important:

- has the event deprived the other side of the entire benefit of the contract? *Krell v Henry* (1903) and *Herne Bay Steam Boat Co v Hutton* (1903) are useful contrasting decisions on this area; and

- what is the meaning of 'self-induced' frustration? The case of *The Super Servant Two* (1990) is an interesting one to add to the older decision in *Maritime National Fish Ltd v Ocean Trawlers Ltd* (1935).

On the consequences of frustration, you will need to be familiar with:

- the decision in the *Fibrosa* case (1943);

- the provisions of s 1(2) and (3) of the **Law Reform (Frustrated Contracts) Act 1943**; and

- the decision in *BP Exploration v Hunt* (1982).

The *BP Exploration v Hunt* decision and its implications is probably the most difficult area within the topic of frustration. It is not an easy case to understand, but some work on it will pay dividends, in that whenever you need to discuss s 1(3) of the Act your answer will be greatly improved if you can make some attempt to explain the effects of the decision.

Checklist

You should be familiar with the following areas:

- the historical development of the doctrine of frustration;
- the definition of a 'frustrating event';
- the meaning of 'self-induced' frustration;
- the effects of frustration at common law;
- the effects and limitations of the *Fibrosa* case; and
- the **Law Reform (Frustrated Contracts) Act** 1943 – its effects and limitations.

Question 35

Martina owns two houses in Loughchester. In May, she entered into a contract with Loughchester University for it to rent the houses for the coming academic year for use as student accommodation. The University paid Martina £750 straight away, with the rent to be paid to Martina by the University monthly in arrears. Martina then engaged Roger Roofers Ltd to carry out repairs on the roofs of the houses, to be completed by 23 September, in time for the arrival of the students. She paid Roger Roofers £1,000, with the balance of £3,000 to be paid on completion of the work. Consider the effect on Martina's contracts of the following events.

(a) On 1 September, when Roger Roofers had completed work on the first house, but not started on the second, the second house was struck by lightning, causing a fire that destroyed both houses.

(b) As in (a), but only the second house was destroyed. The first house escaped damage.

(c) As a consequence of an unexpected restriction on student numbers imposed by the government, Loughchester University recruited fewer students for its courses than it had expected and had a surplus of accommodation. It told Martina on 20 September that it would not need to use her houses, and regarded their contract as at an end. It also requested the repayment of the £750 already paid.

Answer plan

There are two contracts to be considered: the one between Martina and the University, and the one between Martina and Roger Roofers. In each case, you will need to consider whether the events that have occurred in each of the three situations have led to the frustration of the contract. If there is frustration, you will need to go on to consider the effects of the **Law Reform (Frustrated Contracts) Act 1943** on the parties' obligations.

The suggested order of treatment is:

- introduction – outlining the concept of 'frustration';
- situation (a) – both contracts have been frustrated. As regards the University contract, note that a contract for the lease of land can now be frustrated, as confirmed by *National Carriers Ltd v Panalpina (Northern) Ltd* (1981). In relation to the roofing contract, you will need to consider the application of the 1943 Act, and in particular s 1(3);
- situation (b) – the roofing contract has again probably been frustrated. The application of s 1(3) of the 1943 Act may, however, be different in this situation. Has the University contract been frustrated? Since it can still be performed in part, it may be that it has not – cf *Herne Bay Steamboat Co v Hutton* (1903); and
- situation (c) – is the non-availability of students a frustrating event? Although government intervention can frustrate a contract, in this situation the University's non-allocation of students to Martina's houses may well be treated as 'self-induced frustration', in which case Martina will be able to claim against the University for breach of contract.

Answer

This problem is concerned with the doctrine of frustration, which arises where an external event, which is not the responsibility of either party, renders further performance of the contract impossible, or at least radically different from what had been contracted for.

The kind of events that have been recognised as giving rise to frustration include natural disasters (*Taylor v Caldwell* (1863)), government interference (*BP Exploration v Hunt* (1982)), supervening illegality (*Denny, Mott and Dickson v James Fraser* (1944)), strikes (*The Nema* (1982)) and ill health (*Condor v Barron Knights* (1966)).

The approach of the common law, when it finally recognised the possibility of frustration in *Taylor v Caldwell*, was simply to say that all future obligations were discharged. Money paid was irrecoverable (*Chandler v Webster* (1904)), as was compensation for benefits provided but for which payment was not yet due (*Appleby v Myers* (1867)). This was mitigated to some extent by the decision in *Fibrosa Spolka Akcyjna v Fairbairn Lawson Combe Barbour Ltd* (1943), in which the House of Lords held that money paid could be recovered if there was a total failure of consideration. Further flexibility as regards the consequences of frustration was introduced by the **Law Reform (Frustrated Contracts) Act** 1943, which applies to most, although not all, contracts. There are, however, still some areas in which the rules can operate harshly. In particular, although in certain circumstances **s** 2(3) of the **Act** allows recovery for benefits conferred prior to the frustrating event, the approach to this section adopted in *BP Exploration v Hunt* means that the scope for such recovery is narrower than might be thought at first sight.

Turning to the facts of the problem, there are two contracts that need to be considered in each of the three situations – the one between Martina and the University, and the one between Martina and Roger Roofers Ltd. We are told very little about the contents of these contracts. It is assumed, however, that neither of them contains any provisions directly relevant to the circumstances that have arisen, and that the situations will be dealt with simply by the common law rules and the provisions of the 1943 **Act**.

Situation (a)

In the first situation, the two houses have been destroyed. This is clearly an event that is capable of frustrating the contracts. The destruction of the subject matter is one of the clearest examples of frustration, and was in fact what was involved in the first case in which the principle was recognised by the English courts – that is, *Taylor v Caldwell* (1863). As regards the contract with the University, at one time it was thought that a contract for the lease of land could not be frustrated – *Cricklewood Property Investment Trust v Leighton's Investment Trusts Ltd* (1945). This view was rejected, however, by the House of Lords in *National Carriers Ltd v Panalpina (Northern) Ltd* (1981), in which the majority held that there was no reason in logic or law why a lease could not be frustrated if the intended use of the land became impossible. That would seem to apply here, since the use of the land for the accommodation of students can no longer take place. Although the decision in *National Carriers* might be said to be obiter, in that the House held that on the facts the contract was not frustrated, there is no reason to doubt that it would be followed where necessary. What is the consequence of the contract being frustrated? The University's obligation to pay rent will be discharged. Can it recover the £750 that it has already paid? This is dealt with by **s** 1(2) of the 1943 **Act**. This provides that money paid prior to a frustrating event can be recovered. It is subject to the proviso, however, that if the party to whom the money was paid has incurred expenses, such amount as the court considers just may be retained to cover these. Martina will no doubt wish to argue that she has spent money preparing the houses for student accommodation, and that she should therefore be able to retain the £750. In *Gamerco SA v ICM/Fair Warning Agency* (1995), it was made clear, however, that just because expenses have been incurred this does not automatically mean that retention of money paid will be allowed. The court should take a broad view, looking at all of the circumstances, before deciding what is a just result. On the facts given, there does not seem to be any particular reason why Martina should not be allowed to retain some or all of the £500 towards her expenses. It should be noted, however, that s 1(2) does not allow her to be awarded more than the £750 that has already been paid, even if her expenses exceed this amount.

In relation to the contract with Roger Roofers, this again will be frustrated, in that the work cannot be completed. Martina will wish to recover the £1,000 that she has paid. This would not have been possible under the common law, since there was not here a total failure of consideration, as required by the *Fibrosa* case. Roger Roofers had done half the work on the contract. As we have seen, however, s 1(2) does allow for recovery of the £1,000, subject to the Roger Roofers' expenses. In this situation, it is likely that Roger Roofers will wish to claim that its expenses far exceed the £1,000 and that the full amount should be retained. Moreover, it may wish to argue under s 1(3) that it has conferred a valuable benefit on Martina, by the work done on the first house, and that it would be just for Roger Roofers to be awarded a sum to compensate for this. Under the common law this would not have been possible, because the decision in *Appleby v Myers* (1867) confirmed that where the obligation to pay for work does not arise until after the frustrating event, no compensation for work done is recoverable. Although at first sight s 1(3) appears to alter this position, the way in which the section was interpreted by Goff J in *BP Exploration v Hunt* means that it probably will not do so. Goff J held that the reference in s 1(3) to a 'valuable benefit' referred to a benefit assessed in the light of the frustrating event. If the consequence of the frustrating event was that the benefit was destroyed, then nothing could be recovered in relation to it. The object of the Act was to prevent un-just enrichment, rather than to apportion losses. If the party concerned had not been 'enriched' at the end of the day, there was no need for the Act to intervene. Applying this approach here, it means that Roger Roofers will not be able to recover anything under s 1(3), despite the fact that it has done half the work under the contract.

Situation (b)

This again involves the destruction of the subject matter, and therefore potentially frustration of the contract. In relation to the contract with the University, however, the contract is not completely impossible. One house survives, and there is no reason why it could not be used to accommodate students. The question is, therefore, whether the contract has become 'radically different' from what was intended by the parties (see *Davis Contractors Ltd v Fareham* (1956)). A comparison might be drawn with *Herne Bay Steam Boat Co v Hutton* (1903), in which the hiring of a boat to tour the royal fleet and to watch the King's review of it was held not to be frustrated when the review was cancelled. The fleet remained, so it was possible for the tour to go ahead. Although the circumstances here are different, it might still be argued that enough of the contract survives for it not to be frustrated. Martina, on the other hand, will wish to argue that the contract is frustrated, since otherwise she may be liable for breach in providing only one house, rather than two. On balance, it is suggested that the contract is in fact 'radically different', since only half of it can be performed. If this is so, then the position will be the same as in situation (a) as regards the application of the 1943 Act.

The position with regard to Roger Roofers is much clearer. Since the completion of its work is impossible, the contract is frustrated. There is an important difference from situation (a) here, however, in that this time the house on which the roofing work has been completed has survived the frustrating event. This means that Roger Roofers will have a strong argument for some compensation under s 1(3) of the 1943 Act. Martina has obtained a valuable benefit in that she now has a house with a repaired roof. If she were allowed to retain this without paying anything to Roger Roofers, she would be 'unjustly enriched'. On this occasion, it is likely that a court would consider it just that she should pay something to Roger Roofers in addition to the £1,000 already paid. Since presumably about half the work has been done, the starting point might well be a further £1,000, to bring her payment up to half the contract price. The courts' discretion is broad, however, and can take into account all of the circumstances in deciding what is the appropriate sum to be awarded.

Situation (c)

The alleged frustrating event here is the government's restriction on student numbers. This only affects Martina's contract with the University, so we do not need to consider Roger Roofers' contract here. There is no doubt that government intervention can lead to the frustration of a contract as, for example, in *Metropolitan Water Board v Dick Kerr* (1918), which involved the requisitioning of property in war time. The problem for the University here is that it has some students requiring accommodation, but has allocated them to premises other than Martina's houses. In this respect, the case seems similar to *Maritime National Fish Ltd v Ocean Trawlers Ltd* (1935), in which a company obtained fewer trawling licences than it had hoped for, and failed to allocate one of them to a boat hired from the other party. It was held here that the alleged 'frustration' was in fact 'self-induced', because the company had decided which trawlers should have a licence. Even if the decision involves deciding which of two contracts to break, as in *The Super Servant Two* (1990), the courts have still held that the fact that it was in the hands of one of the parties to decide whether the contract went ahead or not meant that the contract was not frustrated. It seems, therefore, that Martina has a strong case here for arguing that her contract with the University has not been frustrated by the government's action. She is entitled to retain the £750 already paid, and indeed can sue the University for breach of contract in relation to the rent that she was due to be paid.

Question 36

Answer both parts.

(a) 'The decision in the *Fibrosa* case meant that the reform contained in **s 1(2)** of the **Law Reform (Frustrated Contracts) Act (1943)** was unnecessary.'

Discuss.

(b) 'If the facts of *Appleby v Myers* (1867) were to occur again today, the outcome would be exactly the same.'

Do you agree?

Answer plan

Both parts of this question are concerned with the doctrine of frustration. The particular area they raise is the consequences of frustration, and the impact of the **Law Reform (Frustrated Contracts) Act 1943**. It is not necessary in answering these questions to give a full account of the whole doctrine of frustration. The concentration should be on the particular issues raised, as follows.

Part (a)

- What was the common law position on the effects of frustration prior to the decision in *Fibrosa Spolka Akcyjna v Fairbairn* (1943)?

- What was the effect of *Fibrosa*? That is, it allowed, in certain situations, the recovery of money paid under a contract that became frustrated.

- How does the 1943 Act deal with this situation? That is, the situations in which **s 1(2)** allows recovery.

- What are the differences between *Fibrosa* and **s 1(2)**?

Part (b)

- What happened in *Appleby v Myers* (1867)? That is, no recovery for the benefit of work done.

- How does the 1943 Act deal with this? That is, **s 1(3)** – recovery for a 'valuable benefit'.

- Does **s 1(3)** meet the criticisms of *Appleby v Myers*? Here, the decision of *BP Exploration v Hunt* (1982) will need to be considered in some detail.

Answer

Part (a)

This question is concerned with the consequences of a contract being frustrated – that is, coming to an end, as a result of some external factor that is not the fault of either party. The common law, once the possibility of frustration had been accepted (*Taylor v Caldwell* (1863), reversing the line taken in *Paradine v Jane* (1647)), took the view that the loss must lie where it fell at the time of the frustrating event. All actions taken up to that point were to have legal effect, since the contract was at that time still subsisting. Once the contract was frustrated, however, rights and liabilities were frozen at that point. In particular, money paid or payable under a frustrated contract before the time of frustration could not be recovered.

The strict application of this rule led to some anomalous results, with the position of the parties depending on the precise wording of their contract. Virtually identical factual situations could result in very different legal consequences. The cases of *Krell v Henry* (1903) and *Chandler v Webster* (1904) were both concerned with the hire of a room to view the coronation procession of King Edward VII. The procession was cancelled due to the King's ill health, and both contracts were held to be frustrated. In *Krell v Henry*, the hirer had paid a deposit, with the balance payable after the event. In *Chandler v Webster*, however, the full amount was payable before the contract was frustrated (although in fact only part of the amount had been paid). The result of applying the rule outlined above was that in *Krell* the hirer lost his deposit, but was not obliged to pay the balance of the hire, whereas in *Chandler* the hirer not only received no refund of the money already paid, but had to pay the balance as well, even though he had received no benefit under the contract.

This consequence of the strict rule, with its clear potential for injustice, was reconsidered by the House of Lords in *Fibrosa Spolka Akcyjna v Fairbairn* (1943). Here, an English company had a contract to sell machinery to a Polish company. A proportion of the price had been paid in advance, and further payment was due.

The outbreak of the Second World War led to the contract being frustrated. Under the rule applied in *Chandler v Webster*, the Polish company would not have been able to recover anything, and would have had to pay the amount that was due prior to the frustration. The House of Lords, however, overruled *Chandler*, and held that the Polish company was not only relieved of payment of the outstanding sum, but could also recover the money that had actually been paid. The reason for the decision was that here there had been a 'total failure of consideration'. In other words, the buyers had received nothing at all in exchange for their money. In such a situation, the House felt that they should be able to be put back into the position they were in prior to the contract. *Fibrosa* was an improvement on *Chandler*, but it still left two potential areas for injustice to arise. First, the approach could only be used where the failure of consideration was total. If the buyers had received any part of the performance, no matter how small, the rule would not apply, and they would have to pay everything due prior to the frustration. Second, the rule could operate harshly on the other side. The English company in the case, for example, was left without any compensation for expenses that it might have incurred in connection with the contract prior to the frustration.

The **Law Reform (Frustrated Contracts) Act 1943** addressed both these issues in **s 1(2)**. This section states that whenever a contract to which the Act applies is frustrated, money paid under it is to be returned, and money payable shall cease to be so. This applies even where there is no total failure of consideration – that is, where some performance has been tendered. This deals with the first deficiency in the *Fibrosa* rule. Second, however, s 1(2) allows the party to whom the sums were paid or payable to retain, or recover, an amount to cover expenses incurred in relation to the contract. The operation of this is subject to the supervision of the court, which is to allow it to operate only to the extent to which it is just to do so.[1] In *Gamerco SA v ICM/Fair Warning Agency* (1995), for example, although some expenses had been incurred, the plaintiffs' losses were so substantial that in the circumstances the judge made no deduction in ordering the return of the full amount which they had paid.

Was the 1943 Act unnecessary? Clearly not. The *Fibrosa* decision, while a step in the right direction, did not go far enough. The further reform contained in the 1943 Act was necessary to meet the two limitations to the decision outlined above. It has done so in a way that, on the whole, seems fair and sensible.

Part (b)

The case of *Appleby v Myers* (1867) concerned a contract for the manufacture of machinery by the plaintiffs on the defendants' premises. Payment was due on completion of the work. When some of the work had been done, the factory and the partly constructed machinery were destroyed by fire. The contract was clearly frustrated, but could the plaintiffs recover any compensation for the work that they had done? The answer was 'no'. The common law approach to frustration was, as has been indicated above, that losses should lie where they fall at the time of the frustrating event, so there was no basis for a claim by the plaintiffs.

The 1943 Act attempted to deal with this situation in s 1(3), which states that where a party to a frustrated contract has obtained a 'valuable benefit' before the time of discharge, the other party can obtain compensation for this. As with s 1(2), this is subject to the supervision of the court, which must decide what is the just amount in the light of all of the circumstances of the case.

At first sight, this appears to provide a remedy for the plaintiff in *Appleby v Myers*.

The work that they had done could be argued to constitute a 'valuable benefit', for which compensation could be paid. On closer inspection, however, the position is not so simple. How could the defendants be said to have received any benefit when (a) the machinery was not completed, and (b) after the fire it was totally worthless?

These issues were considered in some detail by Goff J, as he then was, in the only reported case on the 1943 Act, *BP Exploration v Hunt* (1982). Looking carefully at the statutory wording, he came to the conclusion that 'benefit' means the 'end product' of what the plaintiff has provided, not the value of the work itself. This is supported by the requirement in **s 1(3)** for the court to take account of the effect on the benefit of the circumstances of the frustration. Using an example similar to the facts of *Appleby v Myers*, he came to the conclusion that a claimant who has carried out work that has been destroyed by fire cannot claim any compensation for this. The defendant has in the end received no benefit, because all of the work has been destroyed.

Goff J's interpretation of the section is not the only possible one,[2] but it has not been criticised or doubted in any subsequent decision, and so we must take it as representing the current law on this issue. If that is the case, then the statement in the question is correct, and *Appleby v Myers* would be decided the same way today as it was in 1867.

Think points

1 What is the position if the expenses exceed what has been paid? No more than what has been paid can be recovered. If, for example, on a contract worth £5,000 a deposit of £500 has been paid, but the other party has incurred expenses of £750, the maximum that can be recovered is £500. The remaining £250 is irrecoverable, unless **s 1(3)**, which deals with the conferring of 'valuable benefits', can be brought into play.

2 What other approaches are possible? Treitel, for example, argues forcefully that the issue of the effect on the benefit of the frustrating circumstances should be taken to refer to the assessment of the 'just sum' rather than the valuation of the benefit: *The Law of Contract*, 12th edn, 2007, p 979; cf Stone, *The Modern Law of Contract*, 7th edn, 2008, p 527–9.

Question 37

Raminder has entered into a contract to have a combined central heating and air conditioning system installed into his house by Coolflo Ltd, at a cost of £9,000. He pays £1,000 and the work starts. Consider the rights and liabilities of Raminder and Coolflo in relation to this contract if the following alternative events occur when the work is two-thirds complete.

(a) Raminder's house accidentally catches fire, and is totally destroyed.

(b) The government announces that, because of a scare about legionnaires' disease, air conditioning systems of the kind that Raminder is having installed will become illegal, with immediate effect. The change will not, however, affect the central heating part of the system.

(c) The firm making parts that are essential to complete the system goes out of business, and there is no other source of supply. Coolflo uses the few remaining parts that it has to complete a system for another customer.

Answer plan

In answering this question, it is necessary to ask the following questions in relation to each event:

- is the contract frustrated?
- if so, what are the effects on the parties?

In part (a), there is no doubt that the contract is frustrated. The concentration will therefore be on the second question – that is, what are the effects on the parties? One particular issue that will need discussing is whether Coolflo can claim anything under s 1(3) of the **Law Reform (Frustrated Contracts) Act 1943**. The views of Lord Goff, as expressed in *BP Exploration v Hunt* (1982), suggest that it will not be able to do so.

Part (b) requires discussion of government intervention making the performance (or part of it) illegal (cf *Denny, Mott and Dickson v James Fraser* (1944)). It must also be considered whether a sufficient amount of the contract survives (that is, the central heating system) for the principle in *Herne Bay Steam Boat Co v Hutton* (1903) to apply, and thus prevent frustration. If the contract is frustrated, there is more chance here that s 1(3) will allow Coolflo some compensation for the work done.

In part (c), the central issue is that of 'self-induced' frustration (cf *Maritime National Fish v Ocean Trawlers* (1935)). To what extent can it be said that it is a result of Coolflo's own actions that it is unable to complete the contract? (Cf *The Super Servant Two* (1990).)

Note that it will not be necessary to repeat discussion of similar points in the different parts. Reference back to earlier discussion is quite acceptable.

Answer

This question is concerned with the doctrine of frustration. This provides that where, as a result of events outside the control of the parties, a contract becomes impossible (for example, *Taylor v Caldwell* (1863)), or at least radically different from what had been agreed (*Davis Contractors Ltd v Fareham UDC* (1956)), it will come to an end. All future obligations will cease, and there may be some redistribution between the parties to take account of money, property or services that have been transferred prior to the frustrating event. This process is governed by a combination of common law rules and the provisions of the **Law Reform (Frustrated Contracts) Act 1943**.

The three alternative situations will now be considered in turn.

Part (a)

There is no doubt that destruction of the subject matter of the contract can result in frustration. Indeed, the first case to recognise the doctrine, *Taylor v Caldwell*, involved such a situation. A music hall had been hired for some performances, but burnt down before they began. It was held that the contract was frustrated, and that all future obligations were discharged. There seems little doubt that the same will apply as between Raminder and Coolflo, so that there will be no further responsibilities under the contract.

More difficulty arises, however, in relation to the £1,000 that Raminder has already paid, and the fact that Coolflo has completed two-thirds of the work. Under the common law, money paid under a frustrated contract cannot generally be recovered (*Chandler v Webster* (1904)). The one exception is where there has been a total failure of consideration on the part of the recipient of the money. Here, since the House of Lords' decision in the *Fibrosa* case, the courts will allow recovery of what has been paid. If there has been any performance, however, this is not possible. Coolflo has certainly performed part of the contract, and Raminder will not therefore be able to recover his £1,000 under common law. The strict approach of the common law is, however, mitigated by the provisions of the **Law Reform (Frustrated Contracts) Act 1943**, and in particular s 1(2). This provides that, where money has been paid under a contract that is then frustrated, it is recoverable. The other party, however, may deduct expenses, up to the value of what was paid.

This is subject to what a court may think is just and reasonable in the circumstances. In *Gamerco SA v ICM/Fair Warning Agency* (1995), for example, although some expenses had been incurred, the plaintiffs' losses were so substantial that in the circumstances the judge made no deduction in ordering the return of the full amount that they had paid. There is nothing in the facts to indicate that this discretion should be exercised against Coolflo here. Coolflo, therefore, may well be able to argue that it should retain all or part of Raminder's £1,000 to cover expenses.

The maximum amount that Coolflo will be able to retain under **s** 1(2) is £1,000. We are told, however, that it has performed two-thirds of a contract for which the total price is £9,000. It may well wish to argue, therefore, that it should be entitled to more than this, because of the work that has been done. The only basis for such a claim is **s** 1(3) of the **1943 Act**. This provides that where a 'valuable benefit' has been conferred by one party on the other before the time of discharge, the court can award a sum that it considers just in all of the circumstances to compensate for this. The precise meaning of this section fell to be considered in *BP Exploration v Hunt* (1982). At issue was the question of whether the 'valuable benefit' had to be considered as it stood before, or after, the frustrating event. In Goff J's opinion (and the appeal courts did not disagree), the answer is that the benefit must be considered after the frustrating event.[1] Thus, he felt that if a building on which work has been done is destroyed by fire, then nothing can be awarded under **s** 1(3). The work is in the end of no value, and so cannot be considered a 'valuable benefit'. Applying this to the problem – that is, almost exactly the position here – assuming that Goff J's view prevails (and there is no judicial authority which contradicts it), Coolflo will not be entitled to any compensation under **s** 1(3). The most that Coolflo will be entitled to on the facts in part (a) is therefore £1,000.

Part (b)

The alleged frustrating event here is the government ban on the system being used for the air conditioning. There is no doubt that government action which renders the performance of a contract illegal can be regarded as frustrating the contract. In *Denny, Mott and Dickson v James Fraser* (1944), the contract concerned trade in timber. This was made illegal in 1939 and, as a consequence, the whole contract was held to be frustrated. The only difficulty here is that the contract for the air conditioning and the central heating seems to be 'entire'. That is, it is not severable, and one payment is to be made to cover all the work. The central heating system remains legal. Can it be said that, nevertheless, the contract as a whole is frustrated? A relevant authority is *Herne Bay Steamboat Co v Hutton* (1903). Here, the contract was for the hire of a boat to go for a day's cruise around the royal fleet, and to watch the King's review of it. The King's illness meant that the review was cancelled. The contract was held not to be frustrated, however, because it still had some purpose. The tour of the fleet was something worth doing in its own right, and so the effect on the contract was not sufficiently fundamental to frustrate it. Using this case, it might be argued that because the installation of the central heating system can go ahead there is still some point to the contract, and it is therefore not frustrated. Alternatively, it might be argued that the answer to the question 'will the performance be radically different from what the parties agreed?' should be 'yes'. The situation is distinguishable from *Herne Bay*, in which the use of the boat was still possible, although there was less to see. Nor is it like the *Suez Canal* cases, such as *Tsakiroglou & Co v Noblee Thorl* (1962), in which the closure of the canal made performance more difficult and more expensive. Here, an important element of the contract cannot be performed at all.[2] The argument is finely balanced, but it is submitted that it should be regarded as being frustrated. If this is so, then the consequences of frustration must be considered. The common law provisions, and s 1(2) of the 1943 Act, will operate in exactly the same way as in (a). There is an argument here, however, that Coolflo should be able to recover something under s 1(3), at least as far as the central heating system is concerned. The work that has been done on this can presumably be completed under a new contract with Coolflo, or someone else, and so can be regarded as a 'valuable benefit'. It would then be up to the court to decide what amounted to a just sum to be awarded for this benefit.

Part (c)

In this case, it is the unavailability of parts essential to the completion of the system that may be said to frustrate the contract. If it is true that there is no other source of supply, and no other way of adapting parts to complete it, then this is the type of event that might bring the doctrine of frustration into play. We are told, however, that Coolflo has, in fact, used parts of the required type to complete another system. This almost certainly means that it will not be able to plead frustration of the contract with Raminder. The relevant authorities are *Maritime National Fish v Ocean Trawlers* (1935) and *The Super Servant Two* (1990). In the former case, the hirers of a trawler decided to use certain fishing licences that they had obtained for boats other than the one hired. The licences were essential for them to be able to use the hired boat. They therefore alleged that the contract was frustrated. It was held that this was not the case, because it was their decision as to which boats should be licensed, and the so-called frustration was therefore 'self-induced'. This case left open the issue of whether a party who is left with the option of choosing which of two contracts to break, because of some potentially frustrating event, would also be unable to use the doctrine. In *The Super Servant Two*, the sinking of one of only two vessels capable of performing a contract meant that the defendants had to decide whether to perform their contract with the plaintiffs, or perform another contract to which the other suitable vessel was already assigned. It was held by the Court of Appeal that the fact that the defendants chose to perform the other contract meant that the 'frustration' of the contract with the plaintiffs was 'self-induced', and so did not operate to relieve the defendants of their obligations. The same argument would apply to Coolflo. It has decided to use the parts for the other contract. Its contract with Raminder will not therefore be frustrated. On the contrary, Coolflo will be in breach of contract for failure to complete, and Raminder will be able to sue for damages.

Think points

1 What is the basis for this approach? It derives from the idea that the Act is concerned not with distributing losses, but preventing unjust enrichment. How does that apply here? Raminder ends up with nothing of value from the work that Coolflo has done, because it has been destroyed in the fire. So Raminder is not unjustly enriched, and should not have to make any payment to Coolflo.

2 Might the precise terms of the contract make a difference here? Does the contract provide simply for the installation of 'an air conditioning system', or for a system of the particular type that has been made illegal? If the former, then it is arguable that it is like the *Suez Canal* cases: Coolflo can still install a system, but this will be more difficult and more expensive for it. The answer given in the text assumes that the contract does specify the particular system.

CHAPTER 11

PERFORMANCE AND BREACH

▌INTRODUCTION

The topics of performance and breach have links with two other areas. First, the issue of whether a particular term is a 'condition' or a 'warranty' ties in with discussion of the contents of the contract (dealt with in Chapter 5). Indeed, contract texts will often deal with the issue at that point. Second, the question of what the consequences are of breaking a contract, and in particular whether there is a right to treat the contract as repudiated, has obvious connections with the whole topic of remedies (which is covered in Chapter 12). Questions may well, therefore, overlap with these other two areas.

The main issues dealt with in this chapter are:

- the distinction between conditions, warranties, and innominate terms – how the courts decide into which category to put a particular term, and why this is important; and

- the distinction between 'entire' and 'severable' contracts or obligations, as in, for example, *Cutter v Powell* (1795), and the doctrine of 'substantial performance', as in *Hoenig v Isaacs* (1952).

The first of these issues is a complex one, requiring you to deal with questions of the parties' intentions, and how these should be assessed, as well as looking at the requirements of the commercial world. The case law is not straightforward, with different courts apparently taking differing approaches. You need to understand where the difficulties lie, but you cannot hope to explain them all satisfactorily in the space available.

The topic of what amounts to performance of a contract is probably easier, in that the case law is less complicated. There is some uncertainty as to what precisely is the difference between incomplete performance and complete but defective performance, but this is an issue that turns as much on the facts of the situation as on any clear principles of law.

Checklist

You should be familiar with the following areas:

- the distinction between 'conditions' and 'warranties' – categorisation under common law and statute;
- the consequences of breach of either type of term;
- the meaning of 'innominate' terms, and the effects of breach;
- the distinction between 'entire' and 'severable' contracts or obligations; and
- the doctrine of 'substantial performance'.

Question 38

'There are . . . many contractual undertakings of a more complex character which cannot be categorised as being "conditions" or "warranties".' (Diplock LJ, in *Hong Kong Fir Shipping Co Ltd v Kawasaki Kisen Kaisha* (1962))

Following the recognition of the category of 'innominate' or 'intermediate' terms in the *Hong Kong Fir* case, would it not be better to place all contractual terms in this category, and thus give the courts greater flexibility in dealing with breaches of contract?

Answer plan

The approach to answering this question is quite straightforward. First, the meaning of the terms 'condition' and 'warranty' should be explained, and their significance. This, of course, relates to the consequences of breach, with a breach of condition giving the right to repudiate as well as to claim damages. Next, the reason for the recognition of the intermediate category should be explained. The main argument comes from the need to recognise that some terms can be broken in a variety of ways, some more serious than others.

The second part of the answer, with the explanations of the terminology out of the way, will need to concentrate on the particular issue raised in the question. There are at least two arguments in favour of retaining the categories of condition and warranty:

- certainty – particularly in commercial contracts it may be important to be able to predict the effect of a breach on a contract, without having to wait to see what the precise consequences of it are; and

- consumer protection – the labelling of some terms as 'conditions' in the **Sale of Goods Act** 1979, for example, provides a strong remedy for consumers who have been sold defective goods.

The conclusion is likely to be that, although the 'innominate' term category allows a desirable degree of flexibility in some situations, there is still scope for applying the more rigid approach derived from classifying terms as conditions and warranties.

Answer

The English law of contract recognises that not all breaches of contract are of equal seriousness. Some will be so serious that they will in effect bring the contract to an end, or should entitle the innocent party to do so. Others will be capable of being adequately dealt with simply by an award of damages to cover losses. For example, in a contract for the hire of a room, failure by the hirer to pay the rent may well mean that the contract can be terminated. On the other hand, failure by the landlord to fulfil an obligation to clean the windows every month would be likely to result only in a remedy in damages.[1] This question is concerned with the methods by which the courts decide which breaches of contract will lead to which consequences.

One of the approaches that has been used is to label particular terms in a contract as conditions or warranties. A condition is an important term of the contract, any breach of which will lead to the right to repudiate. A warranty is a less significant term, any breach of which will only ever give a right to damages. One of the clearest examples of this use of terminology is to be found in the **Sale of Goods Act 1979**, in which the various implied terms as to title, quality, etc, are specifically labelled as either conditions or warranties. In other contracts, it may be more difficult to decide into which category a term should fall.

The courts will sometimes take the view that it is accepted in the commercial world that certain clauses, or types of clause, should be regarded as conditions. In *Bunge Corp v Tradax Export SA* (1981), for example, it was stated that clauses relating to the time for performance in mercantile contracts should usually be treated as conditions. In the absence of such guidance from custom, however, the court is left with trying to decide the importance of the term. Lord Diplock suggested in *Hong Kong Fir Shipping Co Ltd v Kawasaki Kisen Kaisha* (1962) that a condition was a clause, the breach of which would deprive the other party of 'substantially the whole benefit' of the contract. Later cases have not followed this, however, preferring to apply a vaguer test of whether the term is central to the contract. This will depend to some extent on the intentions of the parties when they made the contract. If they have actually spelt out in the agreement that a particular term is a condition, and stated that breach of it will give rise to a right to terminate the contract, then it is likely that the courts will give effect to that intention. Simply labelling a term as a condition, however, is not necessarily conclusive. In *Schuler AG v Wickman Machine Tool Sales Ltd* (1973), the parties had stated that it was a 'condition' of the agreement that the defendants should make weekly visits to six named firms over a period of four and a half years. If this clause was truly a condition, the effect would be that failure to make any one of those visits would amount to a repudiatory breach, giving the plaintiffs the right to terminate the contract. The House of Lords refused to accept that this was what the parties had intended when they made the contract. Despite the fact that the label 'condition' had been used, the House ruled that this clause had to be treated as either a warranty or an innominate term. The decision does not mean that the labels used by the parties are unimportant. They clearly give a strong indication of what the parties may have intended. However, where the result would be as surprising as it would have been in *Schuler v Wickman*, the courts will be prepared to substitute their own interpretation of the intention of the parties.[2]

One problem with the classification of terms into conditions and warranties is that it is an 'all or nothing' approach. If a term is a condition, any breach of it, no matter how apparently trivial, will give the other party the right to terminate. Conversely, if it is a warranty, no breach of the term, no matter what the consequences, will do more than give a remedy in damages. This was the problem confronted by the Court of Appeal in *Hong Kong Fir Shipping Co Ltd v Kawasaki Kisen Kaisha*. The clause that the Court was considering was the obligation of 'seaworthiness' in a time charter. This obligation could be broken in any number of ways. For example, the failure to have proper medical supplies on board would render the vessel 'unseaworthy' just as much as if the whole ship was in danger of sinking at any moment. Some of the possible breaches would be of a kind that could clearly be remedied very easily, or if not remedied could be adequately compensated for by an award of damages. Other breaches of the term, however, would go to the root of the contract, and justify termination. Faced with this situation, the Court of Appeal, with Diplock LJ giving the fullest analysis, decided that there were certain intermediate terms where the question of the right to terminate would depend on the consequences of the breach of contract. In other words, the Court's focus of attention shifts from the making of the contract and the parties' intentions at that time, to the breach that has in fact occurred, and the consequences of it. If those consequences are that the contract is substantially affected by the breach, then the innocent party will have the right to terminate. On the facts of the case before it, the Court held that the breach was not sufficiently serious to be treated in the same way as a breach of condition, and that the charterers had no right to terminate.

The approach taken in *Hong Kong Fir* has been followed in later cases. Would it not be sensible, then, to do as the question suggests, and apply it as the general rule for all contractual terms? The advantage of doing so would of course be, as the question suggests, the greater flexibility that this would allow. The courts would be able to look at the position as between the parties and provide a remedy appropriate to the seriousness of the breach. It is true, as well, that in some circumstances fairly unmeritorious claims of breach of condition have allowed a party to escape from a contract. For example, in *Arcos Ltd v Ronaasen & Son* (1933), there was a sale of goods contract for the supply of some wooden staves to be used in making barrels. The staves supplied were of a thickness one-sixteenth of an inch different from the contractual description of 'half an inch'. Compliance with description is a condition under s 13 of the **Sale of Goods Act 1979**. The buyers were held to be entitled to reject the staves, despite the fact that they would have been perfectly usable for making the barrels.[3] An approach based on 'innominate' terms would almost certainly have come up with a different result. It is clear, however, that even outside the area of the labels applied by the **Sale of Goods Act**, the concept of the condition and the warranty has survived.

A good example of this is the case of *The Mihalis Angelos* (1970). The clause being considered here was that of a vessel being 'expected ready to load' at a particular date. It was held that this was a condition, in the strict sense, and that the charterers were able to terminate for delay without needing to show that the breach had serious consequences. The reasons for adopting the approach given in this case are of more general application. It was pointed out that in the commercial world there are great advantages in certainty. Parties to a contract like to know what the consequences of their actions are going to be. If they break a contract, will the other side be able to terminate or not? If a party terminates for breach, will it run the risk that a court will subsequently say that it had no right to do so? The categorisation of terms into conditions and warranties enables clear predictions to be given, and reduces the degree of uncertainty. This in turn will improve efficiency, and should reduce costs. The suggestion is that, for the business community, the benefits of certainty outweigh the risks of a certain amount of injustice.

There is a second argument for conditions and warranties, which relates to the consumer contract. This is that it is better in the context of trying to establish standards of quality in consumer contracts, which is one of the aims of the **Sale of Goods Act 1979** implied terms, to have strict rules that make the supplier liable if the goods do not meet a particular standard. The consumer who buys an item that turns out to be defective will generally wish to return it and reclaim his or her money. It is better in this situation to impose a strict liability on the supplier, rather than leave the issue of the availability of termination to be decided on a case-by-case basis depending on the seriousness of the breach. Such an approach would undoubtedly work to the advantage of the supplier, who, through standard form contracts or superior bargaining power, would very likely be able to force the consumer to accept a lesser remedy than is available under the law at the moment.

The case of *Hong Kong Fir* was a significant development in the law relating to the consequences of breach of contract. It has opened up the possibility of a flexible approach that in many cases will make it easier to do justice between the parties. It does not provide the right answer for all situations, however. The parties themselves should have the freedom, if they wish, to construct their contract in such a way as to benefit from the certainty provided by the concepts of 'condition' and 'warranty'. Moreover, the consumer continues to need strong remedies available against the supplier of goods that turn out to be defective.

Think points

1 Are there cases that could be used to illustrate this point? *Poussard v Spiers* (1876) and *Bettini v Gye* (1876) provide a useful contrast between the two types of clause.

2 A more recent example of a similar approach is the decision of the Court of Appeal in *Rice v Great Yarmouth BC* (2000).

3 Would the same result be reached today? Probably not, because the position under the **Sale of Goods Act 1979** has been affected by the addition in 1994 of **s 15A**, which removes the right to rescind for minor breaches of **ss 13** or **14** in non-consumer contracts, if the breach is so slight that it would be unreasonable to do so.

Question 39

In September, Arthur bought a large and draughty house, which had a greenhouse in the garden. He engaged Confirm Ltd to fit double glazing to each of the 60 windows in the house, at a price of £500 per window. The total price of £30,000 was to be payable on completion of the contract. He also engaged Tom, a local glazier, to fit new glass, 5 mm thick, to the greenhouse, at a price of £3,000, again payable on completion of the work.

On 30 October of the same year, Confirm informed Arthur that its work had been completed, but, upon inspecting it later the same day, Arthur discovered that one of the windows had not been double-glazed at all, and that 30 of them still let in draughts. At the same time, Arthur noticed that Tom had completed work on the greenhouse, but found, on inspecting some spare panes of glass, that they were only 4 mm thick.

Confirm, while agreeing that further work needs to be done, is insisting on a payment of £14,500 in relation to the 29 windows that are satisfactory before doing any further work. Arthur is insisting that all of the work must be completed in accordance with the contract before he makes any payment.

Advise Arthur as to his rights under his contracts with Confirm and Tom.

Answer plan

The first part of this problem, dealing with the contract between Arthur and Confirm, is concerned with performance, and when the contract price is earned. The issues are:

- is the contract 'entire', as in *Cutter v Powell* (1795) and *Sumpter v Hedges* (1898), or is it severable?
- if it is entire, has there been 'substantial performance', entitling Confirm to some payment, as in *Hoenig v Isaacs* (1952)?

The second contract, that between Arthur and Tom, raises the issue of the remedies for breach. The use of the incorrect thickness of glass will amount to a breach of one of the implied terms under the **Supply of Goods and Services Act 1982**. The issue is then whether Arthur is entitled to repudiate the contract for this breach, or whether he can only claim damages (or a reduction in price) from Tom.

Answer

Arthur has made two contracts, neither of which has been performed to his satisfaction. Slightly different issues relating to performance and remedies arise in relation to each of them, however, and so they will be looked at separately. Looking first at the contract with Confirm, it is seeking payment for the work it has done towards the double glazing contract. Arthur is resisting until all of the work is complete. Whether he is entitled to do so will depend on whether his contract with Confirm is regarded as an 'entire' contract (as in *Sumpter v Hedges* (1898), for example) or severable, and on whether what Confirm has done can be regarded as 'substantial performance' (as in *Hoenig v Isaacs* (1952)).

Is the contract with Confirm an 'entire' contract?[1] A good example of the concept of the entire contract is the case of *Cutter v Powell* (1795). This concerned a contract under which a sailor was contracted to serve on a ship sailing from Jamaica to Liverpool, for a sum of 30 guineas. He died before the voyage was completed, and his widow sued for his wages for the time he had served. It was held that she could not recover anything, because the contract was an entire one. In other words, the obligation to pay the 30 guineas only arose when the voyage was completed. There was no obligation to pay wages on a periodic basis.[2] The same approach was taken in *Sumpter v Hedges* in relation to a building contract, where the work was left incomplete and was finished by the owner. It was held that the builder was not entitled to any payment for the work he had done, because the contract was an entire one.

Applying this to the present case, the answer is not clear-cut. It is possible to identify a price for each window double-glazed but, on the other hand, it is stated that the entire sum is payable on completion. What was the intention of the parties? It seems likely that it was intended to be an entire contract. The position would clearly have been different if payment was to be made in stages, according to the number of windows completed, but that is not the situation here. It is submitted that, although it is possible to put a value on the proportion of the work completed by Confirm, because the contract was made on the basis of a price per window, the statement about payment on completion should override this and preclude a claim of the kind that Confirm is making.[3]

This does not conclude this part of the question, however. In certain situations, the entire contracts rule can operate harshly, and it has to some extent been mitigated by the development of the rule of 'substantial performance'. This was recognised in the case of *Hoenig v Isaacs*. This case concerned a contract to furnish and decorate a flat for a fixed sum. When the work was completed, it was found to be defective in various ways, although it would only have taken a small sum to put the matters right. The defendant refused to pay anything, because the plaintiff had failed to complete what should be regarded as an entire contract. It was held that there had been 'substantial performance' of the contract, despite the fact that it was defective in various ways. The plaintiff was allowed to recover the contract price, less the amount that it would take to put the defects right. The distinction that needs to be drawn is between a contract that is completed, albeit defectively, and one that has not been completed at all. In *Bolton v Mahadeva* (1972), an argument for substantial performance failed. The contract was for the installation of a central heating system. The system as fitted gave out much less heat than it should have done, and caused fumes in one of the rooms. It was held that there was not substantial performance. Although the complete system had been fitted, it did not fulfil its primary function of heating the house, and so the installer was not allowed to recover.

Looking at what has been done in this case, has there been substantial performance? On the one hand, all but one of the windows have had double glazing fitted. On the other, half the windows are still defective in that they do not keep out the draughts, which was presumably a primary reason for installing the double glazing. The answer will depend on whether the case is regarded as being closer to the situation in *Hoenig v Isaacs*, or that in *Bolton v Mahadeva*. It is submitted that the extent of the defects in this case, affecting over half the windows, means that the case is closer to *Bolton v Mahadeva* and that therefore the contract should not be regarded as being substantially performed.

Thus, as regards the contract with Confirm, the advice to Arthur should be that he is not obliged to make any payment to it, but can retain the full contract price, pending Confirm's substantial completion of the contract.

The problem with Tom's contract with Arthur is rather different. The issue here is not a question of entire or severable contracts, or substantial performance. Assuming that the glass that Tom has used for reglazing the greenhouse is 4 mm rather than 5 mm thick, as specified in the contract, there is no doubt that there is a breach. The question is, what are the effects of this breach on the contract?

By virtue of s 3 of the **Supply of Goods and Services Act 1982**, there is an implied obligation in a contract such as this to supply goods that match their contractual description. Here, the contract description states that the glass should be 5 mm thick, whereas that which has been fitted is only 4 mm thick. There is then a breach of this implied obligation. Moreover, the obligation is stated by the Act to be a 'condition' of the contract. The consequences of breaking a condition are that this amounts to a repudiatory breach of contract, entitling the other side to reject performance and treat the contract as at an end. It might be argued by Tom that the difference between what he has supplied and what he should have supplied is small, and that the glass fitted will do its job just as well as the slightly thicker panes. All that he should be obliged to do is to deduct from the contract price an amount equivalent to the difference in price of the two types of material. The courts, however, have approached the issue of breaches of such implied conditions strictly. In *Arcos v Ronaasen* (1933), for example, they were considering the implied condition as to description in a sale of goods contract. The contract was for the supply of wooden staves for making barrels, which were supposed to be half an inch thick. Those supplied, although perfectly satisfactory for making barrels, were one-sixteenth of an inch out. The court held that they did not match their description, and that the buyer was therefore entitled to reject them.

Similarly, in *Re Moore & Co and Landauer & Co* (1921), the fact that tins of fruit were supplied in cases containing 24 tins each, as opposed to 30 tins each as specified in the contract, was held to be sufficient to entitle the buyer to reject the whole consignment. In some later cases, this very technical approach has been disapproved, and s 15A of the **Sale of Goods Act 1979** and s 5A of the **Supply of Goods and Services Act 1982** now restrict the right of a business purchaser to reject for minor breaches of this kind. Since Arthur is a consumer purchaser, however, he can still rely on the principles set out in *Arcos v Ronaasen* and *Moore and Landauer*. Moreover, the use of the incorrect thickness of the glass seems more significant than the deviations in those cases. Although the thinner glass will serve just as well in allowing light into the greenhouse, it will not, for example, provide such good insulation, which may be important to Arthur.

It seems, therefore, that Arthur is entitled to treat the contract as repudiated by Tom's breach. This means that he can refuse to pay anything, and can indeed insist that Tom removes all of the glass that he has installed. If Tom wants to be paid, he will have to do all of the work again, using the correct thickness of glass. On the other hand, Arthur does not have to do this. Where there is a repudiatory breach, the other party always has the choice of whether to terminate or not. It may be that Arthur will decide that the 1 mm difference is not sufficient reason to go to all of the trouble of having the work done again. Instead, he could, by way of damages, set off against the contract price both the difference in the cost of the glass and any other additional expenses, for example, extra heating, that might arise from having the thinner glass installed. This may well be his preferred solution.

It seems, then, that Arthur is in a strong position in relation to both these contracts. He is entitled to insist on full performance, without making any payment, and is thus in a good bargaining position as regards reaching any compromise with either Confirm or Tom.

Think points

1 Is it right to talk, as the courts regularly do, in terms of entire *contracts*? Is it the whole contract that is entire, or only some of the obligations? Some commentators suggest that the courts should be considering entire or divisible *obligations*: see further Stone, *The Modern Law of Contract*, 7th edn, 2008, pp 539, 541–2.

2 One reason for this apparently rather harsh decision seems to have been that the sum of 30 guineas was higher than the normal rate for such a voyage. The sailor was regarded as having taken the opportunity of earning more than normal against the risk of receiving nothing if the voyage was not completed. Does this provide a good reason for the decision, do you think? Would the sailor's widow think so?

3 Would it be appropriate here to introduce a reference to *Williams v Roffey* (1989), in which the revised version of the contract did seem to be on the basis of a payment per flat completed, thus changing what appeared originally to be an entire contract into one containing divisible obligations? There would appear to be analogies to be drawn, if space allowed.

Question 40

In August 2007, Sprocket Ltd entered into a contract with Quikclean Ltd, under which Quikclean agreed to provide cleaning services at Sprocket's office premises for a period of five years. The cleaning was to take place each day between 7 pm and 9 pm. The contract stated in clause 8 that: 'In the event of Quikclean's failure to clean all offices as required, Sprocket Ltd will be entitled to terminate the contract with immediate effect.' On ten occasions between August 2007 and July 2008,

Quikclean's cleaners failed to turn up to clean Sprocket's offices. Quikclean blamed this on a staffing problem, and claimed in July 2008 that the problem had now been solved. On 9 August 2008, Sprocket found that the managing director's office had not been cleaned, although of all the other offices had been. Sprocket thereupon purported to terminate Quikclean's contract, relying on clause 8.

Advise Quikclean.

Would your answer be different if the problem was that Quikclean's employees had left the premises insecure, so that vandals had gained entry and started a fire, which caused extensive damage to Sprocket's premises?

Answer plan

This question is concerned with the rights of an innocent party to terminate a contract following a breach by the other party. The issues that need to be discussed include the differences between conditions, warranties and innominate terms, and the situations in which a breach will be held to be serious enough to justify termination of the contract. The suggested order of treatment is as follows:

- introduction to the issues;
- consideration of the status of clause 8 of the contract – does it mean that every breach of contract can be treated as a breach of 'condition'? Relevant cases are *Schuler v Wickman Machine Tool Sales Ltd* (1973) and *Rice v Great Yarmouth Borough Council* (2000);
- if clause 8 does not have this effect, when will the right to terminate arise? Again, *Rice v Great Yarmouth Borough Council* will be relevant; and
- consideration of the alternative scenario – discussion of the principles derived from the case of *Hong Kong Fir Shipping Co v Kawasaki Kisen Kaisha* (1964) will be relevant here.

Answer

This question is concerned with the rights of an innocent party to terminate a contract for breach. There are two ways in which such a right may arise. In some situations, the party may have broken a term that is of particular importance. The courts will treat this as a breach of 'condition', giving rise to the right to terminate, whatever the effects of the particular breach that has occurred. An example of this type of term is the implied condition of correspondence with description under the **Sale of Goods Act 1979**. Where the clause concerned is not a condition, it may be a warranty (breach of which will not give rise to a right to terminate, whatever the consequences) or an innominate term (in respect of which the right to terminate will depend on the effects of the breach).[1] A serious breach of an innominate term is therefore the second way in which a right to terminate may arise.

In this case, Sprocket has purported to terminate for what seems to be a fairly minor breach: that is, the failure to clean one office. It is probable, however, that this will need to be looked at in the light of the overall dealings between the parties, and Quikclean's earlier breaches.

The courts' starting point is generally an attempt to discern the intentions of the parties. To that end, they will look closely at precisely what the parties have said in the contract itself. If, for example, they have labelled a particular clause as a 'condition', then this may be an indication that they intended any breach to give rise to the right to terminate. Such labelling is not conclusive, however, as is shown by the case of *Schuler AG v Wickman Machine Tool Sales Ltd* (1973). The contract in this case contained a clause, described as a condition, which required that representatives of Wickman should visit six potential named customers of Schuler's goods each week throughout the duration of the contract. Wickman's representatives missed some visits, and Schuler purported to terminate for breach of condition. The House of Lords held that they were not entitled to do so. They said that it was necessary to look beyond the label used by the parties, even though this was relevant evidence of their intentions, and to consider the consequences of categorising a term as a condition. The effect would be that any breach, however small, would entitle the other side to terminate. In relation to the contract under consideration, they could not accept that failure to make only one of several thousand visits could have been intended to be grounds for termination. In that case, the label of 'condition' was used. In the problem, that is not the case. Instead, the clause specifically states that there should be a right to terminate for a 'failure to clean all offices'. In *Rice v Great Yarmouth Borough Council* (2000), the Court of Appeal had to consider a clause of this kind in relation to a contract for the provision of maintenance services to a local authority. The Court adopted a similar approach to that taken in *Schuler v Wickman*, and held that it could not have been the parties' intention that any breach of contract, no matter how minor, should lead to the right to terminate. The clause had to be interpreted within the overall context of the contract and in line with common sense. It was only where there was a breach or accumulation of breaches serious enough to be regarded as repudiatory that the right to terminate would arise.

Applying this approach to the problem, we have a clause that, if read literally, means that a failure to clean only one office on only one occasion would lead to a right to terminate the whole contract. It seems unlikely that a court would regard this as accurately representing the parties' intentions. It will be appropriate to advise Quikclean, therefore, that it is unlikely that its failure to clean one office on 8 August 2008 would in itself entitle Sprocket to terminate the contract. That is not the end of the story, however. Although clause 8 almost certainly does not have the effect of turning every breach of contract into a breach of condition, a breach or accumulation of breaches that is sufficiently serious will give a right to terminate. There are two possibilities to consider here. The office that has not been cleaned is that of the managing director. We do not know exactly what state it was in, or what the managing director's schedule was for 9 August. Suppose that the office had been used for a social occasion on the afternoon of 8 August; suppose also that the managing director had early meetings on 9 August with important clients who needed to be impressed and there was no other appropriate office that could be used. In that situation, it is just possible that a court would regard the effect of the breach on 8 August as being sufficiently serious to justify termination. This would be adopting the approach taken in *Hong Kong Fir Shipping Co v Kawasaki Kisen Kaisha* (1962), which will be discussed further below, in connection with the alternative set of facts.

The other possibility is that Sprocket can refer back to the previous breaches by Quikclean (which appear to have been more serious) and argue that, taken together with the breach of 8 August 2008, termination is justified. In other words, the breach of 8 August would be treated as 'the last straw': not sufficient in itself to justify termination, but adding to the accumulated breaches of the previous year. This was the approach taken by the Court of Appeal in *Rice v Great Yarmouth*. In that case, the contract was to last four years. The Court suggested that it was relevant to look at the contractor's performance over a full year, with a view to judging whether the council had been deprived of a substantial part of what it had contracted for. In that context, previous breaches were relevant as indicating what might be likely to happen in the future. If it was likely that there would continue to be problems, then this would add to the arguments justifying termination. On the facts, however, the Court refused to interfere with the judge's decision that the contractor's breaches were not sufficiently serious to justify termination.

It seems likely that a similar conclusion would be drawn from the facts in the problem. The fact that there had been a failure of performance on ten days out of, say, 250 working days during the previous year is unlikely to be regarded as depriving Sprocket of a substantial part of what it had contracted for. The breaches can surely be adequately dealt with by the payment of compensation, or a reduction in charges for the future. A far greater degree of unreliability would be needed to justify the immediate termination of the contract.

Turning to the alternative situation, Quikclean's staff have here failed to secure the premises, and this has led to severe damage to Sprocket's offices. It is assumed that it was an express or implied term of the contract that Quikclean's staff were responsible for ensuring that the building was secure when they left. Quikclean will therefore be in breach of contract. There is not, however, apparently any provision equivalent to clause 8, purporting to set out the consequences of such a breach.

It will fall to the courts to decide, therefore, whether this is to be treated as a breach of a condition, a warranty or an innominate term. It is possible that it could be argued that keeping the building secure is sufficiently important that any breach should entitle the other side to terminate the contract. If that is the case, then Sprocket will be justified in bringing the contract to an end immediately. On the other hand, it might be argued that the obligation as regards security is more like the term as to 'seaworthiness' in *Hong Kong Fir Shipping Co v Kawasaki Kisen Kaisha*. In this case, it was held that the term as to seaworthiness was neither a condition nor a warranty, but an intermediate or 'innominate' term. In relation to such terms, the question of whether the innocent party can terminate for breach depends on the seriousness of the breach and its consequences. If that approach is adopted in the dispute between Sprocket and Quikclean, however, it still seems that the arguments will go in Sprocket's favour. The failure to secure the building has had serious consequences, with significant damage having been caused to Sprocket's premises. This will no doubt have caused disruption to Sprocket's business. In the circumstances, even if the term as to keeping the building secure is treated as an innominate term rather than a condition, the particular breach that has occurred is sufficiently serious to entitle Sprocket to terminate the contract with immediate effect.

Think point

1 Could it be argued that there are in effect only two categories of term – conditions and innominate terms? This has been suggested, for example, by Reynolds (1981) 97 LQR 541, but does not seem to have found favour with other commentators or the courts. See also Stone, *The Modern Law of Contract*, 7th edn, 2008, p 554.

CHAPTER 12

REMEDIES

INTRODUCTION

There are two main remedies for breach of contract: namely, damages and specific performance. Questions 41 and 43 concentrate on the former, and Question 42 deals with both.

The issues that arise in damages questions tend to centre around the principles used to decide what type of damages to award, rather than how the precise figure to be awarded is arrived at. Thus, the questions will raise issues about:

- the principle behind the award – that is, generally compensation rather than punishment, putting the parties into the position they would have been in had the contract been performed properly;

- the difference between the expectation interest and the reliance interest;

- the possibility of a 'restitutionary' remedy (not based on compensation), as recognised by the House of Lords in *Attorney General v Blake* (2000);

- the rule of remoteness – what is meant by a loss being 'within the reasonable contemplation of the parties' (*The Heron II* (1969))? The recent House of Lords' decision in *Jackson v Royal Bank of Scotland* (2005) will need discussion. Again, some comparison with the tortious rule of remoteness may be called for; and

- the situations in which non-pecuniary losses may be recoverable – as reviewed by the House of Lords in *Farley v Skinner* (2001).

There are relatively few questions that can be asked about specific performance. Again, the question is more likely to be an essay than a problem, and will almost certainly involve some variation on the issues raised in Question 42 – that is:

- what is the basis for the award of an order of specific performance?

- in what situations will the courts regard it as being an appropriate remedy?

The possibility of using an injunction as a contractual remedy may also arise (although not in Question 42).

Checklist

You should be familiar with the following areas:

- the award of damages – general principles of compensation;
- the meaning of, and distinction between, 'expectation', 'reliance' and 'restitutionary' interests;
- the rule of remoteness, its development and current status;
- the situations in which non-pecuniary losses may be recoverable; and
- the availability of specific performance.

Question 41

Explain how the rules of remoteness and mitigation affect the damages that are recoverable for breach of contract, and evaluate whether they impose effective limits on what may be recovered.

Answer plan

This is a straightforward essay dealing with damages, and the limitations on their recovery. The most difficult part is the requirement to provide an evaluation of the effectiveness of the mitigation and remoteness rules. A thorough knowledge of these rules and associated case law will be necessary to answer this question.

The following order of treatment is suggested:

- an outline of the basic rules relating to the recovery of contract damages;
- a description of the rules of remoteness, taking into account the recent House of Lords' decision in *Jackson v Royal Bank of Scotland* (2005);
- a description of the rules as to mitigation; and
- an evaluation of the rules of remoteness and mitigation.

Answer

The object of contract damages is to put the parties into the position they would have been in had the breach of contract not occurred, and the contract had therefore been performed in accordance with its terms. This approach is to be found in *Robinson v Harman* (1848) and has more recently been confirmed by the House of Lords in *Farley v Skinner* (2001). The claimant is therefore allowed to recover compensation for benefits that would have flowed from the contract. This is referred to as allowing the claimant to recover the 'expectation interest'. In some situations, however, damages based on expenditure (the 'reliance interest') or recovery of property transferred ('restitution') may be used.

Two particular problems may arise in relation to the calculation of damages, whatever primary measure is used. First, can the claimant recover in relation to *any* consequence that as a matter of fact is caused by the breach? Second, to what extent is the claimant entitled to sit back and watch losses accumulate following a breach? Does the claimant have any obligation to take steps to reduce the losses?

These two problems are addressed in English law by the rules relating to remoteness, and mitigation. These will be considered in turn, and then some evaluation of their effectiveness will be attempted.

The type of situation with which the rule of remoteness is intended to deal is as follows. Suppose A books a taxi to take him to a meeting with a potential client, due to start at 10 am. The taxi fails to turn up, and A is very late for his meeting. The client is very annoyed, and decides not to allocate a £1m contract to A. The taxi firm is clearly in breach of contract. If the contract had been performed as promised, A would probably have gained the £1m contract. Should the taxi firm be liable for the loss of the contract? The common sense answer must be 'no' – but how does the law arrive at that conclusion? This is where the rule of remoteness comes into play.

The origin of this rule as far as contract is concerned (a similar rule applies in tort) is the nineteenth-century case of *Hadley v Baxendale* (1854). This involved a contract for the transport of a broken mill shaft. The mill was out of action for longer than anticipated because of delays in the carriage of the shaft. The mill owner sought to recover all of the consequent losses. The court stated the rule as being that a claimant could recover for all losses arising in the 'usual course of things' from the breach, or those that were in the 'reasonable contemplation' of the parties at the time of the contract as the probable result of the breach. Applying this to the case before it, the court held that it would not normally have been assumed that the absence of this particular shaft would stop the mill entirely. In the usual course of things, therefore, no loss would have been suffered. Nor were the defendants aware of the fact that in this case delay in the return of the shaft would have these consequences. The damages were too remote.

The rule set out in *Hadley v Baxendale* has been subsequently interpreted further. In *Victoria Laundry (Windsor) v Newman Industries* (1949), the breach of contract related to the delay in the delivery of a boiler. The plaintiffs had entered into some particularly lucrative dyeing contracts with a government ministry, and they sought to recover the losses on these contracts. The court held that they could recover for the normal level of business losses that would follow from the delay in delivery, but not for those relating to the ministry contracts. The defendants were not aware of these contracts and the losses were therefore too remote. This case illustrates clearly the operation of the two parts of the *Hadley v Baxendale* rule.

The Heron II (1969) focused on the degree of risk that was necessary before a loss could be recovered. When was a risk within the 'reasonable contemplation of the parties'? Did it have to be 'probable', 'very likely' or just 'likely' to result? The House was clear that the test was stricter than that applying in tort, which is based on what is 'reasonably foreseeable'. Although there is no very clear statement, it seems that the test should be whether the result was 'not unlikely' to occur.

Once a particular type of loss is within the parties' contemplation, then it seems that all losses of that type will be recoverable. This was the outcome of the decision in *Parsons v Uttley Ingham* (1978). The breach of contract was likely to cause harm to the plaintiff's pigs; the fact that it actually caused the death of a significant number did not make the loss too remote.

The most recent House of Lords consideration of the remoteness rules was in *Jackson v Royal Bank of Scotland* (2005). The defendant bank, in breach of its contractual duty of confidentiality, revealed to one of the claimant's customers the level of mark-up being charged on goods supplied. The customer terminated their contract with the claimant, who sought compensation for lost business from the bank. The question related to how many years of business could be said to have been lost. The House of Lords clearly took the view that there were two separate parts to the rule in *Hadley v Baxendale*.[1] This case fell under the first – losses arising in the usual course of things. The Court of Appeal had held, however, that the claimants' losses should be restricted by the circumstances existing at the time of the breach, and limited the loss of forward business to one year's worth. The House of Lords disagreed. It emphasised that any consideration of what was or was not too remote had to be based on the parties' state of knowledge at the time of the contract, not the time of breach. Once it had been found that the loss arose under the first limb of *Hadley v Baxendale*, there was no reason to interfere with the trial judge's finding that four years of lost business was recoverable. The second limiting factor in relation to damages that needs to be considered is that of mitigation. This is the rule that prevents a claimant simply allowing losses to accumulate, when action could have been taken to limit them. The basic principle is derived from the case of *British Westinghouse Electric and Manufacturing Co v Underground Electric Railways Co of London* (1912). The obligation, as set out there by the House of Lords, is to take all reasonable steps to mitigate the loss. What steps will be 'reasonable'? That will be a question of fact to be decided in the circumstances of each case. It is clear, however, that in a contract for the sale of goods, if goods are not delivered, the buyer will be expected to try to acquire equivalent goods fairly quickly. If such goods are available, then the damages recoverable will be limited to the difference between the contract price and the price paid to acquire the substitute goods.[2] If a party in breach makes a reasonable offer of substitute performance, this should normally be accepted, as in *Payzu Ltd v Saunders* (1919).

The most difficult issue in this area arises in relation to anticipatory breach. If a party has indicated before the time for performance that it is not going to perform, does the other party have an obligation to mitigate immediately, or can it wait until the time for performance has passed? In *White and Carter (Councils) v McGregor* (1962), the answer, somewhat surprisingly, was the latter. The defendant cancelled a contract for advertising space, before any work had been done. The plaintiffs went ahead and produced and ran the adverts. They were held to be entitled to recover the full sum due under the contract. Later cases have, however, tried to limit the scope of this decision, so that the claimant must have a 'legitimate interest' that will justify acting in continuing with the contract. No such interest was found in *The Alaskan Trader* (1984), for example. The area remains one of some uncertainty, however.

In conclusion, the rule of remoteness, based on reasonable contemplation, does seem to provide a satisfactory basis for deciding what damages are recoverable. There is some uncertainty about the precise degree of 'likelihood' that is required, but otherwise the rules seem to operate without any major problem, and broadly to achieve justice between the parties. Similarly, the rules on mitigation, again based around what is 'reasonable', are largely satisfactory. The only difficult area is that of anticipatory breach. A strong move away from the approach taken in *White and Carter (Councils) v McGregor* would probably be the most satisfactory development in this area.

Think points

1 Could it be argued that there is in fact only one rule? That is, losses are recoverable if they are at the time of contract foreseen by the parties as likely to result from the breach.

2 What is the position if the market price is below the contract price? The buyer will only be able to recover nominal damages.

Question 42

(a) How do the courts decide whether to grant an order of specific performance? Are the criteria used sensible?

(b) Paperfine Ltd is a printing business. It makes a contract with Mekanix Ltd to repair one of its printing machines, at a cost of £200. Mekanix's employee negligently reassembles the machine incorrectly, so that the first time it is used a drive shaft breaks, and the machine is then beyond repair. The cost of replacing it is £7,500, and Paperfine is unable to obtain a replacement for three weeks. During this period it is estimated that the lack of the machine has reduced the firm's profits by £500 per week. Moreover, the firm misses out on the chance to bid for a very lucrative contract, which would have produced a profit of £6,000.

Advise Paperfine as to the damages it can claim for Mekanix's breach of contract.

Answer plan

The two parts of this question are entirely distinct. While both are concerned with remedies, they raise totally different issues, and so need to be tackled virtually as two short questions rather than one long one.

Part (a)

The first part of this answer will be purely descriptive. Following a brief introduction explaining the nature of the remedy, it is simply a question of outlining the bases on which the courts will exercise their discretion to grant an order, such as the adequacy, or otherwise, of damages, and the requirement of mutuality. Some critical analysis of these criteria must then be made. This is probably most easily done by making comments on each of the criteria as it is discussed, and then giving a brief summing up at the end. The quality of the argument, rather than the specific points made, will be most important here.

Part (b)

This is concerned with the issue of remoteness. It will be necessary to outline the principle from *Hadley v Baxendale* (1854), and describe its development through the cases. There is little doubt that the cost of the replacement, and some lost profits, will be recoverable. The main issue is whether the chance to bid for the lucrative contract can be taken into account. If Mekanix has actual knowledge of this, or it is within its reasonable contemplation, then the issue becomes one of assessing the value to be placed on the 'loss of a chance' (as in *Chaplin v Hicks* (1911)).

Answer

Part (a)

The order of specific performance is an equitable remedy, whereby the court orders one of the parties to perform his or her side of the contract. Disobedience to the order will result in the party being in contempt of court, and thus liable to fines or imprisonment. The fact that the remedy developed in the courts of Chancery means that it is intended to complement the common law remedy of damages. It also means that it is a discretionary remedy. The claimant cannot claim specific performance as of right (unlike damages); it is up to the court to decide whether the remedy is appropriate.

In exercising this discretion, the courts have developed a number of guiding principles, which form the 'criteria' referred to in the question. The first of these is the question of the adequacy of damages, as held in *Harnett v Yielding* (1805). As has been mentioned, the common law remedy of damages is available as of right, but it will not always provide a just result. If, for example, the contract concerns a valuable original painting, a disappointed purchaser will not be properly compensated by money.[1] Conversely, if the seller has failed to supply goods that are easily available elsewhere, even if at a higher price, the claimant buyer is unlikely to be granted an order of specific performance. The provision of damages in the form of money to buy equivalent goods will be a perfectly adequate remedy.

Another example where damages may be inadequate is if there is no real financial loss, so that only nominal damages are available. This will apply where, for example, the benefit of performance is to be received by a third party. This was the position in *Beswick v Beswick* (1968), in which the nephew was ordered to perform the contract made with his uncle, for the benefit of his aunt.[2] The principle of considering the adequacy of damages is clearly sensible. It is questionable, however, whether the way in which it is applied in relation to contracts for the sale of land is justifiable. The courts take the view that each piece of land is unique, so that specific performance is always available for this type of contract. It is hard to see that this really applies in relation to a standard plot on a housing development, for example. In many cases, it is submitted, a disappointed purchaser could be adequately compensated by damages, although it is admitted that there would be many others where an order for performance would be appropriate. A second criterion for exercising the discretion is whether or not the performance will require close supervision. If it will, then the court will be reluctant to grant the order, as in *Co-operative Insurance Society Ltd v Argyll Stores (Holdings) Ltd* (1998), which concerned a covenant to keep a supermarket open during specified hours.

Nor will the court normally grant an order in relation to a contract for personal services. This basic principle is sensible, in that there is no point in trying to get people to work together if they are clearly incompatible. In some circumstances, however, for example, where the breach of contract is not a result of any breakdown of the relationship between the parties, an order may still be appropriate. This was the case in *Hill v Parsons* (1972) (dismissal as a result of union pressure) and *Powell v Brent LBC* (1987) (defect in appointments procedure). This principle is therefore acceptable, provided that it is not applied rigidly.

The courts also look to 'mutuality' in deciding whether to make an order. This means that they will be reluctant to order performance against the defendant, unless such an order would also be available against the claimant. This might arise, for example, where the claimant is a minor. The time to assess the position, however, is at the time of trial (*Price v Strange* (1978)), and if the claimant has by this stage performed (even though he or she could not have been compelled to do so), the order may be granted.

Disproportionate hardship to the defendant as a result of the making of an order will result in the discretion being exercised against it. Thus, in *Denne v Light* (1857), the making of the order in relation to the sale of a piece of land would have left the defendant without any access to his plot. Specific performance was therefore refused.

Finally, the origin of the remedy in the Chancery courts inevitably means that it will only be used where it is 'equitable' to do so. In addition to the above criteria, some of which may also be said to be concerned with 'doing equity', there is a general requirement that the claimant has acted equitably. As the equitable maxim puts it, 'he who seeks equity must do equity'. Thus, a claimant who has made unfair use of a strong bargaining position (*Shell v Lostock Garages* (1977)), or who has taken advantage of the defendant's ignorance or mistake (*Walters v Morgan* (1861)), will not be granted an order for performance. This flexibility that the courts allow themselves to do justice on the facts of the case seems entirely sensible, although, as with any such approach, it carries with it a lack of predictability of the outcome of any particular set of facts.

Overall, then, the rules relating to the use of the remedy of specific performance are satisfactory. The only area in which there is room for criticism is in relation to contracts for the sale of land. Here, in contrast to the flexible approach taken elsewhere, a rather rigid rule applies, for which there is little obvious justification.

Part (b)

Mekanix is in breach of contract, as a result of its employee's negligence, and Paperfine is seeking damages. The basic objective that the courts will generally try to achieve is to put the innocent party into the position that he or she would have been in had the contract been performed properly (*Robinson v Harman* (1848)). This 'expectation interest' is what Paperfine will be seeking. The difficulty is in deciding exactly what should come under this heading, particularly in the way of lost profits.

Taking the most straightforward issue first, we are told that the defective assembly has led to the machine needing to be replaced. If that is right, then there seems little doubt that Mekanix will have to pay for the replacement. This loss is a direct result of its employee's negligence. Paperfine will of course be under an obligation to mitigate its loss: *British Westinghouse Electric Manufacturing Co v Underground Electric Railways Co of London* (1912). This means that it must take reasonable steps to acquire the cheapest replacement machine of equivalent quality, as quickly as possible. It is assumed that the price of £7,500 is the best deal available, and that therefore Mekanix will be liable to pay this amount. We must then consider the losses that follow as a consequence of this breach – that is, the lost profits. Such losses are recoverable, provided that they are caused by the breach and are not too remote. Looking first at the loss of £500 per week, there appears to be little argument that this has been caused by the breach. Is the loss too remote? The contractual rules of remoteness derive from the case of *Hadley v Baxendale* (1854), which concerned a delay in the delivery of a drive shaft. The principle to be applied was said to be that the defendant was liable for all losses that flowed from the breach in the natural course of events, plus those that may reasonably be supposed to have been in the contemplation of the parties at the time of the contract as the likely consequence of a breach.

Subsequent interpretation of this rule in *Victoria Laundry (Windsor) v Newman* (1949) and *The Heron II* (1969) shows that there is in effect one test: given the parties' state of knowledge at the time of the contract, was the loss one that should reasonably have been within their contemplation as a consequence of the type of breach that has occurred? Knowledge of everyday matters will be assumed, but where the loss results from some particular intricacy of the claimant's business, awareness of this will not be assumed. Thus, in *Balfour Beatty Construction (Scotland) Ltd v Scottish Power plc* (1994), it could not be assumed that the defendant would be aware of the fact that the claimant's construction project required a 'continuous pour' of concrete, and that disruption of this halfway through would mean that it would have to start again from the beginning.

Applying this to the problem, the fact that a machine being put out of service would result in some loss to Paperfine's profits was surely within the reasonable contemplation of the parties at the time of the contract. As long as some loss under this heading is contemplated, the precise figure does not have to be foreseen *(Parsons v Uttley Ingham* (1978)). Mekanix will therefore have to pay the £1,500 lost profits for the period until the replacement machine is obtained.

The loss relating to the missed chance to bid for a very lucrative contract is more remote. In *Victoria Laundry (Windsor) v Newman*, the plaintiffs were not allowed to recover for some particularly lucrative contracts of which the defendants were unaware. The possibility of recovery under this heading, then, will depend on the knowledge of Mekanix at the time of the original contract.[3] Did it know that Paperfine had a chance of this special deal? If, as seems likely, it did not, then Paperfine will not be able to recover under this heading. Even if Mekanix did know about the deal, Paperfine will not be able to recover the full £6,000 that it might have made on it. We are told that it missed out on the 'chance to bid'. Courts are prepared to award compensation for the 'loss of a chance'. In *Chaplin v Hicks* (1911), the plaintiff was prevented from taking part in an audition for a show. She was awarded a proportion of what she might have earned, had she been successful. So, here, the best that Paperfine will be able to do is to recover some proportion of the £6,000, assessed according to the court's view of its chances of actually landing the contract.

Paperfine will be likely, therefore, to recover a total of £9,000: £7,500 to replace the machine, and £1,500 for lost profits. It is unlikely that it will be able to recover any part of the £6,000 on the special contract, unless Mekanix knew about this when the original contract to repair the machine was made.

Think points

1 Unless, perhaps, the sole reason for the purchase is investment?

2 What if damages are nominal because equivalent goods are easily available at or below the contract price? This will not be a reason for granting specific performance.

3 Why is knowledge at the time of the breach not sufficient? The parties need to be able to appreciate the risks at the time of the contract, because this may affect the contractual terms, and the taking out of insurance.

Question 43

In January 2008, Peggy made a contract with the Regency Hotel in Leighborough, booking it for the wedding reception of her daughter, Samantha, to be held on 10 August 2008, at a price of £6,000. Samantha particularly wanted the reception to be at the Regency because of its extensive grounds, enabling much of the reception to take place out of doors. Two weeks prior to the wedding, when Peggy rang the Regency to check on certain arrangements, she was told that there had been a mistake over the dates. When Peggy made the contract, the hotel had in fact already been booked for another event on 10 August. On learning this, Peggy immediately attempted to find another location for the reception. The only two possibilities were a local public house, the King George, which could offer a function room and limited catering for £4,500, and the Majestic Hotel in the middle of Leighborough. The Majestic was able to offer an equivalent provision to the Regency, but at a price of £7,500. Peggy booked the Majestic, and the reception took place there. It went smoothly, but Samantha was very disappointed at the change in venue because the

Majestic had no grounds, and the whole event had to take place indoors. As a result of all of the worry and extra work caused by the change of venue, Peggy suffered a breakdown, and three months later was still receiving treatment for depression.

Advise Peggy, on the basis that the Regency Hotel has accepted that the mistake over the booking was entirely its fault.

Answer plan

Since the Regency Hotel has admitted that it is at fault, the issue that needs to be considered here is the extent of the damages that Peggy may be able to recover. The two main issues that need discussion are the questions of mitigation and non-pecuniary loss. As regards mitigation, the principles set out in *British Westinghouse Electric Manufacturing Co v Underground Electric Railways Co of London* (1912) will need consideration. On non-pecuniary losses, the most important authority is the recent House of Lords' decision in *Farley v Skinner* (2001).

The suggested order of treatment is:

- a statement of the general principles relating to damages;
- consideration of whether the 'extra' £1,500 paid to the Majestic is recoverable – this will in part depend on whether Peggy could be said to have taken reasonable steps to mitigate her losses. Should she, for example, have taken the cheaper alternative offered by the King George?
- a statement of general principles relating to non-pecuniary loss;
- consideration of whether Peggy can recover for Samantha's disappointment – this will include the question of recovering damages on behalf of another – see *Jackson v Horizon Holidays* (1975);
- consideration of whether Peggy can recover damages for her breakdown and continuing depression – applying the principles set out in *Farley v Skinner*;
- a conclusion.

Answer

The Regency Hotel has accepted that the mix-up over the bookings was its fault. It is therefore in breach of contract in failing to provide the reception that it had promised in its contract with Peggy of January 2008.[1] The question is then what damages Peggy can recover as a consequence of this breach.

The general principle of contract damages is that they are intended to put the innocent party into the position that would have resulted had the contract been performed properly – *Robinson v Harman* (1848). So, in this case we need to look at what the position would have been had the Regency Hotel performed its contract, and the extent to which Peggy is worse off as a result of its failure to do so.

The first way in which Peggy has suffered a loss is that she has had to pay the Majestic Hotel £7,500, whereas she would only have had to pay the Regency £6,000. It is assumed in this discussion that the Regency has repaid any deposit that Peggy may have paid. If not, then this should be included in the loss. Subject to this, Peggy's loss appears to be £1,500. The right to claim contract damages is, however, subject to an obligation on the innocent party to mitigate the loss. Allowing the loss to increase without taking steps to limit it, or taking action that contributes to its size, is not permitted. Any loss that is attributable to a failure to mitigate will not be allowed. The principles were set out in *British Westinghouse Electric Manufacturing Co v Underground Electric Railways Co of London* (1912), in which it was stated that the claimant is under a duty to take reasonable steps to limit the losses flowing from a breach of contract. What is the relevance of this to Peggy's claim? It is possible that the Regency Hotel may wish to argue that Peggy should have taken the cheaper alternative that was available to her – that is, the offer of the King George public house to provide the reception for £4,500. If that argument was successful, then Peggy's economic loss would be reduced to nil. She could have obtained alternative provision for less than the contract price. It is important to remember, however, that the obligation is to take reasonable steps to mitigate. The question is therefore whether it would have been reasonable for Peggy to take the King George's offer. It is likely that the function room at a public house would provide less elegant sur-roundings for the reception than could be provided by a hotel. Moreover, it seems that the King George could only offer 'limited catering'. This suggests, again, that it would not be providing something equivalent to what the Regency had offered. The Majestic, on the other hand, was able to provide an 'equivalent' service. For this reason, Peggy's action in deciding to reject the offer from the King George would be likely to be regarded as reasonable. She should, therefore, be able to recover the full £1,500 additional payment that she has had to make.

The facts do not reveal any other financial losses flowing from the Regency's breach, so this seems to be the total of the damages that Peggy can claim under this head.

The other losses for which Peggy may wish to claim fall into the category of 'non-pecuniary losses' – that is, the disappointment, including that of her daughter, in having to change the venue, and her breakdown and continuing mental illness. The recovery of this type of loss in a contractual action is generally regarded as being exceptional – contracts are concerned with economic transactions, and compensation for the resulting economic losses is the limit of what should be recoverable.

Particularly in commercial contracts, the view is taken that the disappointment or distress that may result from a breach is irrecoverable – as stated in *Addis v*

Gramophone (1909). This approach has been modified, however, in some circumstances, particularly in relation to contracts involving consumers. The current position was recently reconsidered by the House of Lords in *Farley v Skinner* (2001).

In *Farley v Skinner*, the House of Lords confirmed that there were two types of situation in which non-pecuniary losses (other than those arising from consequential physical injury resulting from a breach of contract) could be recoverable. The first category is where the object of the contract, or a significant part of it, is to provide 'pleasure' or 'enjoyment' to the other party. Thus, where the contract is to provide a holiday, as in *Jarvis v Swans Tours* (1973) or *Jackson v Horizon Holidays* (1975), damages may be recoverable for the disappointment resulting from the fact that the defendant's breach of contract meant that the holiday did not match expectations. A case bearing some resemblance to the problem is the Scottish decision in *Diesen v Samson* (1971), in which damages were recovered under this head for the failure to take photographs of a wedding. In *Farley v Skinner* itself, this was extended to the failure of a surveyor to take proper steps in relation to a specific contractual obligation to investigate whether a house that the claimant was planning to buy was affected by aircraft noise.

Applying this to the problem, there seems little doubt that a contract to provide a wedding reception would come into the category of contracts to provide pleasure and enjoyment. It seems, therefore, that Peggy will be able to recover compensation for any disappointment she may have suffered as a result of the enforced change of venue. The person most affected in this way, however, seems to be Samantha. She, of course, is not a party to the contract between Peggy and the Regency. It has been recognised, however, that in certain types of case, a claimant who has made a contract designed to provide pleasure to a group of people may be able to recover compensation for the disappointment of the rest of the group. This was the view of the House of Lords in *Woodar v Wimpey* (1980), in explaining the Court of Appeal's decision in *Jackson v Horizon Holidays*, in which a father was allowed to recover damages for the disappointment suffered by the rest of the family in relation to an unsatisfactory holiday. One of the examples given in *Woodar v Wimpey* was that of a person booking a meal in a restaurant. It would seem likely that the situation of booking a wedding reception would be treated in the same way, and that the disappointment of the bride in particular should be able to be taken into account in assessing damages.

The second category of situations where non-pecuniary damages can be recovered is where some physical inconvenience causes discomfort or distress. In *Farley v Skinner*, for example, it was held that the claimant could claim compensation for the fact that his occupation of the house that he had bought was adversely affected by the noise of aircraft. It does not seem, however, that this will apply here. As was made clear in *Farley v Skinner*, there can be no recovery under this heading, even if the claimant has suffered a complete mental breakdown, if there is no physical discomfort arising directly from the breach of contract. The failure to provide the wedding reception has not involved discomfort of this kind. As regards Peggy's breakdown and mental illness, therefore, it seems that recovery for this will only be possible if it can be attached to the first category of non-pecuniary loss – that is, that it is a consequence of her unhappiness at the effect that the breach of contract has had on the wedding arrangements. In the circumstances, it seems likely that a court would look sympathetically on such an argument.

Whichever category of non-pecuniary loss is involved, this will, of course, be subject to the normal 'remoteness' rules – that is, was a loss of the type suffered within the reasonable contemplation of the parties at the time of the contract as a likely consequence of the breach (*The Heron II* (1969))? Again, it is likely that a court would find this test to be satisfied in this case. The late cancellation of wedding arrangements is very likely to cause distress to all involved.

Finally, there is the question of the amount recoverable for non-pecuniary losses. In *Ruxley Electronics v Forsyth* (1996), the plaintiff was awarded £2,500 for 'loss of amenity' when his swimming pool was built to the wrong depth. In *Farley v Skinner*, £10,000 was awarded for the problems relating to the aircraft noise. In both cases, the House of Lords, while upholding the awards, suggested that they were on the high side. In general, awards for non-pecuniary loss in contracts will be modest. Given the overall cost of the contract in this case, an award in hundreds rather than thousands of pounds would be most likely.

In conclusion, therefore, Peggy should be able to recover £1,500 for the economic loss involved in having to find an alternative venue for her daughter's wedding reception. As regards the non-pecuniary losses that they have suffered, some recovery should be possible under this heading as well, but the sum involved is likely to be small.

Think point

1 It might be pointed out here that it is strictly speaking an 'anticipatory breach', in that the Regency Hotel indicates before performance is due that it will not be able to perform its obligations. On the facts, however, this does not seem to raise any particular problems in relation to remedies. For further discussion of this type of breach, see Stone, *The Modern Law of Contract*, 7th edn, 2008, pp 558–9.

CHAPTER 13

QUASI-CONTRACT AND RESTITUTION

INTRODUCTION

The topic of quasi-contract, or, as it is more commonly known nowadays, restitution, is on the margins of contract law, and many courses will not touch on it, although it is a topic that is of increasing practical importance. By definition, the situations are ones in which there is no contract governing the relationship. This will generally be either because a contract that was made is ineffective, as a result of a mistake or illegality, or some other vitiating factor, or because the parties, while negotiating towards a contract, never in fact managed to formalise their agreement.

Both questions in this chapter raise similar issues, although the first does so in essay form, and the second by way of a problem. The issues that are likely to come up in any question relating to this area are:

- the ways in which money can be recovered, where it has been paid in pursuance of an ineffective contract; and

- the extent to which compensation can be recovered for work that has been done outside the framework of a contract (the *quantum meruit* claim).

The area is not an easy one, because the basis of the law has never been very clear, and it tends to stray across other topics, such as mistake and frustration. The fact that in some respects the law is in a process of development adds to the uncertainty. If, however, the main types of action and the basic authorities are grasped, there is no reason to shy away from answering a question on this topic. One of the reasons why this topic is often not dealt with in a contract course is that the law of 'restitution' is now emerging as a topic in its own right. This follows the pioneering work done in this area by Lord Goff and Professor Gareth Jones in their book, *The Law of Restitution*, 5th edn, 1998, and developed subsequently, in particular by Professor Peter Birks (for example, in *An Introduction to the Law of Restitution*, 1989).

Checklist

You should be familiar with the following areas:

- the definition of 'quasi-contract' and 'restitution';

- the historical development of the area;
- the situations currently governed by the two concepts;
- the recovery of money on the basis of a total failure of consideration;
- the recovery of money paid on the basis of a mistake (including the change in the position relating to mistakes of law resulting from the case of *Kleinwort Benson Ltd v Lincoln City Council* (1998)); and
- the availability of compensation on a *quantum meruit* basis, in particular, where a contract has failed to materialise.

Question 44

'It is clear that any civilised system of law is bound to provide remedies for what has been called unjust enrichment, or unjust benefit, that is, to prevent a man from retaining the money of, or some benefit derived from, another which it is against his conscience he should keep.' (Lord Wright in *Fibrosa Spolka Akcyjna v Fairbairn Lawson Combe Barbour Ltd* (1943))

How does English law attempt to provide such remedies? Does it do so satisfactorily?

Answer plan

This is a very broad essay question, which requires you to summarise the main rules relating to 'quasi-contract' or 'restitution', and to make some critical comments about them. There are two aspects that need consideration:

- actions to recover money (paid to either the defendant or a third party); and
- actions to recover compensation for some benefit conferred on the defendant (that is, a *quantum meruit* claim).

The best way to tackle this is to give a brief outline of each possible action, and then to describe some examples from the cases.

The commentary on the area is likely to raise difficulties arising from the fact that this is still a developing area of law, and one within which, as a result, there are still uncertainties about exactly how it applies and which situations it covers.

Answer

English law has been slow to develop remedies of the kind mentioned by Lord Wright. This is in part because the kinds of situations in which such remedies are necessary do not fall easily into the categories of either contract or tort, although they may have some connection with either or both. Where money has been paid under a contract that turns out to be void, for example, no action on the contract is possible, because no contract exists. Similarly, work done in prospect of an agreement that has been promised, but does not materialise, again cannot be compensated for by a contract since, by definition, no contract has ever been finalised. Moreover, in the absence of fraud or, in some circumstances, negligence, no tortious action will be possible either. Certain remedies do exist, however, and there is a growing acceptance amongst both judges and academic writers that this area is best regarded, for the purposes of analysis, as falling outside both tort and contract, and under a separate heading of 'restitution'. What are the remedies that have so far been recognised? We need to look at them under two headings: first, remedies to recover money that has been paid; and second, remedies to compensate for benefits conferred.

In respect of the recovery of money paid, one clear example of a situation in which the courts will allow recovery is where there is a contract, but there has been a total failure of consideration. This was the situation in *Fibrosa Spolka Akcyjna v Fairbairn Lawson Combe Barbour Ltd* (1943), in which the contract was frustrated. The House of Lords held that, because the plaintiffs had received no part of what they had contracted for, they were entitled to reclaim all of the money they had paid towards the contract. This approach has been applied controversially in relation to sale of goods contracts where the seller has no title to the goods. In *Rowland v Divall* (1923), the plaintiff was a car dealer who bought a car from the defendant. Neither party knew that the car had previously been stolen. The plaintiff resold the car to X from whom, after some months, the true owner reclaimed it. The plaintiff repaid the purchase price to X and sued the defendant for the price he had paid to him. Despite the fact that the car was now valued at considerably less than the plaintiff had paid, he was allowed to recover the full amount, because there had been a total failure of consideration. The essence of the sale of goods contract was the transfer of legal title to the goods, and this the defendant had failed to do. The decision, which was to some extent understandable on the basis that the plaintiff, as a dealer, was primarily interested in rights of ownership that he could resell, was applied in a different situation in *Butterworth v Kingsway Motors* (1954). In this case, the plaintiff was a private individual who had used the car for nearly a year before it was discovered that it had been sold in breach of a hire purchase agreement. The defendant, who was again innocent of the defect in title, was nevertheless compelled to repay the full purchase price to the plaintiff. The plaintiff had thus had the free use of the car for nearly a year.

Money will also be recoverable where it is paid under a mistake of fact. The mistake must be as to a fact that, if true, would have obliged the claimant to pay the money: *Aiken v Short* (1856). Contracts that are void for a common mistake of fact will come into this category. The rule will apply more generally, however, as is shown by *Norwich Union Fire Insurance Society Ltd v Price Ltd* (1934). An insurer paid out on a claim in the belief that a cargo of fruit had been damaged at sea. In fact, it had been sold because it was becoming overripe. The insurer was able to recover the payment as having been made on the basis of a mistake of fact. Of course, recovery will not be possible if the person making the payment is aware of the mistake, but it seems that the fact that they perhaps should have been aware of it is not enough. This is illustrated by *Kelly v Solari* (1841), in which an insurance company paid out on a life policy, having overlooked the fact that the final premium had not been paid. The company was allowed to recover its payment.

Although, in general, the cases on mistake of fact have involved legal obligations, it seems that this may not be necessary. In *Larner v LCC* (1949), it was held that payments made under a mistake of fact that if true would have created a 'moral' rather than a legal obligation to pay could be recovered.[1]

Until recently, it was the position that there could be no recovery in relation to money paid under a mistake of law. This has now changed as a result of the decision of the House of Lords in *Kleinwort Benson Ltd v Lincoln City Council* (1998). The House could see no reason why there should not be recovery where the recipient would otherwise be unjustly enriched. If the recipients of the money had changed their position in reliance on the payment, this might preclude recovery. On the other hand, the fact that the mistake was based on a view of the law, which appeared to be settled at the time, but which the courts later ruled was incorrect, would not prevent recovery. However, the only subsequent reported decision on the application of this new principle, *Nurdin and Peacock plc v DB Ramsden & Co Ltd* (1999), involved payments made on the basis of incorrect legal advice.

A further situation in which recovery of money may be possible is where the claimant has paid money to a third party for which the defendant is liable. In *Exall v Partridge* (1799), for example, Exall paid the arrears of rent owed by Partridge, in order to prevent Exall's carriage, which he had left on Partridge's premises, being seized by bailiffs. The money must be paid under an obligation or constraint, rather than voluntarily, for this action to succeed: *Macclesfield Corp v Great Central Railway* (1911). Moreover, the defendant must have been under a legal obligation to pay the money. In *Metropolitan Police District Receiver v Croydon Corp* (1957), a police authority had paid the wages of an injured policeman, as it was obliged to do under statute. The policeman sued and recovered damages for negligence from the defendants. These damages did not include any element for lost wages, because these had been paid by the police authority. The police authority sought to recover the amount of the wages from the defendants. It was held that it could not succeed, because the defendants had no legal liability as regards the wages of the policeman, only as regards his losses. Since he had been paid his wages, he had suffered no loss in this respect.

We must now turn to the situation in which the claimant is trying to recover not a particular sum of money paid, but compensation for some benefit conferred on the defendant. The claim will be for a *quantum meruit* payment – that is, a sum equivalent to the value of the benefit conferred. Such a claim may, of course, arise within a contract where no price has been fixed for work to be done. Generally, the defendant will be expected to pay a 'reasonable' price. A *quantum meruit* claim can have a wider scope than this, however, and has been recognised in some cases as existing independently of any contract. A good example is *Planché v Colburn* (1831). The plaintiff had agreed to write a book for the defendant. After the plaintiff had done a considerable amount of work, the defendant pulled out of the project. It was held that, independent of any contract, the plaintiff should be able to recover on a *quantum meruit* basis. There was no longer any contract in existence, and the plaintiff should not be deprived of the 'fruit of his labour'. A payment of 50 guineas was ordered.

A further situation in which such a sum may be recovered is where services have been performed under a void contract. It was noted above that money paid under such a contract is recoverable. It is, therefore, not surprising that an action for compensation for work done may also be successful. An example of this is the case of *Craven-Ellis v Canons Ltd* (1936). The plaintiff had been appointed managing director of a company under a procedure that was invalid. He sought to recover either the money due under his contract with the company, or on a *quantum meruit* basis. It was held that he could not recover under the contract, since it was void, but he was allowed to recover reasonable remuneration for the work he had done.

By analogy with this, it has also been recognised in more recent cases that work done under an anticipated contract that never actually comes into existence may be compensated in a similar way. In *British Steel Corp v Cleveland Bridge and Engineering Co* (1984), Robert Goff J held that the plaintiffs were entitled to reasonable compensation for work done, at the defendants' request, in manufacturing items that were to be used in the construction of a building.

Although there had been extensive negotiations, no contract had ever been finalised. The action succeeded as a restitutionary *quantum meruit* claim.[2] The above outline shows that in a number of areas English law has found sufficient flexibility to provide compensation so as to avoid unjust enrichment or unjust benefit. To this extent, it is fulfilling the requirement that Lord Wright laid down for 'any civilised system of law'. It cannot be said, however, that the result is wholly satisfactory. The area has developed piecemeal and, as is inevitably the case with the common law, in response to particular problems. As a result, there are gaps and inconsistencies in what it provides. The actions for recovery of money paid, for example, are much better developed than those for compensation for work done. There is also only a very slow development of general principles to provide a framework for future development. Only when this has been achieved will it be possible to say that the law in this area is 'satisfactory'.

Think points

1 Cheshire, Fifoot and Furmston suggested that, as a result of this, the test is not whether there would have been a legal obligation to pay, but rather whether the mistake was 'sufficiently serious': *Law of Contract*, 14th edn, 2001, p 727; cf Stone, *The Modern Law of Contract*, 7th edn, 2008, p 616.

2 The decision in *Trentham v Archital Luxfer* (1993), relaxing the courts' approach to finding a contract where performance has been completed, means that situations of this kind are now more likely to be dealt with in contract, as opposed to restitution.

Question 45

In January 2008, Exmouth University acquired a large site, containing a derelict factory, on which it proposed to build a new hall of residence. In connection with this project, it took the following steps.

(a) It engaged a firm of architects, Shark & Co, to draw up plans for the new building. The contract price was to be £12,000, with a deposit of 7.5 per cent payable immediately. Dim, the University's finance officer, incorrectly calculated the deposit as £1,800 instead of £900 and paid the larger amount to Shark.

(b) It offered the job of clearing the site to tender. The lowest tender (£28,000) was received from Crush & Co, and the University decided to contract with it. Negotiations on the details of the contract were slow, but in the meantime the University allowed Crush onto the site to start work.

(c) It bought 20,000 used bricks from Facers Ltd, at a price of £20,000. Several hundred of the bricks were used immediately to repair buildings on the University's main site. The rest were to be used for the warden's accommodation at the new hall.

In June 2008, Shark, whose business was in difficulties, terminated its contract with the University, having produced only an outline sketch of the hall. Crush's work was proceeding so slowly (although 25 per cent of the site had been cleared) that the University told it to leave the site, as it was going to offer the clearance contract to another firm. Finally, the bricks turned out to have been stolen (although Facers was ignorant of this) and were reclaimed by the true owner. The market price of such bricks is now 80 p per brick.

Discuss.

Answer plan

There are three main elements to this rather complicated problem, relating to the three different contracts. All raise issues of quasi-contract, or restitution. The matters for consideration are:

- can the University recover the deposit paid to Shark on the basis of a total failure of consideration (as in *Fibrosa Spolka Akcyjna v Fairbairn Lawson Combe Barbour Ltd* (1943))? If not, can it recover the £900 overpayment, as money paid under a mistake of fact (*Kelly v Solari* (1841))?

- can Crush recover any compensation for the work it has done in clearing the site, on a *quantum meruit* basis (*British Steel Corp v Cleveland Bridge and Engineering Co Ltd* (1984))?

- can the University recover the price of the bricks from Facers, on the basis that as it had no title to sell, there was a total failure of consideration (*Rowland v Divall* (1923))?

Answer

The problems with the three arrangements or contracts that the University has entered into in connection with its new hall of residence all raise issues relating to the area of quasi-contract, or restitution.

Looking first at the contract with Shark, since its business is in difficulties, suing for damages for breach of contract may well not be worthwhile. Instead, the University may wish simply to try to recover the money that it has paid – that is, the £1,800. It is well established in English law that, in appropriate circumstances, money paid towards a contract that is terminated may be recovered. In *Fibrosa Spolka Akcyjna v Fairbairn Lawson Combe Barbour Ltd* (1943), for example, a contract for the manufacture of machinery was frustrated by the outbreak of war. The plaintiffs were allowed to recover all of the money that they had paid, because it was held that they had received nothing of what they had contracted for, and therefore there had been a total failure of consideration. If, however, there has been some performance that has conferred a benefit on the other side, then the action will fail.

In *Whincup v Hughes* (1871), the fact that one year of a six-year apprenticeship contract had been served before the master died prevented the recovery of a premium paid by the apprentice. In the problem, then, the difficulty for the University is that, although the full drawings required have not been produced, Shark has provided an outline sketch. It would seem likely that, although this may not be of much value to the University, it is sufficient to prevent the action for recovery on the basis of a total failure of consideration being successful.

If this is the case, the University may alternatively wish to recover the overpayment of £900 that resulted from the miscalculation of the finance officer. Again, it is well established that a payment made on the basis of a mistake of fact is recoverable. In *Cooper v Phibbs* (1867), for example, the plaintiff had paid money in relation to the rent of property that in fact already belonged to him. He was allowed to recover. In this case, there is clearly a mistake of fact as to the amount of money due. The only query is whether the University is entitled to rely on this, since it results from the mistake of one of its officers. The answer would seem to be 'yes'. In *Kelly v Solari* (1841), the careless oversight by an insurance company of the fact that an instalment of the premium had not been paid was nevertheless held to allow the company to recover the money that it had paid out on the policy. The carelessness of the finance officer in miscalculating the amount due would therefore seem to be irrelevant. The University should be able to recover its £900.

The next agreement to consider is that with Crush. The problem here is that, although the two parties are negotiating towards an agreement, no contract has ever been made. Nevertheless, Crush has done 25 per cent of the work required, and may well feel that it should receive some compensation, such as 25 per cent of the £28,000 that it tendered. Crush's claim would be a quasi-contractual one for a *quantum meruit* payment. The courts have insisted that 'an agreement to agree' does not give rise to legal obligations: *Courtney & Fairbain v Tolaini Bros (Hotels) Ltd* (1975). A *quantum meruit* claim has, however, been recognised as possible where services have either been requested or have been freely accepted by the other party, as in *William Lacey (Hounslow) Ltd v Davis* (1957). In that case, the plaintiffs had prepared plans and estimates on the assumption that they would receive a building contract. This work went beyond what would normally be expected, and was done at the defendant's request. The plaintiffs were allowed to recover a reasonable sum for the work done. Similarly, in *British Steel Corp v Cleveland Bridge and Engineering Co Ltd* (1984), the plaintiffs were allowed to recover on a *quantum meruit* basis for the manufacture and delivery of a number of steel nodes, required for the construction contract by the defendants. No contract was ever finalised, and moreover the defendants claimed that there were problems with the time and order of delivery of the nodes. The plaintiffs were, however, allowed to recover a reasonable sum for the work they had done.[1] Can Crush similarly claim for the work it has done in clearing the site? For Crush to succeed, the work will have had to be of some benefit to the University, and either done at the University's request or have been freely accepted by it. Despite the fact that the work has been done very slowly, 25 per cent of the work has been done. It will now presumably cost the University less to have the work completed.[2] We are also told that the University 'allowed Crush onto the site to start work'. This indicates at least free acceptance of what was being done, if not that the work was done at the University's request. It seems, then, that Crush will be able to claim some compensation. What it receives need not have any necessary connection to the contract price, but 25 per cent of £28,000 (that is, £7,000) is presumably in practice going to be the most likely sum to be awarded.

The third problem arises with the contract for the bricks. They turn out to be stolen, and are reclaimed by the true owner. It is well established in the cases on the sale of goods to which the seller has no title that the buyer can generally claim repayment of the purchase price, on the basis that there has been a total failure of consideration. This was held to be the case in *Rowland v Divall* (1923), and was followed in *Butterworth v Kingsway Motors* (1954). In both cases, the contracts concerned cars that were sold between two innocent parties who were in ignorance of the fact that earlier the car had been stolen, or sold in breach of a hire purchase agreement. The eventual buyer was allowed to recover the full purchase price even though there was a considerable lapse of time between the contract and the discovery of the defect in title. On this basis, it would seem that although Facers sold the bricks to the University in good faith, because it had no title to them, it would be liable to repay the full £20,000. The University would then apparently be able to buy a similar load of bricks for £16,000, and thus end up £4,000 better off. There is a problem, however, in that some of the bricks have already been used to repair buildings on the main site. One of the conditions for using the *Rowland v Divall* approach is that the buyer should be in a position to return the goods. If, by his actions, the buyer has made it impossible for them to be returned, then this right of action will be lost. In this case, it would seem unlikely that the bricks already used in the repairs could be returned. If that is so, then the University would not be able to succeed in its claim to recover the £20,000. What is its position if it is sued in conversion by the true owner of the bricks? It will have to return those bricks that it can, and pay compensation for having converted the rest (or simply compensate the owner for the conversion of the full 20,000). The University will, however, be able to recover a contribution from Facers under the **Civil Liability (Contribution) Act 1978**.

To summarise the position, then, the most likely outcomes of the three situations would be: (a) that the University would be able to recover simply the £900 overpayment from Shark; (b) that Crush would be able to recover on a *quantum meruit* basis for the work that it has done in clearing the site; and (c) that the University will be liable to the true owner of the bricks, but will be able to recover a contribution towards any compensation paid from Facers. The University is unlikely, however, to be able to reclaim the full purchase price of the bricks from Facers.

Think points

1 The two parties may not be in an equal position as regards a restitutionary claim of this kind, as is shown by the fact that in this case the defendant's counterclaim in relation to the late delivery and the fact that the nodes were delivered in the wrong order was not successful. Is this fair?

2 It might be worth considering here what the effect on Crush's claim would be if the University could not get the rest of the work done without paying out at least another £28,000. Would Crush's work then be of any benefit to it? To put it another way, would there be any 'unjust enrichment' at Crush's expense?

CHAPTER 14

AGENCY

▌INTRODUCTION

A full-blown consideration of the topic of agency is more properly the concern of a commercial law course, rather than one on the general law of contract. It is not uncommon, however, to find some treatment of agency in contract law. There are probably two reasons for this. One is that the concept is an important exception to the doctrine of privity. It will often be dealt with in this context. Another reason is that the basic concepts of agency are used in other areas of the law (company law is a good example) and so some basic understanding of them is desirable. Even within the mainstream of contract, cases such as *The Eurymedon* (1975), which involve the use of agency concepts, such as ratification, are difficult to understand properly without some grasp of the essence of agency itself.

The main issues dealt with in two of the questions in this chapter (that is, Questions 46 and 48) relate to the decision of when a principal will be liable, or be able to sue, on a contract made by the agent without authority. The concepts that need to be understood are: the different types of authority, and in particular ostensible authority (also commonly known as 'apparent authority'); usual or customary authority may also be important in some situations; and ratification – what it means, when it can be used and what its effects are. In both areas, the effect of **s 36C** of the **Companies Act 1985** on the rights and liabilities of promoters of as yet unincorporated companies needs to be noted. Question 47 concentrates on the rather different issue of an agent's rights and liabilities vis-à-vis the third party. The concept of the undisclosed principal is important here. The roles of the collateral contract and the implied warranty of authority also need to be noted.

Checklist

You should be familiar with the following areas:

- the general concept of agency, and its relationship to the doctrine of privity;
- the concepts of implied, usual and apparent authority;
- the concept of the 'undisclosed principal';

- ratification – its availability and effects;
- the duties of the agent as regards the principal;
- the rights and obligations between agent and third party; and
- the implied warranty of authority.

Question 46

Pristine Premises plc provides a floor-cleaning service for business premises. It employs Adam as its agent in the south-west of England. Adam has authority to sign contracts on behalf of Pristine Premises plc, but is under instructions not to commit Pristine Premises plc to more than three regular contracts at one time in any town that involve cleaning over weekends, because of the difficulty in finding staff to work at these times. Sally owns a small restaurant in Exeter that deals mainly with the lunchtime office trade, and is not open at weekends. She wants the carpets cleaned once a month. Adam tells her that Pristine Premises plc already has three weekend contracts in Exeter, but that he will 'see what can be done'. Sally tells him that he can have a free meal in the restaurant if Pristine Premises plc will take the contract. Without having consulted Pristine Premises plc, Adam telephones Sally a week later and says that the contract has been approved. When he takes the contract into Sally's restaurant for her to sign it, she presents him with a case of expensive wine, as a 'thank you' for his efforts.

Advise Pristine Premises plc as to:

(a) whether it is bound by the contract with Sally, or, if not, whether it can take it over;

(b) what action it can take against Adam.

Answer plan

There are two aspects to this question.

Part (a) is concerned with authority, and when an agent's acts will bind the principal. It also asks you to discuss the power of the principal to ratify unauthorised contracts.

Part (b) is concerned with obligations of an agent, and the remedies of the principal for breach of such obligations.

As regards part (a), the suggested order of treatment is as follows.

- Authority:
  - state the principles relating to an agent's actual and apparent authority;
  - state the requirements for apparent authority, as set out in *Rama Corp and Proved Tin and General Investments* (1952);
  - deal with the issue that the representation of authority must come from the principal (*Armagas Ltd v Mundogas Ltd* (1986)), and the way in which this has been interpreted in *First Energy (UK) Ltd v Hungarian International Bank Ltd* (1993); and
  - apply the above to the facts of the problem.
- Ratification:
  - state the requirements for ratification of a contract;
  - apply the above to the facts of the problem.

As regards part (b), the suggested order of treatment is:

- state the obligations of an agent towards the principal, including –
  - the duty to obey instructions;
  - the fiduciary duties (such as not to take bribes, or make a secret profit);
- consider the remedies available to the principal for a breach of duty;
- apply the above to the facts of the problem.

Answer

Adam is the agent of Pristine Premises Plc, and as such has certain powers and responsibilities. Part (a) of this question is primarily concerned with his power to bind his principal to a contract that has not been specifically authorised. Part (b) deals with the agent's responsibilities, and the principal's remedies when these are not met.

(a) There are two main types of authority that an agent may have – actual and apparent. Actual authority is determined by the express and implied powers given to the agent under his or her agreement with the principal. Here, Adam has express authority to make contracts for Pristine Premises, subject to the limitation on the number of weekend contracts in any one town. This is Adam's 'actual authority' and, provided that he keeps within it, Pristine Premises will be bound to any transaction that Adam makes on its behalf.

Apparent authority is different, in that it is a concept designed to protect third parties, rather than to deal with the relationship between principal and agent. Apparent authority arises when an agent has no actual authority to make a particular transaction, but it reasonably appears to the third party that the agent does have such authority. The requirements for apparent authority to arise were set out in *Rama Corp Ltd v Proved Tin and General Investments* (1952). They consist of: (i) a representation of authority; (ii) reliance on the representation by the third party; and (iii) an alteration of position by the third party as a result of such reliance.

These requirements are fairly straightforward, but there has been some case law dealing with the first element – the need for a representation of authority. The question that has arisen is whether the representation of authority has to come from the principal, or whether it can come from the agent. The restatement of the requirements for apparent authority by Diplock LJ in *Freeman & Lockyer v Buckhurst Properties (Mangal) Ltd* (1964) indicated that the statement must come from the principal, rather than the agent, and this was confirmed by the House of Lords in *Armagas Ltd v Mundogas Ltd* (1986). If this line were to be taken as between Adam and Pristine Premises, it would appear that Pristine Premises should be able to escape from the agreement, because the representation of Adam's authority comes from Adam himself, when he telephones Sally to say that the contract has been approved. Cases subsequent to *Armagas v Mundogas* have, however, made the position less clear-cut. For example, in *First Energy (UK) Ltd v Hungarian International Bank Ltd* (1993), the manager of a branch office of the principal told the third party that a credit facility had been granted. The third party was aware that granting such a facility was beyond the manager's authority. It was held by the Court of Appeal, however, that the manager had, by virtue of his position in the principal bank, apparent authority to communicate decisions of the head office. In other words, although he had no authority (actual or apparent) to grant a credit facility, he did have apparent authority to state that head office had approved the grant of such a facility. The bank was therefore bound by the contract that the manager made with the third party.

Applying this to the problem, Sally's argument will be that Adam had apparent authority to communicate a decision by Pristine Premises to approve the contract, and that therefore it is bound by the transaction. It is important to remember, however, that the decision in the *First Energy* case depended on the agent's status as a branch manager. By putting him in the position of branch manager, the principal was 'representing' that he had authority to communicate head office decisions. In Adam's case, he is simply employed as an agent to make particular contracts, and has no other status in Pristine Premises. On this basis, it may well be that the approach taken in *Armagas v Mundogas* should be applied here. Adam made a representation as to his authority, but this should not be attributable to Pristine Premises. On this basis, Sally will not be able to enforce the contract against Pristine Premises, and will be left to take action against Adam for any losses, on the basis of a breach of the implied warranty of authority.

If Pristine Premises is not bound by the contract with Sally, can it nevertheless take it over? This depends on the rules relating to ratification. These are, first, that the agent must have been purporting to act for a principal. Thus, if the agent appears to be acting on his or her own behalf, there is no scope for later ratification: *Keighley Maxted & Co v Durant* (1901).

Second, the principal must have been in existence at the time of the alleged contract. This requirement means that, for example, a contract made on behalf of an unincorporated company cannot be ratified by that company when it subsequently comes into existence: *Kelner v Baxter* (1866). Thirdly, the principal must have capacity, both at the time of the alleged contract, and at the time of ratification.

None of these requirements seem to cause any problems here, so if Pristine Premises wishes to take over the contract with Sally it can do so, by ratifying the agreement. This will be effective even if Sally has by that time decided that she does not want to go ahead, since ratification is retrospective, meaning that the contract is deemed to have been binding from the moment at which Adam purported to enter into it: *Bolton Partners v Lambert* (1998).

(b) This is concerned with the obligations of an agent towards his or her principal. The main obligations of an agent are:

(i) to obey instructions – see, for example, *Fraser v BN Furman (Productions) Ltd* (1967);

(ii) to act with due care and skill;

(iii) fiduciary duties, including the duty to avoid a conflict of interest, the duty not to make a secret profit, and the duty not to take a bribe – see, for example, *Bristol and West Building Society v Mothew* (1996).

In this problem there does not seem to be an issue with (ii) – Adam's competence is not in issue. There are, however, potential breaches of (i) and (iii).

Clearly Adam was under instructions not to make more than three contracts in one town involving weekend work. He has purported to do so in relation to the contract with Sally, and so has not followed his instructions. The remedies for Pristine Premises are similar to those for any breach of contract. It can terminate the agency agreement, and seek damages for any losses caused by the breach of instructions. In this case, if Pristine Premises is held to the contract with Sally, on the basis of apparent authority (as discussed above), it could potentially recover from Adam the expense of finding additional staff to work weekends, over and above the three contracts already in existence.

As regards fiduciary duties, the ones that are particularly relevant here are the duty to avoid conflicts of interest and the duty not to take bribes. Sally has offered Adam a free meal if he arranges the contract, and has also given him an expensive case of wine. The first of these gives rise to a potential conflict of interest – Adam may be motivated by the prospect of a free meal to act in a way that conflicts with the interests of Pristine Premises (cf *Armstrong v Jackson* (1917), in which a stockbroker sold his own shares to a client). The gift of the case of wine may be a bribe. The definition of a bribe is to be found in *Industries and General Mortgage Co v Lewis* (1949) and includes any payment made to the agent by a third party, with knowledge of the agency, and which is not disclosed by the third party to the principal. There is no need to show any fraudulent intention.

On this basis both the offer of the free meal and the gift of the wine could constitute a bribe. If so, this entitles the principal to dismiss the agent, and to recover the bribe from the agent, or from the third party, if not yet paid: *Mahesan v Malaysia Government Officers' Co-operative Housing Society Ltd* (1979). Thus in this case, Pristine Premises could dismiss Adam and recover the value of the meal that has been offered, and the case of wine. Alternatively it can sue Adam and Sally in tort for any losses it has suffered as a result of the breach of duty by Adam. On the facts, there are no clear losses, so recovery of the value of the bribes would seem to be the better course of action.

Question 47

To what extent is it true to say that once an agent has brought his principal and a third party into a contractual relationship the agent drops out, and has no rights or liabilities as against the third party?

Answer plan

This question requires you to know and explain the exceptions to the general rule that an agent is neither liable under, nor entitled to enforce, a contract that he makes on behalf of his principal. It goes a little further than that, however, in that there are some actions that may be taken by the third party against the agent which are not strictly speaking based on the contract. Examples are liability on a collateral contract, or liability for breach of the implied warranty of authority. The issues to be discussed are:

- intention to contract personally;
- custom;
- undisclosed principal;
- principal non-existent;
- collateral contract; and
- implied warranty of authority.

It may also be useful to say a little about the power of the third party to choose whom to sue in a situation in which both principal and agent may be potentially liable.

Answer

There is no doubt that it is true to say that in the normal course of events, once the principal and third party have made a binding contract, the agent has no further rights or liabilities against the third party. The agent may of course have outstanding claims on, or obligations towards, the principal, but that is a separate issue, arising from their continuing relationship rather than the specific contract that has resulted from the agent's activities. It is also true, however, that in certain situations the agent will have rights and liabilities either alongside, or in place of, the principal, and it is to those exceptions that we now turn. Some of them relate to rights and liabilities on the contract itself; some are independent of the contract.

The first exception that must be considered is where the parties themselves intend that the agent should have personal rights or liabilities. At one time, much stress seemed to be placed on the exact form in which the contract was signed, for example, to sign 'as solicitors' left the agent liable, whereas to sign 'on behalf of' or '*per pro*' was taken to indicate an intention that the agent should not be liable. The modern approach, set out by Brandon J in *The Swan* (1968), suggests that it is a question of looking carefully at the contract and the surrounding circumstances to try to determine the intention of the parties.[1] *The Swan* involved a one-man company, JD Rodger Ltd, which had hired a boat belonging to JD Rodger himself, who was a director of the company. The company gave instructions, through JD Rodger, for repairs to be carried out. It was held that, in all of the circumstances, although the order for the work had been signed simply as 'Director' (which carried no implication of personal liability), JD Rodger, the agent, was personally liable. It was natural for the ship repairers to assume that the shipowner would accept personal liability.

It is also clear that if there is a custom or trade usage that agents are personally liable or entitled, the courts will give effect to it, provided that it is consistent with the express terms of the contract and the surrounding circumstances. Where the principal is undisclosed, then it is only fair that the third party, who thinks that the agent is the other party, should be able to take action against the agent. Once this is established, it must also be fair to allow the reciprocal right to the agent.

There may also be rights and liabilities where there is in fact no principal standing behind the agent. This might occur in two ways. It may be that the agent is in fact the principal and is simply pretending to act as an agent. Second, the principal may not be in existence at the time the contract is made.

If the agent is simply pretending to be acting for a principal (real or imaginary), while really acting on his own behalf, then there is no doubt that he will be liable on the contract. He will also be able to enforce the contract, provided that he gives due notice of the fact that he was acting on his own behalf, and the contract is not one in which the personal characteristics of the other party are important, as they would be, for example, in an employment contract or an underwriting contract: *Collins v Associated Greyhound Racecourses Ltd* (1930).[2]

More difficulty can arise where the principal was not in existence at the time of the contract. This can happen in relation to contracts made on behalf of a company that has yet to be incorporated. The common law approach was demonstrated by *Kelner v Baxter* (1866), in which it was held that the promoters were personally liable for the contract. This has now been given statutory force by **s 36C(1)** of the **Companies Act 1985**. The terms of the section deal only with liability, rather than ability to enforce. At common law, the only authority in this area was *Newborne v Sensolid* (1954), in which the decision against allowing the agent to enforce turned on a very pedantic argument about the precise form of the signature on the contract. This kind of technical argument has been disapproved of in later cases, and in particular by the Court of Appeal in *Phonogram v Lane* (1982). The balance of opinion seems to be that, following the statutory intervention noted above, the agent should be able to sue as well as being liable, where a contract is made on behalf of a company not yet incorporated. That was also the view taken by the majority of the Court of Appeal in *Braymist Ltd v Wise Finance Co Ltd* (2002), although with the limitation that the third party may have a right to escape from the contract if the identity of the other contracting party is important.

The situations we have looked at so far have involved the agent being liable on the contract itself. There are two situations, however, in which the agent may have a separate type of liability to the third party. The first is where there is a collateral contract between the agent and the third party. The kind of situation in which this could arise is exemplified by the case of *Andrews v Hopkinson* (1957). The plaintiff wanted to acquire a car on hire purchase. The dealer said: 'It's a good little bus. I would stake my life on it.' The plaintiff entered into a hire purchase contract with a finance company for the car, arranged through the dealer. When the car turned out to be defective, it was held that the plaintiff, although at first sight having no contractual remedy against the dealer, could in fact sue him on the basis of a collateral contract. At the time, the dealer was held not to be the agent of the finance company, but that has now been changed by **s 56** of the **Consumer Credit Act 1974**. The case illustrates how a statement made by an agent that encouraged the third party to enter into the contract could make the agent liable for breach of a collateral contract.

The final way in which the agent may be liable to the third party is for breach of the implied warranty of authority. This will occur where the agent has held himself out as having authority from the principal, when in fact he does not. Of course, in some circumstances, the principal may nevertheless be liable for the contract on the basis of usual or ostensible authority. If the principal is not liable, however, the agent will be liable for breach of this implied warranty. The remedies that the third party will be able to recover, however, are limited to what could in practice have been recovered from the principal. Thus, if the principal is insolvent, it may not be worth suing the agent for breach of the implied warranty. The existence of the warranty does not depend on the agent's awareness of the lack of authority. This was established in *Collen v Wright* (1857) and taken to its logical extreme in *Yonge v Toynbee* (1910). In the latter case, the warranty was held to operate against a solicitor who had continued to act for a client who, unknown to the solicitor, had become mentally incapacitated (which had the automatic effect of terminating the solicitor's authority). The fact that the solicitor had acted in good faith throughout was regarded as irrelevant.

A final issue that may need consideration is the position in which the third party has the possibility of suing either the agent or the principal. Judgment cannot, of course, be enforced against both, but suppose that judgment has been obtained against the principal, who turns out to be unable to pay. Can the third party then sue the agent in respect of the same loss? Or does he have to make a choice at an earlier stage? The rules are not very clear. It used to be the case that once judgment was obtained against either principal or agent, that precluded any action against the other. That was changed, however, by the **Civil Liability (Contribution) Act 1978**, so that there is no longer any automatic effect of this kind. In all situations now, the test is whether the third party has 'elected' to sue one party. If so, this will bar any action against the other. The problem is in deciding what amounts to an 'election'. In *Clarkson Booker Ltd v Andjel* (1964), it was held that what was required was a 'truly unequivocal act'. It might have been thought that the institution of proceedings was such an act, but the Court of Appeal thought that this was only prima facie so. The election to be binding must be made with knowledge of all of the relevant facts. In the case before them, the third party had issued a writ against the principal, but had subsequently discovered that the principal was insolvent. It was held that because they were not in possession of the full facts, the issue of the writ against the principal was not a binding election. Proceedings could be started against the agent. The question of the precise requirements for an election remains unclear.

As we have seen, there is a variety of ways in which the agent may have rights against and liabilities towards a third party. Most of the rules seem to operate in a reasonably satisfactory way. Some criticism might be made, however, of the rather strict approach to the implied warranty of authority. Moreover, as has just been pointed out, the rules relating to 'election' are in considerable need of clarification.

Think points

1 Is the test objective or subjective? As in most other areas of contract law, it is objective – that is, the question is not what the two individuals actually intended, but what 'two reasonable businessmen making a contract of that nature, in those terms, and in those surrounding circumstances, must be taken to have intended' (Brandon J in *The Swan* (1968)).

2 In this case, the problem was that an undisclosed principal wanted to take over the contract, but is there any reason why it should not also apply where the agent is wanting to step into the shoes of the supposed principal?

Question 48

Sasha has decided to start a new business selling high-quality dresses by mail order. She has asked her friend, Kristen, who is a designer, to assist her. Sasha goes to Venture Finance Ltd to seek funding for her project. She makes an appointment to see Colin, Venture Finance's regional manager. She has approached Colin in the past for support for other business ideas, and knows that he can approve loans of up to £60,000 without approval from his superiors. Sasha visits Colin with Kristen. They initially ask for £60,000, but realise, in working through the project with Colin, that more capital is needed. Sasha eventually applies for £80,000. Three weeks later, Sasha receives a letter from Colin, in which he says that he can confirm that the loan will be available. A copy of this letter is sent by Colin to Kristen. As a result, Kristen sells £5,000 worth of shares that she has promised Sasha she will contribute to the business. Sasha and Kristen use this money to buy equipment for the business.

Two weeks later, however, Sasha receives a letter from the Head Office of Venture Finance telling her that Colin had not sought the proper approval for her loan, and that the money will not be paid.

Advise Sasha and Kristen.

Answer plan

The matters to be discussed in answering this problem are:

- usual authority – that is, can Sasha rely on Colin's 'usual authority' as a regional manager to enforce the loan agreement against Venture Finance?
- ostensible authority – that is, what was Colin's ostensible authority as regards the loan of £80,000?
- if the agreement cannot be enforced against Venture Finance, what remedies might Sasha and Kristen have against Colin himself, for example, for misstatement, or under the implied warranty of authority?

Relevant cases include:

- on ostensible authority – *Freeman & Lockyer v Buckhurst Properties (Mangal) Ltd* (1964); *Armagas v Mundogas* (1986); and *First Energy (UK) Ltd v Hungarian International Bank Ltd* (1993);

- on the implied warranty of authority – *Collen v Wright* (1857); and *Penn v Bristol and West Building Society* (1997).

Answer

This question is concerned with the extent to which agents who act beyond their actual authority can still bind their principals. It also raises the issue of the remedies available against the agent for those who have acted on a false representation of authority.

Sasha and Kristen presumably wish to continue to set up and run their new business. Ideally, therefore, they will wish to argue that Venture Finance is bound by the offer of the loan made by Colin in his letter to Sasha. If this is not possible, however, they will then wish to explore remedies against Colin personally. Colin did not have authority to approve loans of over £60,000, and so has clearly acted in excess of his actual authority. Can Sasha argue that Venture Finance is nevertheless caught by Colin's 'usual' or 'ostensible' authority?

'Usual' authority arises where the principal puts the agent in a position to which it can be said that certain authority attaches. A solicitor, for example, can be said to have usual authority to compromise a claim, as in, for example, *Waugh v Clifford* (1982). Is it possible to argue that Colin, as 'regional manager', would be taken to have usual authority to approve the loan to Sasha? There are two difficulties with this. First, it is by no means clear that it would be possible, as a matter of fact, to establish what the 'usual' authority of a regional manager of a finance company would be. It is, in any case, unlikely that it would include authority to make loans without some limit on their value. Second, and even more importantly in these circumstances, it is clear that Sasha is aware of the limits on Colin's actual authority, as a result of her previous dealings with him. It would therefore be very difficult for her to argue that she was relying on his 'usual' authority when he wrote to her confirming that the loan was approved.

What about the possibility of 'ostensible' authority? The requirements for this were laid down in *Freeman & Lockyer v Buckhurst Park Properties (Mangal) Ltd* (1964). There must be a representation (by words or conduct) from the principal to the third party, which is relied on by the third party and which leads to an alteration of position by the third party. There is no doubt here that Sasha has assumed that Colin had authority, and changed her position by entering into the agreement for the loan. The more difficult question is whether the assumption was created by any representation from Venture Finance to Sasha. There was clearly an implied representation of authority in the letter from Colin to Sasha. Is this enough to bind Venture Finance? The difficulty with such an argument is that the representation of authority must normally come from the principal (that is, Venture Finance) rather than the agent (that is, Colin). This was emphasised by the House of Lords in *Armagas v Mundogas* (1986). In this case, a vice president of a company had indicated that he had authority to agree a deal for the sale and charter back of a ship. His plan was to make a secret profit out of the transactions. When his deceit came to light, the third party argued that the shipowners were bound by the vice president's ostensible authority. The House of Lords disagreed, holding that there was no representation of authority from the principal as opposed to the agent, and that therefore ostensible authority could not arise.

Applying this approach to the facts of our problem would suggest that Sasha cannot rely on Colin's ostensible authority, since the only representation was contained in a letter from Colin himself. The subsequent decision of the Court of Appeal in *First Energy (UK) Ltd v Hungarian International Bank Ltd* (1993) may, however, lead to a different answer. In this case, a branch manager of a bank had, in contravention of limitations on his actual authority, agreed arrangements with a third party for the provision of credit facilities to customers of the third party's business. The third party knew that the manager had no personal authority to enter into such arrangements on behalf of his principal, but assumed, from a letter written by the manager, that the appropriate approvals had been obtained.

Although this appeared to amount to a representation by the agent, and therefore to fall foul of the decision in *Armagas v Mundogas*, the Court of Appeal felt able to distinguish the earlier case. It held that an agent who does not have ostensible authority to enter into a particular transaction may nevertheless have ostensible authority to communicate to a third party that such a transaction has been approved. Part of the reason for this was a feeling that it would be unreasonable to expect a third party to have to check in such situations whether the board, or whatever body within the principal company was appropriate, had in fact given approval to the transaction. If this approach were to be applied here, it would be of assistance to Sasha. The argument would be that it would have been unreasonable for her to have had to check that Colin had in fact sought the approval of his superiors as required. She ought, therefore, to be able to rely on his ostensible authority, as indicated in his letter, and enforce the loan agreement against Venture Finance.

What, on the other hand, is Sasha's position if the *First Energy* approach is not adopted by the court here, and it is held that there was no ostensible authority for Colin to agree to the loan? Although the loan cannot then be enforced, Sasha will clearly be looking to recover compensation from Colin himself. There are two ways in which this might be possible. First, there is the possibility of an action in tort for deceit, or negligent misstatement under the *Hedley Byrne v Heller* (1964) principle, as modified in *Caparo v Dickman* (1990).[1] If Colin is found to have made a statement as to the fact that the transaction had been authorised, which he knew was false or which he made without proper care, this could give rise to an action for damages.

Second, Sasha may seek to rely on the 'implied warranty of authority' that is given by all agents when they purport to contract on behalf of a principal (as in, for example, *Collen v Wright* (1857)). This might enable her to recover all of the losses that she has suffered as a result of the fact that Colin was acting without authority. It is possible to obtain either expectation or reliance damages under this action. It is available even if the representation of authority is innocent, or completely inadvertent. Thus, in *Yonge v Toynbee* (1910), it applied where the principal had become a certified lunatic, thus ending any authority, even though the agent was quite unaware that this had happened. It is therefore quite a powerful remedy, which Sasha may well be able to use.

What about Kristen? She has sold her shares in reliance on Colin's letter, and used the money to buy equipment. This may well have resulted in some loss to her (if, for example, the shares have subsequently increased in value). It would seem that she could bring an action in deceit (assuming that Colin's misstatement was deliberate or reckless), since it is clear that Colin's misrepresentation was made to her and she acted on it. Similarly, an action for negligent misstatement would also be possible, provided that Kristen could be said to be owed a duty of care by Colin, under the principles of *Caparo v Dickman*. This would not seem to be too difficult on the facts. Colin's letter was copied to Kristen and she was, therefore, within the group whom Colin could have expected to rely on the statements contained in it. Provided that Kristen's action in selling her shares could be said to be reasonably foreseeable, she will be able to claim for damages for her losses consequent upon this.

Could Kristen also claim under the breach of the implied warranty of authority? It might be thought that this would not be applicable, since Kristen was not in the end someone whom Colin was purporting to bring into a contractual relationship with his principal. The decision in *Penn v Bristol and West Building Society* (1997), however, suggests that this may not be an obstacle. In this case, a solicitor agent's innocent misrepresentation of authority to a building society was held to give rise to liability for breach of the implied warranty, even though the building society's loss resulted not from attempting to contract with the solicitor's principal, but from lending money to someone who was entering into such a contract. It was held to be sufficient that the representation of authority had been made to the building society and that it had acted on it to its detriment. Applying that to the situation in the problem, the representation of authority was clearly made to Kristen, and she has acted on it to her detriment by selling her shares. On this basis, Kristen, like Sasha, could seek damages for breach of the implied warranty of authority from Colin.

The possibilities for Sasha and Kristen, therefore, look good. Sasha may well be able to rely on Colin's ostensible authority, and so enforce the loan agreement with Venture Finance. If, however, this is not possible, she will be able to recover compensation from Colin either in tort or for breach of the implied warranty of authority. Kristen will not be able to enforce the loan but, if Colin has acted without authority, she will have the same possibilities of action against him as are available to Sasha.

Think point

1 Why would an action under the **Misrepresentation Act** 1967 not be possible here? The remedies under the Act only apply as between the parties to a contract, and there is no contract between Sasha and Colin.

CHAPTER 15

SALE OF GOODS

▌INTRODUCTION

As with agency, the full consideration of the topic of sale of goods belongs more properly in a commercial law (or perhaps a consumer law) course. We have already seen, however, that it is difficult to escape the **Sale of Goods Act** 1979, and aspects of it have already been touched on in the questions on exemption clauses (Question 23).

Within a contract course, the most likely topic to be discussed is liability under the implied terms in **ss 12–15**. The **Sale of Goods Act** 1979 is regularly used as an example of statutorily implied terms, and this discussion may well lead into a general consideration of the content of those terms. The terms concerning title (**s 12**) and sale by sample (**s 15**) will be considered less frequently than the terms relating to quality. If sale of goods is part of your contract course, you are likely to need to have a good understanding of:

- **s 13** (compliance with description);
- **s 14(2)** (satisfactory quality); and
- **s 14(3)** (fitness for a particular purpose).

It is important to understand the relationship between these three sections, and to remember that **s 13** is the only one that applies to sales which are not in the course of a business. In particular, it is important to remember that although 'fitness for purpose' is referred to by **s 14(2B)** as one of the factors that is relevant in deciding whether goods are of 'satisfactory quality', this is quite distinct from the 'fitness for a particular purpose' covered by **s 14(3)**. There is considerable case law on **ss 13** and **14(3)** which needs to be understood; the case law on **s 14(2)** is less helpful because it is all concerned with the concept of 'merchantable' quality that was used prior to 1994, when it was replaced with 'satisfactory' quality, with an amended definition. Some knowledge of the pre-1994 cases will nevertheless be useful.

The other area about which you may be asked, and which is covered in Question 49, is the 'passing of property'. The rules relating to this are of considerable practical importance, as the answer to Question 49 indicates. Provided that you are familiar with **ss 16–20** of the Act, and apply them carefully, there should be no difficulties with questions in this area. There is less case law than on the implied terms, so it is easier to deal with the most important authorities (for which, see the answer to Question 49).

Checklist

You should be familiar with the following areas:

- the scope of the implied terms under **ss 12–15** of the **Sale of Goods Act 1979**;
- the meaning of 'sale by description' – **s 13**;
- the meaning of 'satisfactory quality' – **s 14(2)**;
- the meaning of 'fitness for a particular purpose' – **s 14(3)**;
- the remedies for breach;
- the passing of property – general principles (**ss 16–20**) and the importance of determining when property passes; and
- the special rules for the passing of property under **s 18**.

Question 49

When, according to the **Sale of Goods Act 1979**, does ownership of goods pass under a sale of goods contract? Why is it important to pinpoint this time?

Answer plan

To answer this question, you will need to know your way around **ss 16–20** of the **Sale of Goods Act 1979** and the related case law. Ownership is of course described as 'property' in the Act, so we are dealing with the rules for the 'passing of property'. The main features are:

- goods must be 'ascertained' – **s 16**;
- intentions of the parties are important – **s 17**; and
- in the absence of express intentions, the rules contained in **s 18** apply, so that, for example, in a contract for the sale of specific goods, property will often pass at the time of the contract (**r 1**). If the contract is for unascertained or future goods, however, property will not pass until

there has been an 'unconditional appropriation' of relevant goods to the contract (**r 5**).

Not all of the rules in **s 18** will need to be discussed in detail. The answer should, however, demonstrate that you have a general grasp of their scope and provisions. The second part of the question asks why it may be important to pinpoint the time when property passes. There are three main reasons:

- if one of the parties becomes insolvent, it may be vital to discover who owns the goods;

- if goods are lost or damaged, generally speaking, it will be the owner who will be able to take action against anyone responsible, or alternatively will have to bear the loss – **s 20** (passing of risk); and

- it is only when the property has passed that an action for the price can be maintained – **s 49**.

Answer

The **Sale of Goods Act** 1979 uses two words to denote rights of ownership: namely, 'title' and 'property'. 'Title' is mainly concerned with the right to sell the goods, as in the implied condition in **s 12**. Where the transfer of ownership rights is concerned, the Act refers to the 'passing of property'. The rules relating to this are set out in **ss 16–18** of the Act.

Section 16 states that property cannot pass unless the goods are 'ascertained'. This means that, if the contract is, for example, for the purchase of '5,000 size four widgets', no property will pass until the widgets relevant to the contract are 'ascertained'. Similarly, if you go into an electrical store and order a particular model of washing machine, property cannot pass until the actual machine that you are going to buy has been identified. The way in which this will operate is discussed further below in connection with **s 18, r 5**.

Where goods are ascertained – that is, it is clear at the time of the contract which particular items are being sold or are specific, as in, for example, the sale of a second-hand car – then **s 17** says that property will pass when the parties intend it to pass. Thus, the intentions of the parties are paramount and will override any other rules. The intentions must, however, be expressed prior to the time when the contract was made.

In *Dennant v Skinner* (1948), the successful bidder in an auction wanted to pay by cheque. The seller agreed, provided that the buyer signed a document saying that property would not pass until the cheque was cleared. It was held that this expression of intention as to the passing of property came too late, since the contract was concluded when the auctioneer knocked the lot down to the buyer. In many cases, of course, the parties do not bother to express any intention as to when property should pass, and in that situation the Act provides a set of rules, set out in **s 18**, to determine what should happen. There are five rules in all.

Rule 1 deals with the situation in which the contract is for the sale of specific goods in a deliverable state. It states that in this case property passes when the contract is made. The time of payment or delivery is irrelevant. If, for example, a person agrees to buy a second-hand car on a Monday, which is to be collected and paid for on the Wednesday, property passes on the Monday, and the buyer becomes the owner of the car from that point. This becomes even more important when the position as to 'risk' (discussed below) is considered.

Rules 2 and **3** again deal with specific goods, but relate to the situation in which something further needs to be done, either to put the goods into a deliverable state (**r 2**) or to determine the price (**r 3**). In both cases, property will not pass until what is required has been done, and the buyer has notice of that fact. So, for example, if the contract is for a load of grain in a ship, it may need to be put into bags to be deliverable (**r 2**), or if the load is bought at a price per tonne, it will be necessary to weigh it to determine the exact contract price (**r 3**).

Rule 4 deals with the particular problems of sales that are on an 'on approval' or 'sale or return' basis. It provides guidelines for deciding when it should be deemed that the goods are going to be retained. Once it is clear that the goods are to be kept by the buyer, property will pass immediately. This presumably means, for example, that if several cases of wine are bought on a sale-or-return basis for use at a party, the property in each bottle will pass as soon as it is opened.

The final rule, **r 5**, deals with the problem of unascertained or future goods. It thus covers both the order for generic goods that are already in existence (as in the '5,000 size four widgets' mentioned above) and goods that have to be manufactured, or grown, for the contract. **Rule 5** says that property passes when goods matching the contract description, and in a deliverable state, are 'unconditionally appropriated' to the contract by either party 'with the assent' of the other. There are two problems that may arise with this rule. First, what is meant by 'unconditional appropriation'? Second, what is meant by 'assent'? Looking first at 'unconditional appropriation', there is a further provision in the second part of **r 5**, which indicates that this may be satisfied by delivery of the goods to a carrier. The goods will need also to be 'ascertained' at this stage, however, in order to fulfil the requirements of **s 16**. Thus, in *Healey v Howlett & Sons* (1917), the contract was for 20 boxes of fish. The seller put 190 boxes onto a train, with instructions that 20 were to be delivered to the seller. It was held in this case that delivery to the carrier did not amount to an unconditional appropriation. Such appropriation could only occur when the defendant's 20 boxes were separated from the rest of the 190.

Other than this, the Act gives no guidance on what amounts to unconditional appropriation. In *Carlos Federspiel & Co SA v Charles Twigg & Co Ltd* (1957), it was emphasised that the assignment of the goods to a particular contract had to be intended to be irrevocable. Moreover, it was relevant to ask whether the seller had done the 'last act' that he was obliged to do. Thus, in *Aldridge v Johnson* (1857), grain had been bagged in accordance with the buyer's order and was awaiting collection by the buyer. Property was held to have passed. In the *Carlos Federspiel* case, however, although the goods had been packed, the seller had the obligation to ship them. Since the seller had not taken this last step, it was held that property had not passed.

As to assent, this may be express or implied, and may be given before or after the appropriation has taken place. It is clearly not necessary for the other party to be notified and to agree specifically. In fact, the approach seems to be that provided that what has been done is what was reasonably to be expected, then assent will be implied.

We must now turn to the second issue raised in the question – that is, why is it important to fix the time at which property passes? There are a number of reasons. First, it may be that one of the parties becomes insolvent. If the seller becomes insolvent prior to delivery, or the buyer after delivery but before payment, the other party will be in a much stronger position if they can establish a proprietary claim over the goods. The problem has arisen most commonly in relation to the insolvency of the buyer, and s 19 specifically recognises the seller's right to 'reserve the right of disposal' of the goods until payment has been made. Such a reservation by the seller is taken to be an indication that property is not to have been intended to pass. This works satisfactorily where the goods are still in their original state in the hands of the buyer or seller. More difficulties arise where the goods have been resold or have been used in some manufacturing process. Here, there have been elaborate attempts to protect the seller's position by so-called *Romalpa* clauses. These cannot be discussed in detail here, but their development indicates the importance of the issue 'when does property pass?'.

The second reason why it may be important to identify when property passes is that, as a result of **s 20** of the **Sale of Goods Act 1979**, 'risk' usually passes with property. Thus, if goods are lost or damaged, it is the owner who will be responsible, and will have the obligation of insuring them. If property has not passed to the buyer, then the seller will have to provide the buyer with replacement goods. If property has passed, the buyer will be obliged to pay for the goods, and will have to bear the loss of repairing or replacing them. Moreover, if someone else (such as a carrier) can be identified as being at fault, only the owner of the goods will have a right to take a tortious action against them: *Leigh & Sillivan Ltd v Aliakmon Shipping Co Ltd (The Aliakmon)* (1986).

Finally, **s 49** of the Act makes it clear that it is only where property has passed that the seller may maintain an action for the price against the buyer. The rules relating to the transfer of ownership in a sale of goods contract are fairly clearly defined by the **Sale of Goods Act 1979** provisions. Some uncertainties, such as what exactly is meant by 'unconditional appropriation', remain, but generally the parties in a sale of goods contract will know where they stand. This is important since, as has been indicated, the issue of if and when property has passed can be of vital importance in determining the rights and liabilities between buyer and seller.

Question 50

Gordon owns a restaurant that is situated on the seafront of the popular holiday resort of Scarlington, on the north-east coast of England. He finds that the effect of the sea air and severe winter weather means that the wooden frontage of his restaurant needs repainting every year. He reads in a magazine an advertisement for new paint called 'Wetherall', produced by the Miracle Paint Company. The advertisement states that, although it is expensive, the paint will outlast any other paint in the market. Gordon rings a local builder's merchant, Brix Ltd, and orders eight 5-litre cans of Wetherall. Advise Gordon as to his possible rights of action against Brix Ltd in each of the following alternative situations.

(a) On delivery, the paint is supplied in sixteen cans of 2.5 litres each. Gordon has just decided to sell his restaurant and so does not want to bother repainting it. He wishes to know whether he is entitled to reject the paint.

(b) Gordon engages a local decorator to apply the Wetherall in accordance to the instructions on the tin. After six months, however, the paint is starting to deteriorate. An independent report has discovered that while Wetherall lasts better than other paints in most situations, it performs poorly where there is a high level of salt in the air (as is the case in Scarlington).

(c) Would it make any difference to your answer in (b) if Gordon had told Brix Ltd the precise purpose for which he required the paint? .

Answer plan

This question is concerned with the implied terms as to description and quality under ss 13 and 14 of the Sale of Goods Act 1979. Note that you are only asked to deal with Gordon's possible actions against Brix Ltd, so you do not need to consider any possible actions that Gordon might have against the Miracle Paint Company. The issues you will need to look at are:

• in relation to situation (a), does the supply of the tins in 2.5-litre, rather than 5-litre, cans breach the implied term as to description under **s** 13? The amendment to the law in this area contained in **s 15A** of the **Sale of Goods Act 1979** will need to be considered;

- in relation to situation (b), does the fact that the paint starts to deteriorate quickly mean that it is not of 'satisfactory quality' under **s 14(2)** of the **1979 Act**? Do the statements in the Miracle Paint Company's advertisement have any bearing on this issue?

- alternatively, even if the paint is of 'satisfactory quality', might Gordon have a right of action under **s 14(3)**, in that the paint is not fit for the particular purpose for which he bought it? This will be much easier to establish if the situation as specified in (c) applies – that is, Gordon had made clear to Brix when ordering the paint the situation in which it was going to be used.

Cases that will be relevant to your answer include *Re Moore and Landauer* (1921), *Arcos v Ronaasen* (1933), *Ashington Piggeries v Christopher Hill* (1972) and *Jewson Ltd v Boyhan* (2003).

Answer

This question is concerned with potential liability for breach of certain of the implied terms under the **Sale of Goods Act 1979**. Brix Ltd has sold the paint to Gordon, and so may be liable under these provisions. The Miracle Paint Company is not a party to this contract, and so can have no liability to Gordon under the **Sale of Goods Act**.

Part (a)

The first of the implied terms to consider is **s 13**, which states that it is a condition of a sale of goods contract that where the sale is by description, the goods should comply with that description. The sale in this case is clearly 'by description'. The question is whether the failure to supply the paint in cans of the size specified in the order amounts to a breach of the obligation under **s 13**. Brix Ltd will no doubt wish to argue that the size of the cans is irrelevant. As long as it has supplied the overall correct quantity of paint of the specified make (which it has), then it has complied with the obligation. Moreover, its position would appear to be strengthened by the fact that Gordon is apparently only seeking to get out of a contract that he no longer needs, rather than having any genuine problem with the size of the cans.

There is, however, some case law that would support Gordon's right to reject the paint for breach of the **s 13** implied term. The most directly comparable in factual terms is *Re Moore and Landauer* (1921), in which cans of fruit were supposed to be supplied in cases of 30 tins, but a substantial part of the consignment consisted of cases of 24 tins. This was held to be sufficient of a deviation from the contractual description to allow the buyer to reject all of the goods. The fact that the paint is still perfectly usable for its intended purpose is not crucial either. In *Arcos v Ronaasen* (1933), some of a batch of staves supplied for making barrels were found to be one-sixteenth of an inch bigger than was specified in the contract. Despite the fact that these staves could still have been used for making barrels, the buyer was allowed to reject the whole consignment, because they did not precisely match their contractual description.

The approach taken in these cases has been criticised, in that it allows the buyer to escape from a contract about which he has changed his mind without there being any real justification for doing so. The situation has been altered by parliamentary intervention in the form of **s 15A** of the **Sale of Goods Act**, which was added to the Act in 1994. This provides that, where the buyer does not deal as a consumer, the right to reject for breach of the implied term as to description cannot be exercised where the difference is so small that it would be unreasonable to do so.

The buyer is left to recover damages for any loss resulting from the breach. This would seem likely to apply to Gordon, provided that he is not regarded as 'dealing as a consumer'. This phrase is defined in the same way as the equivalent phrase in the **Unfair Contract Terms Act 1977**. Here the courts have, in *R & B Customs Brokers v UDT* (1998), taken a broad view of what is a 'consumer', deciding that a business that does not regularly deal in the goods which are the subject matter of the contract should be treated as a consumer. On this basis, Gordon would be treated as a consumer and would not be subject to **s 15A**. He would therefore be able to reject the paint, provided that the size of the cans was found to be part of the contractual description.

Part (b)

In this situation, the issue is whether the paint meets the standard required by **s 14** of the **Sale of Goods Act 1979**. **Section 14(2)** imposes an implied condition that goods sold in the course of a business are of 'satisfactory quality'. **Section 14(3)** implies a condition that such goods will be fit for any particular purpose made known to the seller. In this part of the answer, the main focus will be on **s 14(2)**, with **s 14(3)** being discussed in part (c).

The test of 'satisfactory quality' is set out in **s 14(2A)**, and states that goods must be of the standard that a reasonable person would regard as satisfactory in all of the circumstances (including the description of the goods and the price charged). This is then further elucidated by **s 14(2B)**, which gives a list of factors that may be relevant. Of these, the ones that would seem likely to apply to Gordon and Brix are the goods' 'fitness for all the purposes for which goods of the kind in question are commonly bought' and their 'durability'. In the circumstances, the two can be combined into the question. 'Was the paint as durable as it was reasonable to expect when used for any of the purposes for which paint of that kind is commonly bought?' The first issue is that of durability. The paint is clearly sold as exterior paint. How long should such paint normally last, before repainting is required? A reasonable answer would seem to be that, in normal circumstances, exterior paint would be expected to last four to five years. Here the paint has started to deteriorate within six months. At first sight, therefore, the paint would seem to be unsatisfactory. This is particularly so since Miracle Paint has advertised Wetherall as being more durable than other paints. By virtue of **s 14(2D)** of the **Sale of Goods Act 1979**, in a consumer sale (which this probably is, as discussed above), statements in advertising by a manufacturer can be taken into account as one of the relevant circumstances when assessing whether goods are of satisfactory quality. Brix Ltd is likely to try to counter the claim of 'unsatisfactory quality' by arguing that the use to which Gordon put the paint fell outside the purposes to which goods of that kind are commonly put, because of the particularly severe conditions applying in the location of his restaurant. This might be successful, but it would depend on whether the court thought that the conditions were sufficiently unusual to be treated in this way. On balance, it would seem that Gordon has a strong case for arguing that the paint was not of satisfactory quality, and recovering damages for this.

Part (c)

If Gordon had told Brix precisely why he needed the paint, then his case against the company will be even stronger. **Section 14(3)** provides that where the buyer wants goods for a particular purpose, and the buyer is aware of this, then there will be an implied term that the goods will be reasonably fit for that purpose. The only exception will be if the seller can prove that the buyer either did not rely, or that it was unreasonable for him to rely, on the seller's skill and judgment in supplying goods for the purpose.

It is possible that Gordon might be able to rely on **s 14(3)**, even without a specific statement on his part. Since Brix is a local supplier, it should be aware of the conditions in which exterior paint is likely to be used. It may even be aware of who Gordon is, and that he has a restaurant on the seafront. On the other hand, the Court of Appeal has recently emphasised in *Jewson Ltd v Boyhan* (2003) that for **s 14(3)** to apply there must be full knowledge of all of the relevant circumstances. The specific statement by Gordon puts the issue beyond doubt. Clearly, as the independent report makes clear, Wetherall was not suitable for use in the location where Gordon's restaurant is sited. Brix's only defence, therefore, will be to prove that Gordon did not, or that it was unreasonable for him to, rely on Brix's skill and judgment in supplying the paint. On Brix's side in this argument is that Gordon specifically ordered Wetherall by name, rather than asking for an 'exterior paint'. On the other hand, having made his purpose clear, there would seem to be at least some indication that Gordon was expecting Brix to supply a product that was suitable, or at least to say if the product ordered was not suitable. As was made clear in *Ashington Piggeries v Christopher Hill* (1972), even partial reliance on the skill and judgment of the seller is sufficient to bring s 14(3) into play. It seems, therefore, that if Brix was aware of Gordon's purpose, there will be a strong case against it under s 14(3).

In all three situations under consideration, the result seems to be that Gordon (particularly if he is treated as a consumer buyer, rather than a business) has a strong case to either reject the paint (in situation (a)) or to recover damages for the fact that Wetherall has not lived up to its manufacturer's claims for durability (in situations (b) and (c)).

INDEX